Great Sites of the Ancient World

First published in 2020 by Frances Lincoln Publishing,
an imprint of The Quarto Group.
The Old Brewery, 6 Blundell Street
London, N7 9BH,
United Kingdom
T (0)20 7700 6700
www.QuartoKnows.com

A catalogue record for this book is available from the British Library.

ISBN 978-0-7112-5913-3

Ebook ISBN 978-0-7112-5914-0

10 9 8 7 6 5 4 3 2 1

Printed in Singapore

Great Sites of the Ancient World

EDITED BY **PAUL BAHN**

FRANCES LINCOLN

CONTENTS

AFRICA

NEAR EAST AND WESTERN ASIA

FAR EAST AND OCEANIA

INTRODUCTION

This volume's aim is to take the reader on a tour of some of the world's most famous archaeological sites. In doing so, it will show how, through the patient detective work of generations of scholars and researchers, as well as the scientific advances in archaeology, we now know more about the past than ever before.

W hy does archaeology intrigue and even fascinate people? Probably everyone has some kind of interest in the past, even if only that of their own family— as shown by the current craze for having one's DNA analyzed to explore one's geographical origins or the percentage of Neanderthal! But countless people are also interested in the past of our species, of all humankind, and archaeology constitutes our only means of learning about early or vanished cultures, and answering really big questions such as the origins of farming, or of settled life, or of humankind itself.

But—as the archaeologist Glyn Daniel often stressed— archaeology can also be tremendous fun. It features some of the most beautiful artworks and some of the most astounding structures ever created, and often in dramatic or exotic locations that include deserts, jungles, mountains, and islands. Moreover, the emotions aroused by unearthing something that has not seen the light of day for centuries, or even millennia, are hard to describe, whether one is a professional excavator or a metal-detecting enthusiast.

Personally, I first experienced the joys of archaeology through childhood visits to the ruined medieval castles and abbeys of my native Yorkshire, the Roman ruins of northern England, and the megalithic monuments of

Left The fourth-century B.C.E. tholos at Delphi, Greece.

Wessex. Later I was fortunate enough to be taken by my mother—who was equally smitten by the lure of the past—to Pompeii, Rome, and the sites of Greece. But another early and vivid influence came from Hergé's stories of Tintin, especially *The Temple of the Sun* and *Cigars of the Pharaoh*. The impact of fictional characters on young minds should never be underestimated.

Indeed, if asked to name an archaeologist, most people today would probably come up with Indiana Jones; but real archaeology is worlds away from that swashbuckling fictional hero. It is not just about treasure or rich burials, though it is no less exciting for all that. It is true that, decades ago, and more, it was indeed a subject focused on spectacular discoveries and exotic finds, but over the years, as it grew into a serious discipline, and aspired to be scientific, archaeology became increasingly concerned with the more mundane aspects of the past, and with the traces of the lives of ordinary people rather only those of kings, queens, and emperors. It now concentrated not on finding things, but on finding *out* things, on trying to explain when and where and how and why things happened and changed in the past.

Inevitably it can sometimes be tempting for archaeologists to overinterpret, to go beyond the hard evidence into the realms of pure speculation—more often than not, this is done to satisfy the media's thirst for simple answers to complex problems. Today, it is often frowned upon to say "we don't know," let alone "we shall never know," even when these are the correct and honest answers. The hitherto unimagined analytical techniques available to us have led some researchers to a curious optimism that nothing is now unknowable—but unless and until a time machine is invented, it is hard to see how most of our deductions about the past will ever be tested, far less verified.

It is also only comparatively recently that archaeological excavation and museum curation previously conducted without the slightest consultation with, or permission sought from, local groups have begun to be undertaken with a bit more consultation and sensitivity, particularly when indigenous groups (in North America, Australia, or New Zealand, for example) or religious groups (most notably in Israel) have serious objections. This in turn has had profound effects on how sites and collections are displayed and interpreted for the public, and on the explicit and implicit messages that are conveyed in this way.

Because a great deal of groundless nonsense about archaeology and the past is promulgated on TV and the web, it is always worthwhile to produce a book that sets out the "real past," the astonishing variety of human achievements, the end products of our ancestors' sweat and ingenuity. Based on solid evidence, the pages in this volume not only explain what archaeologists do and how they make their deductions, but also, we hope, go a little way toward counteracting the wilder speculation that is sometimes seen.

The Past is Human

Only archaeology can uncover and elucidate the wonders of past times and the astonishing achievements of our forebears. It is still a very young discipline, though, and the contents of this book can only cover a fraction of what has been recovered and learned in a couple of centuries. We have come a long way from the crude, fumbling digs of the nineteenth century, which usually employed laborers armed with pickaxes and shovels (and sometimes even explosives), to rip objects out of the ground without the context that tells us so much. This caused the destruction of vast quantities of crucial and irreplaceable information.

However, we need to judge those early archaeologists in the context of their time. Who, in the nineteenth century, would recognize the slow, painstaking excavations of today, aided by aerial photography, radiocarbon dating, remote sensing, computers, or genetic analysis? It is likely that in another 150 years,

archaeologists will look back on our own efforts as worthy and well-meaning, but primitive and unimaginative. Faced with the incredible pace of technological development, we simply cannot imagine what the ever-growing and improving battery of archaeological and scientific techniques will reveal about our past during the next century, or what information our descendants will be able to extract from the apparently insignificant material traces of the past.

The future therefore looks as exciting as the past. The real joy of archaeology is that it is constantly changing through an endless stream of new discoveries, any one of which can radically alter our picture of the past: it may be a new kind of fossil human, an earlier date for a phenomenon (such as pottery or cremation) or for an event (like the arrival of humans in the New World or Australia), or something completely unexpected like the body of King Richard III turning up under a car park in Leicester—a find that immediately became a major news story all over the world in 2013.

Our Selection of Sites

It is inevitable that a book such as this, which sets out to present the world of archaeology through just one hundred places, is forced to a large extent to feature only the most famous and most visited sites. But we wanted to introduce readers to other places that are doubtless far less known yet of great interest and importance. Above all we sought to feature a wide variety of sites—not just palaces and tombs, but caves and cities, rock art and sanctuaries. Collectively, they span a period from our earliest ancestors to an event as recent as the Battle of the Little Big Horn.

In putting together this collection, aimed at the archaeology aficionado, the armchair enthusiast, and also, of course, the interested traveler, a whole range of factors came into play. First and foremost, the sites selected needed to be of archaeological importance; of interest to the general public rather than merely to a handful of

Above The main entrance of the Angkor Wat complex, Cambodia.

specialists; they had to be accessible to tourists; and also photogenic, for those readers who might never have the chance to see these places—and there are probably not many people out there who have seen, or will ever see, all of the chosen sites during their lifetime!

It was clear from the very start that a hundred or so places was remarkably few for the enormous subject of world archaeology, so each contributor had to make some very tough choices about what should be included from their part of the world. Many of them could easily have presented a hundred sites in their regions—from Egypt, for example, or the Classical World, or the New World civilizations. Where my own speciality, Ice Age art, is concerned, there are still around fifty original decorated caves open to the public, and I would argue that at least twenty of them are world class.

We were determined to be as rational as possible in our allocation of space, and there are inevitable imbalances in both geographical and chronological distribution. Serious archaeology only began relatively recently in Australia and much of Africa, whereas— thanks to historical accident—Europe has been the scene of intensive work for far longer. Conversely, the Paleolithic period, despite constituting 99 percent of the archaeological record in terms of timespan, was assigned only a small part of the book, since so few of its sites really appeal to the tourist.

It is sad that our selection process was made slightly easier by the fact that conflict and terrorism have rendered a number of areas inaccessible to the archaeological tourist at the moment. Several major sites in Syria and Libya— such as Palmyra and Leptis Magna —would certainly have been included in any such compilation. We had originally intended to feature Timbuktu, but tensions that part of the Africa has likewise placed it off-limits for the time being.

The Preservation of Sites
for Generations to Come

It is to be hoped that these conflicts will soon become history in their turn, so that visits can resume to the archaeological treasures that are currently denied to us. At the same time, it is fervently to be hoped that most of the sites in question will emerge unscathed. Sadly, we know that terrible damage has been done to Palmyra and other sites in Syria, as well as to collections in archaeological museums both there and in other countries, such as Iraq and Afghanistan.

However, and with supreme irony, the greatest threats to archaeological sites all over the world come from the people who love them and visit them. Archaeological tourism has never been more popular, and is of enormous importance in many countries such as Egypt, Peru, and China. Yet its very popularity carries the tremendous risk of people loving it to death, by visiting fragile sites and monuments in excessive numbers. At many of the most popular sites such as Stonehenge or Carnac, the general public can no longer enter the monuments because of the potential damage of millions of feet; only a few people can now enter, outside of normal visiting hours and/or at great cost. When I first visited Easter Island in the mid-1980s, I was the only guest in my hotel, and I had almost all the sites to myself, with no restrictions on where one could go or climb. Today there are so many thousands of visitors every year that most of its monuments cannot even be approached too closely.

There are many reasons for this phenomenon all over the world—primarily the increasing affluence of the public, the rapid and constant growth of relatively cheap flights and foreign travel, and, of course, the ready availability of information about sites through popular books and magazines, television documentaries, and the Internet. And as the number of tourists continues to expand—particularly those coming from countries like China, who were unable to travel in the past—it is hard to see how this problem can be solved.

One solution, already used in such cases as the decorated caves of Lascaux, Altamira, and Chauvet is to produce exact replicas for tourists to visit, while the original sites are kept closed for reasons of conservation. Naturally, facsimiles are always poor substitutes for the real thing, but when they are superbly accurate, as in the caves mentioned above, they are well worth a visit. Cynics have pointed out that few people would pay to see a roomful of fake Rembrandts; but if the choice is either to see the replica or to see nothing at all, then surely most would opt for the former! Another solution arising from modern technology is to visit sites and monuments through virtual reality, and this, too, will become more common as restrictions on tourism create the demand. In addition, these hi-tech alternatives will prove invaluable to those who are financially or physically unable to travel to the sites. The new technology will also enable archaeologists to make further progress in reconstructing the past, but in helping to relieve tourist pressure on the more fragile and vulnerable remains of that past it will contribute greatly to its conservation for future generations.

It is imperative that we leave future generations as much of the past as we can, and in good condition—not only by cherishing and protecting known sites, but also by preventing the clandestine robbery and destruction of our precious and irreplaceable heritage. As long as looters and vandals are kept at bay, the prospects for broadening and deepening our understanding of the past will be bright.

Paul G. Bahn

Opposite Hatshepsut's temple, Egypt.

1

NORTH AMERICA

North America presents an astonishing variety of sites, from the spectacular and majestic ruins and pueblos of the Southwest to the enigmatic effigy mounds of Ohio and the great urban complex of Cahokia. But it also features a wide range of equally remarkable places like the evocatively named Head-Smashed-In Buffalo Jump. It provided the first solid evidence for Viking settlement at L'Anse aux Meadows. And at the Little Bighorn there took place one of the world's most famous and tragic battles, which has achieved almost mythical status through books and movies.

Left Mesa Verde National Park in Colorado.

NORTH AMERICA
LOCATIONS

HEAD-SMASHED-IN **BUFFALO JUMP**

TYPE: KILL SITE • **ARCHITECTURAL STYLE:** N/A
LOCATION: ALBERTA, CANADA • **CONSTRUCTION BEGUN:** N/A

The winds seem to blow constantly from the Rocky Mountains, all the way
across the great sea of grass called the Great Plains of North America.
These grasslands were once home to tens of thousands of American bison,
and the indigenous tribes of North America relied on those mighty beasts
for their food, their shelters, their clothing; they wasted very little of the animal.

The bison is a herd animal, and indigenous people devised many ways to kill them. The most spectacular was the buffalo jump, in which hunters carefully shepherded hundreds of bison and, in a controlled stampede, drove them off the edge of a cliff to fall to their deaths. They then processed the carcasses, providing food and raw material for hundreds of people. By one estimate, one could walk along the foothills of the Rockies from Alberta to Colorado and never lose sight of at least one jump.

The Head-Smashed-In Buffalo Jump, located in southern Alberta on the edge of the Rockies, is one of the most splendid examples of the jump. It was in use for close to 6,000 years (the latest use was by the historic Blackfoot tribe). The overall complex comprises four primary elements. First is the gathering basin in the foothills of the Rockies, where hunters would herd small groups of the animal until a critical mass had been reached and they stampeded through lines of stone cairns,

called a drive lane. Women, children, and old men stood along the lines and helped drive the animals to their deaths. The second element is the cliff itself from where the animals fell to their deaths. Then there were the bone beds at the base of the cliff. In the case of Head-Smashed-In these beds are about 40 ft (12 m) deep and provided archaeologists with thousands of broken or complete projectile points that the hunters had used to dispatch any animals that survived the fall. The final element was the processing camp, where members of the tribe processed the animals. They dried and stored the meat, used the hides to provide clothing and coverings for the tipis in which the tribes lived, and they turned bones and ligaments into tools of all kinds.

Successfully completing a jump required a great many people, and their coordination was absolutely essential. The lead-up to the kill was filled with religious ritual and prayer, and unless everything was done correctly the jump could be postponed or canceled. But the payoff for all this was a bounty that provided everything the tribes needed for several months, especially during the harsh winters of the northern Plains.

The name Head-Smashed-In comes from a Blackfoot legend that a hunter wanted to view the kill up close, but got too close and was crushed by the falling bison. A more prosaic explanation is that it was where the buffalo themselves had their heads smashed in. Today the jump is a World Heritage site and boasts a superb five-level interpretive center, and regularly scheduled guided hikes featuring the cliff jump, drive lanes, and spiritual sites. The site is located 11 miles (18 km) northwest of Fort McLeod in southern Alberta.

Opposite Views across the site.

Above Diorama of the buffalo jump in the interpretive center.

Right Reconstruction of a tipi.

THE VIKING SETTLEMENT OF
L'ANSE AUX MEADOWS

TYPE: HABITATION • **ARCHITECTURAL STYLE:** WOOD AND SOD
LOCATION: NEWFOUNDLAND, CANADA • **CONSTRUCTION BEGUN:** ELEVENTH CENTURY C.E.

On a windswept peninsula of Newfoundland lies one of the most remarkable archaeological sites in all of North America: L'Anse aux Meadows. Remains found provide indisputable evidence that the Vikings reached and lived there, if only for a small period.

L'Anse aux Meadows (French for The Bay with Meadows, although it is almost certainly a corruption of the original French name) was discovered by Helge Ingstad (1899–2001) and Anne Stine Ingstad (1918–1997) in 1960, both of whom conducted excavations here during that decade. Parks Canada then conducted further excavations to expand our overall knowledge of the site.

The excavations revealed a Viking settlement of eight houses, probably made of sod on wooden frames. In addition, archaeologists found the remains of a smithy, a charcoal kiln, and a woodworking shop. Only a small number of artifacts were recovered (a few more than a hundred), but they included a bronze pin, a whetstone, and a bone needle—all characteristic items of eleventh-century Viking life. Radiocarbon assays have confirmed this date.

The small number of artifacts found and no evidence of house rebuilding suggests the settlement was short-lived. Possible causes of the abandonment include its distance from Scandinavia, a deteriorating climate caused by the Little Ice Age, or threats from local indigenous groups, collectively termed Skraelings by the Norse.

What archaeological evidence there is fits in nicely with the sagas left by the Norse, however. Originally oral traditions—they were probably written down between 1200 and 1300 C.E.—these sagas, such as *The Saga of Erik the Red* and *The Saga of the Greenlanders*, tell of the Norse voyages west to Iceland, Greenland, and ultimately to a place called Vinland, somewhere along the northeast coast of North America, and tentatively identified as present-day Newfoundland, although that is contested. Leif Erikson, son of Eric the Red, is credited with being the first European to set foot on the continent, although it is probably too much of a stretch to say with certainty that he founded L'Anse aux Meadows.

A National Historic Site and also a UNESCO World Heritage site, L'Anse aux Meadows is located on the tip of the Northern Peninsula about 30 miles (50 km) from the regional airport at the town of St Anthony. At the site itself, raised berms outline the original huts. Parks Canada has reconstructed the village so that the visitor can get a very good idea of what life was like. There is a visitor center, as well as actor re-creations to help visitors enjoy their stay.

Opposite above Reconstructed village at L'Anse aux Meadows.
Opposite below Overview of the site.

THE GREAT HOUSES OF **CHACO CANYON**

TYPE: HABITATIONS AND RELIGIOUS SITES • **ARCHITECTURAL STYLE:** STONE, WOOD, ADOBE PLASTER
LOCATION: NEW MEXICO, USA • **CONSTRUCTION BEGUN:** 800 C.E.

It is hard for the casual visitor to imagine that, in the high desert of northern New Mexico, with its cold winters and blazing hot summers, there arose one of the greatest indigenous cultures of North America. For more than three hundred years, beginning in the 800s C.E., Ancestral Puebloans occupied this wide canyon and developed a culture of great social complexity and community organization, based on the cultivation of plants such as maize and beans and on long-distance trade.

The most prominent sites in the canyon are called Great Houses. These are huge multistory stone buildings consisting of habitation rooms, storage rooms, and ceremonial underground structures called kivas. Pueblo Bonito, the finest example of a Chacoan Great House, was the center of the Chacoan world. Over 600 rooms, thirty-two kivas, and three great kivas, are arranged in a semicircular pattern around a central plaza. Extant walls at the rear of the pueblo stand two to three stories high. So-called great kivas were also built, such as Casa Rinconada. This great kiva stands above ground, unlike others whose roofs were at ground level.

Because of the land's aridity, nothing would have been possible without the construction of complex irrigation systems that both captured and channeled the rainfall onto the fields. Radiating out from the canyon was a series of constructed roads linking the canyon to other Chacoan sites throughout the region, especially to the north and west. The Chacoans traded throughout the wider American Southwest, perhaps as far as modern-day Mexico, and items such as copper bells and macaw feathers attest the far-flung nature of their trade.

The material culture of the Chacoans is exemplified by the beautiful black-on-white pottery they produced. The

Left Chacoan pottery was some of the most beautiful produced by prehistoric Native Americans.

Opposite, from top Casa Rinconada. This great kiva was of great symbolic and ceremonial importance to the Chacoan culture. View of Pueblo Bonito from the Pueblo Alto trail.

potter's wheel was unknown in North America at the time, so Chacoan pottery was made of long "sausages" of clay that were coiled into the desired shape.

There is significant evidence for the importance of astronomical observations to the Chacoans, such as the alignment of the walls of Pueblo Bonito. One of the most enigmatic pieces of evidence is found on nearby Fajada Butte. Researchers found upright slabs of sandstone that cast daggers of light onto two spiral rock carvings. At summer solstice, the light splits the middle of the spiral.

Archaeologists have for decades debated the reasons for the existence of the Chaco Canyon complex. It was

for many years assumed that Chaco was an important trading center. Many archaeologists now believe that the canyon was perhaps not continuously occupied, but rather it served as a center for when far-flung Chacoan communities temporarily came together for ceremonial, religious, and trading purposes. Perhaps it even served as a resource distribution center when times were tough.

By the 1200s, Chaco's importance had declined and new and existing Ancestral Puebloan centers to the north and west, including Mesa Verde, became more prominent.

Today, access to the park, south of Farmington, New Mexico, comprises both paved and dirt roads. Within the park itself is a very informative and helpful visitor center.

MESA VERDE NATIONAL PARK

TYPE: HABITATION AND RELIGIOUS SITES • **ARCHITECTURAL STYLE:** STONE, WOOD, ADOBE PLASTER
LOCATION: COLORADO, USA • **CONSTRUCTION BEGUN:** 600 C.E.

The visitor to Mesa Verde, in southwest Colorado, looks to the north and sees the majestic, towering Rocky Mountains, and to the south the apparently endless high desert of the American Southwest. Mesa Verde seems to dominate its landscape. It also happens to be the scene of one of the best-preserved archaeological sites on the continent: Cliff Palace.

Mesa Verde (Spanish for Green Table) is the collective term for a series of high, flat-topped mesas intersected by deep canyons. From approximately 600 to 1300 C.E. Ancestral Puebloans (formerly called the Anasazi) lived on the mesas, building a variety of structures, hunting and gathering, growing corn and other crops, and leaving behind a spectacular legacy of over 5,000 archaeological sites.

The earliest habitation structures on the mesa date to around 600 C.E. and are called pithouses. These semisubterranean houses, dug 4–5 ft (1.2–1.5 m) deep into the earth, were circular or rectangular in shape. A fire pit provided warmth in the winter and a ventilator shaft allowed fresh air for the fire in. The Ancestral Puebloans

built earthen benches around the edges of the pithouse and upright stone slabs served as quasi room dividers. Smoke escaped through a hole in the roof (made of logs and woven branches covered in adobe, a clay-based plaster.) Later, the Puebloans moved to aboveground, multiroomed structures made from shaped slabs, while pithouse architecture evolved into ceremonial kivas, the center of religious life for the Puebloans, then and now.

During the twelfth century, the Four Corners region (the point of intersection of the states of Colorado, New Mexico, Arizona, and Utah) experienced severe droughts. Gradually, the inhabitants abandoned the region, moving to more amenable climes to the south and west. (It is here that the successors of the Ancestral Puebloans still live, tribes such as the Zuni, Hopi, and Acoma among them). The inhabitants of Mesa Verde remained—at least for a time—possibly because the southerly slope to the mesa tops and the proximity to the Rockies continued to provide a favorable combination of solar radiation and higher precipitation for the growing of corn, their main crop. However, they too were finally forced to leave.

Left Ancestral Pueblo Pottery, 1180–1200 C.E.
Opposite top Cedar Tree Tower and kiva.
Opposite below Balcony House cliff dwelling.

Cliff Palace

It was during the twelfth century that Ancestral Puebloans built a series of dwellings in natural alcoves in the cliff faces. Archaeologists are not sure whether this relocation was due to environmental conditions, threats from outside marauders, or some other factor. There are some 600 cliff dwellings in the park although most of these are not dwellings at all, but rather clusters of one to five small storage rooms.

Cliff Palace is the largest such dwelling. It comprises over 150 individual rooms and over twenty kivas, all made from shaped sandstone blocks, roof beams and wall supports of timber, and adobe, which was plastered onto the walls and roofs. Cliff Palace also boasts some

remarkable wall paintings. Estimates of population size are difficult for archaeologists to make, but probably a population of one hundred or so people at any one time would be a fair estimate. Another well-preserved site, also open to the public, is Balcony House, which consists of thirty-eight rooms and two kivas.

Mesa Verde National Park

The arid desert climate of southwestern Colorado has been a great boon to archaeologists in that it has allowed the preservation of organic material that normally would not have stood the test of time. (In 1888, the ranchers Richard Wetherill and Charlie Mason were the first Europeans to see Cliff Palace, and they said that it looked like its inhabitants had left just the day before.) The well-preserved roof beams also allow archaeologists to date sites using the technique of dendrochronology (tree-ring dating).

Mesa Verde was established in 1906 as a National Park and is extremely visitor-friendly. The visitor center (opened in 2012) is the first point of call. A forty-minute drive from the center takes the visitor to the museum on top of Chapin Mesa. The museum overlooks Spruce Tree House, the third-largest and probably best-preserved cliff dwelling in the park. In the museum, visitors can see many examples of Ancestral Puebloan culture, such as black-on-white pottery (bowls, mugs, ladles), exquisite bone implements, *manos* and *metates* (the ubiquitous stone tools primarily used for grinding corn meal), projectile points, and preserved items such as yucca sandals and baskets. More than 40 miles (64 km) of paved roads crisscross the park, allowing the visitor to experience the complete range of Ancestral Puebloan sites.

Right View across Mesa Verde National Park, established in 1906.

THE BATTLE OF **THE LITTLE BIGHORN**

TYPE: BATTLEFIELD • **ARCHITECTURAL STYLE:** N/A
LOCATION: MONTANA, USA • **CONSTRUCTION BEGUN:** N/A

The gravestones of the troopers stand starkly white against the rolling grasslands of Montana, the peaceful solitude of their resting place at odds with what happened here almost 150 years ago.

It was here, on the banks of the Big Horn River, that General George Armstrong Custer (1839–1876) rode his force of about 600 cavalrymen into history on June 25, 1876. Ordered to capture a large force of Cheyenne, Lakota, and Arapaho encamped on the banks of the river, Custer split his command into three (led by himself, Major Marcus Reno, and Captain Frederick Benteen). Custer and Reno made a two-pronged attack against the encampment. However, Custer had underestimated its size and rather than closing in on the camp in a classic pincer movement, he rode straight into the camp's center. Reno and Benteen took casualties, but Custer's force of 210 cavalrymen was wiped out, and the myth grew that they made a gallant last stand until they fell. But questions about what really happened have always lingered because, of course, all of Custer's men were killed and Benteen and Reno were too far away to see clearly what had happened. The Native Americans left as soon as the battle was concluded.

It is here that archaeology has helped fill in some of the blanks. In 1983 a grassfire swept through the battlefield, allowing archaeologists to conduct a ground survey and some limited excavations. Spent cartridges, bullets, clothing, and guns were recovered, among other artifacts. The skeletal remains of more than thirty cavalrymen were also found.

Forensic analysis of bullets allowed the scientists to trace the paths of the rifles that fired them across the battlefield. From this it seems that the command discipline of the cavalrymen evaporated quickly and the men were hunted down in small groups. Although Last Stand Hill was heavily covered with cartridges, it is still unclear whether this was indeed the place of the last stand. Instead, it is possible that the last stand, if there was such an event, took place in a ravine rather than on a hill.

Remains of cavalrymen themselves have also provided information on how they died. For example, one trooper, about 5 ft 8 in (173 cm) tall and aged about twenty-five, had been shot in the chest and head. His skull was then smashed, arrows shot into him, and his front and back slashed. In other cases, forensic anthropologists have reconstructed the facial contours of individuals to give accurate portrayals of what they looked like in life.

Visitors can reach Little Bighorn Battlefield National Monument via Battlefield Tour Road 756 in Montana. The monument boasts a museum and bookstore. Guided tours are available, as well as self-guided tours.

Opposite Gravestones of fallen US cavalrymen.
Below Iron sculpture by Lakota artist Colleen Cutschall.

THE MOUND LANDSCAPE
OF **CAHOKIA**

TYPE: PLATFORM MOUND, BURIAL MOUNDS • **ARCHITECTURAL STYLE:** COMPACTED EARTH, WOOD • **LOCATION:** ILLINOIS, USA • **CONSTRUCTION BEGUN:** 800 C.E.

Just a few miles east of the sprawling metropolis of St. Louis and the Mississippi River, in a region called the American Bottom, lies the largest pre-Columbian urban complex north of Mexico, Cahokia. Named for the local Native American tribe, this sprawling complex of mounds, homes, and farmland originally covered over 4,000 acres (1,600 ha), with a population possibly as high as 20,000. Cahokia's heyday was between 1000 and 1350 C.E., a period characterized by the Mississippian Culture.

The central, dominating structure here is Monks Mound (so named because, when the antiquarian Henry Brackenridge visited the site in 1811, it was occupied by a group of Trappist monks). It is technically termed a platform mound, because of its flat top. Excavations on the mound's summit revealed the remains of a large building, 100 × 40 ft (30.5 × 12 m) in size, which may have been a temple or the residence of Cahokia's leader. The mound covers more than 14 acres (5.7 ha), and was built in four terraces over several centuries to a maximum height of 100 ft (30.5 m). It required more than seven million cubic feet (two million cubic meters) of earth, which was removed from nearby borrow pits. In front of Monks Mound is a central plaza, approximately 1,000 × 1,300 ft (305 × 396 m) in size. A wooden palisade, two miles (3.2 km) in length, surrounded Cahokia's central area, probably serving as a social rather than a defensive barrier. Surrounding the plaza were smaller platform mounds (supporting the timber-built houses of the lesser elite) and conical and ridgetop mounds that served as burial places. There are more than one hundred extant mounds at Cahokia,

Above The Keller Figurine— a woman performing a corn ceremony.
Right Aerial view of Monks Mound.

but many more outside the park boundaries have undoubtedly been destroyed by urban encroachment.

One spectacular example of a burial mound at Cahokia is Mound 72. Originally about 10 ft (3 m) high and 140 × 70 ft (43 × 21 m) in area, it is actually a composite of smaller mounds that were then integrated into one. Archaeologists excavated more than 250 individual skeletons at the mound, one of which lay on a bed of shell beads. Scattered around were other skeletal remains, all of them with grave goods, including a cache of several hundred finely knapped projectile points.

Just west of Monks Mound are the remains of a series of circles formed of upright wooden posts (identified by the remaining postholes). Archaeo-astronomical investigations have demonstrated that one structure (sometimes called Woodhenge, after its equivalent in southern England), which was rebuilt several times, was aligned with the movement of the sun and may, it is suggested, have served as a calendar.

The Mississippian Culture

Cahokia was part of the Mississippian Culture (800–1400 C.E.). The basic social structure of the culture was a ranked chiefdom—that is, a chief (possibly hereditary) held paramount power, with different social ranks or classes below. Political and economic power was based on the control of widespread trade networks throughout the Southeastern and Eastern United States and beyond, to as far as the Rocky Mountains in the West and the Great Lakes to the North. Beside its mound architecture, Mississippian Culture is characterized by the cultivation of maize, shell-tempered pottery, a social inequality exemplified by the disparity in grave goods, and a distinct settlement hierarchy in which smaller satellite settlements were reliant upon and "fed into" larger settlements such as Cahokia. One very important characteristic of Mississippian Culture is the southeastern Ceremonial Complex (once called the Southern Cult). Dating to between 1000 and 1600 C.E., it is characterized by similarities in artifacts, iconography, and mythology. The complex, which some have identified as a distinct religion, may have originated in Cahokia and then spread—by trade, diffusion, or migration—throughout the Southeast United States as far as Florida to the south, and as far as Texas to the west. A UNESCO World Heritage site, Cahokia is located in Collinsville, Illinois. It is a very tourist-friendly site, with a state-of-the-art interpretive center that offers theater programs, exhibits, and re-creations of life at Cahokia. Guided tours are also available.

Above, from left Mississippian vessel with beaver representation; ear spools from the Kunneman Mound.
Opposite Woodhenge: markers of astronomical sightings.

SERPENT MOUND
THE WORLD'S LARGEST EFFIGY MOUND

TYPE: EFFIGY MOUND • **ARCHITECTURAL STYLE:** COMPACTED EARTH
LOCATION: OHIO, USA • **CONSTRUCTION BEGUN:** 800 B.C.E.

In the US state of Ohio, Serpent Mound sits on an ancient meteorite impact crater dating to the Permian era. As its name implies, the mound is shaped like an undulating serpent, 1,348 ft (411 m) in length and ranging in height from 4 to 5 ft (1.2 to 1.5 m) and in width 20 to 25 ft (6 to 7.6 m). An oval mound forms the serpent's head. Some believe that the oval represents a large eye, others a hollow egg being swallowed by the serpent. The tail is coiled. The mound was constructed of local clay soils reinforced with rocks.

This site was first excavated by the antiquarian/archaeologist Frederic Ward Putnam (1839–1915) in the late-nineteenth century. He found no artifacts in the mound itself, so he was unwilling to make a cultural assignation. However, the mound is close to two conical earthen burial mounds built by people of the Adena Culture (800 B.C.E.–100 C.E.) and to a third burial mound dated to the later Fort Ancient Culture (1000–1500 C.E.).

Additionally, a nearby prehistoric village contained evidence of both cultures. In 1991 radiocarbon dating indicated the mound was 900 years old and therefore attributable to the Fort Ancient Culture. In 2014 more radiocarbon dating attributed the mound to the Adena Culture. These cultures must regularly have repaired the mound as erosion bit into its earthen core, so radiocarbon dates spanning a long period of time are to be expected.

The Adena Culture, centered in southern Ohio, is characterized most prominently by conical burial mounds. The population was scattered around the burial mounds, their settlements comprising a small number of circular wooden huts. They relied on hunting and gathering and the cultivation of such plants as sunflower, pumpkin, and squash. They produced a variety of stone, bone, horn, shell, antler, and ceramic artifacts. Their pottery was either undecorated or decorated with cord or fabric markings.

The Fort Ancient Culture is found along the Ohio River, in Ohio, Kentucky, Indiana, and West Virginia.

Through its history, populations congregated in large settlements with a degree of town planning evidenced by huts surrounding a central plaza. Theirs was apparently an egalitarian society, as indicated by the relative lack of variety in grave goods. Fort Ancient people relied on hunting and gathering, as well as the cultivation of maize, beans, and squash.

The purpose of the Serpent Mound is unknown. There were no burials found in the mound itself, although the proximity of the three burial mounds might suggest that the structure had some significance regarding the afterlife. It has also been posited that the alignment of the mound was based on equinoctial and solstitial events. The mound lies a few hours drive from Cincinnati or Dayton. There is a museum at the site, with information on the mound itself, as well the Adena Culture in general.

Opposite A close-up view of the mound.
Above Aerial view of Serpent Mound.

2

MIDDLE AND SOUTH AMERICA

Middle and South America together constitute one of the world's richest regions archaeologically, with an astounding variety of sites, and they include some of the most famous which are on everyone's must-see list, such as Teotihuacan, Chichén Itzá, Tikal, Copán, Machu Picchu, and the Nazca lines. Some of them impress by their location, others by the sheer scale of their constructions, whether in stone or mud brick. But architecture—cities, pyramids, ball-courts, plazas—is not the only attraction, since there are also sumptuous tombs, fabulous pottery, carved stelae, and breathtaking mural decorations.

Left Maya pyramids at Tikal, Guatemala.

MIDDLE AND
SOUTH AMERICA
LOCATIONS

TEOTIHUACAN CITY OF THE GODS

TYPE: CITY • **ARCHITECTURAL STYLE:** TEMPLES, PALACES, AND APARTMENT COMPOUNDS
LOCATION: NEAR MEXICO CITY, MEXICO • **CONSTRUCTION BEGUN:** FIRST CENTURY B.C.E.

Spreading over 8.5 sq mi (22 sq km), in a narrow valley at the northeast entrance to the Basin of Mexico, Teotihuacan was once the largest urban center in the Americas. Spectacular monumentality and measured standardization are common first impressions of this great city, which dominated Mexico's central highlands between about 1 and 600 C.E.

We do not know the city's original name, but later groups called it the City of the Gods and identified it as the place where ancient deities had gathered to generate the fifth cycle of creation through ritual sacrifice. Its spiritual magnetism was such that, centuries after it had fallen into ruin, its temples still attracted many pilgrims, including the Aztec emperor Moctezuma; indeed, several fifteenth-century ceremonial offerings excavated at the Great Temple of the Aztecs in Tenochtitlan (now Mexico City) contained items looted from Teotihuacan.

The city had a population in excess of 100,000, and the Street of the Dead and the East–West Avenue divided its gridiron plan into four quarters. To design a city unlike any other, Teotihuacan's planners translated time into space by basing the dimensions of major civic-ceremonial architecture on the 260-day ritual calendar, perhaps to proclaim this new metropolis as "the place where time began." They also oriented the grid fifteen and a half degrees east of astronomical north so the setting sun would align directly with the centerline of the Sun Pyramid on August 11, the anniversary of the world's creation in 3114 B.C.E. At the northern end of the Street of the Dead, they constructed the Moon Pyramid to echo the outline of the Cerro Gordo that rises behind it, revealing the metaphorical relationship between pyramid and mountain. At the intersection of the

city's four quarters—considered the location of the vertical fifth direction that links the realms of the underworld, earth, and sky in Mesoamerican cosmology—Teotihuacan's architects built the Ciudadela, the walled compound that frames the Feathered Serpent Temple.

Teotihuacan's early architecture centers on modest groups of three temples that may have served to anchor the different communities that migrated into the valley at the beginning of the Common Era. Shortly thereafter, the city initiated its master plan that included its three largest pyramids: the Moon, the Sun, and the Feathered Serpent Temple. Excavations into these have revealed elaborate dedicatory offerings with ritually sacrificed humans and animals. The Sun Pyramid and the Feathered Serpent Temple stand over deep tunnels, laboriously excavated to hold extravagant offerings of greenstone, obsidian, pyrite, slate, conch shells, rubber balls, figurines, pottery, and other sumptuary items. Originally, these two tunnels may have housed royal tombs, but modern archaeologists have not

Opposite North–south view of the ceremonial core of Teotihuacan. At the bottom is the facade of the Moon Pyramid; 2,300 ft (700 m) farther south, on the left (east) side of the Street of the Dead, is the Sun Pyramid; the quadrangular Ciudadela compound, with the Feathered Serpent Temple, can be seen in the distance.

found any human burials in them, perhaps because they were opened on various occasions in the pre-Hispanic past.

A Unique Residential Setup

To organize its dense population, city planners devised a new type of residence: the apartment compound. Unique to Teotihuacan, these suites of rooms centered on a shared ritual courtyard and were surrounded by a high wall that provided protection and privacy for its residents. These units, which number more than 2,000, varied greatly in elegance and size—ranging from 5,900 to 38,750 sq ft (550 to 3,600 sq m)—and accommodated both locals and migrants from many parts of Mesoamerica.

Today, most of the city's buildings no longer feature the architectural sculpture and vibrant murals that once graced their facades, giving the site a somber appearance. Nonetheless, remnants of elaborate mural paintings remain along the Street of the Dead and, significantly, in its apartment compounds. Unlike the Maya tradition, Teotihuacan's mural art and statuary shun images of rulers, opting instead to display mythical scenes, processions of fantastic animals—often devouring human hearts—and lavishly dressed individuals engaged in ritual acts. No formal writing system is known from Teotihuacan, but enough evidence exists to suggest that this was a literate society.

An Influential Polity

Teotihuacan's influence was felt throughout Mesoamerica. It engaged in long-distance trade in prestige items, including exotic feathers, jade, and even wild animals. Its military presence and its interference in royal succession are detailed in epigraphic texts at Maya sites such as Tikal and Copán, and conversely fragments of Maya-style murals and imported ceramics appear in Teotihuacan's Plaza of the Columns, which may have been the primary palace of the city.

Toward the end of the sixth century, Teotihuacan's political power collapsed. While this disruption may stem from the government's inability to deal with the onset of an intense drought and the arrival of immigrants from the north, the burning of temples and palaces, the destruction of icons, and the looting of offerings strongly suggest an internal ideological rejection of authority. Ballooning over the site at dawn is a memorable experience. Teotihuacan's monumental architecture is best visited early in the morning, reserving high noon to explore the shaded apartment compounds and two site museums.

Opposite The sculpted facade of the Feathered Serpent Temple that dominates the Ciudadela compound.

Above, left Seen from the Pyramid of the Sun, the Pyramid of the Moon is the focal point of the Street of the Dead.

Above, right This mural in the ritual patio of the Tetitla apartment shows Teotihuacan's bountiful Great Goddess.

THE MOUNTAINTOP CITY OF
MONTE ALBÁN

TYPE: CITY • **ARCHITECTURAL STYLE:** TEMPLES, PALACES, AND TOMBS
LOCATION: OAXACA, MEXICO • **CONSTRUCTION BEGUN:** FOURTH CENTURY B.C.E.

Majestically situated on a 1,300 ft- (400 m-) high mountain ridge at
the center of Mexico's Valley of Oaxaca lie the remains of Monte Albán.
This ceremonial center was the capital of the Zapotec state from
500 B.C.E. until it was abandoned some 1,300 years later.

Monte Albán was one of Mesoamerica's first cities, founded, according to some, as a defendable bastion by a coalition of communities in response to increasing conflict. Others argue that its creation reflects the emergence of a religious ideology devised by elites to justify their rights to land, water, and other resources. These are not mutually exclusive, and archaeology has shown that both militarism and religion were essential to the capital's origins and longevity.

Monte Albán's monumental buildings define the Main Plaza, measuring 984 ft (300 m) north–south by 656 ft (200 m) east–west, on the artificially leveled summit. At the northern end of the plaza, a wide staircase leads to the royal palace complex, which covers 12 acres (5 ha) and whose sunken patio could hold over 3,000 individuals; in addition to its administrative, religious, and residential buildings, a small ballcourt was built just off its southeastern corner. At the opposite end of the plaza, the South Platform, 459 ft (140 m) on a side, supports two temples. Platforms also line the east and west edges of the plaza and run down its central axis. At its peak in the mid-seventh century C.E., the city had more than 17,000 inhabitants living on the 2,000 residential terraces that cascade down the mountain's steep slopes.

The city's earliest architecture is largely covered by later constructions; most of what one sees today dates to the sixth and seventh centuries C.E. One important exception is Los Danzantes, located at the southwestern corner of the Main Plaza. Although only a section of the vertical platform wall remains, it was originally faced with irregular stone slabs carved with human figures. Because these male individuals are shown in ungainly poses—and often with mutilated genitals and closed eyes—they have generally been interpreted as sacrificed captives. However, others argue that they are warriors practicing ritual bloodletting. The two monoliths that form the southwestern corner of this building, stelae 12 and 13, preserve the earliest known Zapotec text (ca. 500 C.E.).

As the ceremonial center took its final form in the first centuries C.E., Los Danzantes was dismantled and covered over, and a new public display was created on the strangely oriented arrow-shaped Building J at the southern end of the Main Plaza's central spine. Here, stone slabs engraved with place glyphs, and sometimes an inverted human head, were embedded in the platform walls. Known as the Conquest Stones, these images of place and decapitation focus more on location than specific individual leaders and thus might memorialize more distant military ventures.

Later carved stones, which refer to foreign conquest and political relations with Teotihuacan, were set into the corners of the South Platform. Most show captive warriors, but one presents ruler 12 Jaguar, dressed as the feline he was named for, and seated on a throne that rests upon the city's place glyph. Monuments from the city's final years avoid martial themes and instead deal with noble genealogies and the transfer of entitlements from one generation to the next.

Life at Monte Albán

Zapotec houses consisted of rooms built around a patio with a subfloor tomb. Elite families had lavish funerary chambers decorated with mural paintings portraying venerated ancestors and glyphic data about lineage members. They were well stocked with pottery vessels, including anthropomorphic urns, often fashioned with individuals dressed as one of the many deities of the Zapotec pantheon. Monte Albán's most famous tomb, Tomb 7, was originally built during the city's Classic

period occupation (250–800 C.E.). However, well after the city had been entirely abandoned, it was re-entered from the roof and reused. Its spectacular offerings—jade, amber, and rock crystal artifacts; gold, silver, and turquoise jewelry, and finely carved jaguar bones—were not placed in honor of a single dignitary, but instead the funerary chamber was repurposed in the fourteenth century as an ossuary for the bundled remains of revered ancestors brought to the sacred mountain from faraway regions.

Toward the end of the eighth century, as Monte Albán's population began to relocate to towns on the valley floor, the ceremonial center fell into disrepair. The reasons for the city's abandonment remain unclear. Some scholars suggest that geopolitical changes following the collapse of Teotihuacan may have triggered political and economic problems for the Zapotec capital, but others argue that the disruption stemmed from challenges to royal authority by members of the nobility.

Above View of the site showing its spectacular setting.

TIKAL CITY OF THE MAYA

TYPE: CITY • **ARCHITECTURAL STYLE:** TEMPLES, PALACES, AND BALLCOURTS
LOCATION: PETÉN, GUATEMALA • **CONSTRUCTION BEGUN:** SEVENTH CENTURY B.C.E.

With its temples rising above the forest canopy, Tikal occupies an important watershed in the lush jungles of Guatemala's lowland Petén Province. One of the best-studied sites in the Maya area, the city was first occupied around 800 B.C.E. on what was a key trade route connecting the Usumacinta River drainage with the Caribbean Sea. The site's 988-acre (400-ha) core, which includes its principal monumental architecture, is now the cornerstone of the Tikal National Park, a World Heritage property.

By the first century C.E. Tikal had developed into a low-density agrarian city ruled by the dynasty founded by Yax Ehb' Xook (First Step Shark). Tikal's cultural climax took place after it defeated rival Calakmul in 695 C.E. and initiated a political revival that lasted two centuries. At this time the city's population is estimated to have been around 60,000.

Tikal's Great Plaza, bounded on the east and west by the magnificent Temples I and II respectively, is the ceremonial core of the site. The 154 ft- (47 m-) high Temple I on the east side of the plaza memorializes the tomb of King Jasaw Chan K'awiil I (682–734 C.E.), conqueror of Calakmul. Temple II on the opposite side was raised as a cenotaph to his wife. The North Acropolis, which rises to the north, contains many royal tombs surmounted by commemorative temples. To the south, the Central Acropolis, a maze of forty-six buildings organized around six courtyards, was the royal palace. To the southwest of the Great Plaza is another ceremonial precinct where several of Tikal's early rulers were buried. Known as the Lost World, it is dominated by the

Opposite Tikal's North Acropolis is formed from pyramids with temples that commemorate the tombs of early kings.
Right Found in Tikal's Great Plaza, Stela 9 (475 C.E.) depicts King K'an Chitam ("Precious Peccary").

105 ft- (32 m-) high pyramid with stairways on each side (called radial pyramids) that were once flanked by huge stucco masks. One of the most significant discoveries from this complex is the famous Marcador stone, whose texts document Teotihuacan's takeover of the city in 378 C.E.

Raised causeways—some almost 164 ft (50 m) wide—connect the major temples and building complexes at Tikal. They served both as roadways and water-catchment systems, designed to channel runoff from the plazas into a reservoir on the west side of the Central Acropolis. The city's largest temples, those whose roof combs rise above the forest canopy, are all in the southern section of the site; Temple IV, which stands almost 213 ft (65 m) high, is the most massive, while Temple VI, the Temple of the Inscriptions, bears a long text on the back of its roof comb recounting the city's legendary history. Carved wooden lintels spanned most of the temple rooms. With the exceptions of those from Temples I and III, these superb works of art are now scattered among various museums outside of Guatemala.

The Maya Cosmos

One of the most distinctive types of architectural complex at Tikal is the Twin Pyramid Group. Starting in the sixth century C.E., nine of these were built to commemorate the ending of successive *katun* cycles (7,200 days, almost twenty years). Their layout replicates the Maya cosmos and consists of a raised plaza with two opposing radial pyramids, one at the east end and one at the west. Nine plain altar-stele pairs are lined up in front of the east pyramid. On the south side is a long building with multiple doorways and on the north there is a small roofless enclosure with a carved stele and altar. The east and west pyramids mark the sun's passage across the sky, while the nine doorways of the south building allude to the nine levels of the underworld. The structure on the north is open to the celestial realm, and it is here that the king's sacred monuments were placed.

Above top Tikal's temples soar above the forest canopy of the Guatemalan jungle.

Above The Guatemalan government has provided modern firepits for indigenous pilgrims to make burnt offerings at Tikal and other ancient sites.

Tikal's Stelae

The most common sculptural formats used at Tikal were the stele and altar. A total of 231 of these monuments are known from the site, and of these, seventy are carved with finely dressed kings and queens accompanied by texts chronicling their lineages and their victories. Stela 11 (869 C.E.) is Tikal's last dated monument and marks the beginning of a sharp decline in royal power. Like many other centers in the southern Maya lowlands, ninth-century Tikal had reached the limits of its resources, and when an extended drought struck, the realm was unable to overcome the shortages caused by the climatic shift. All over the region, city after city plummeted into social chaos and, eventually, political collapse. During the next 150 years Tikal was taken over by squatters before being abandoned to the jungle.

The flora and fauna of Tikal Park are as compelling as the ruined city, so plan some extra time to explore. Tickets are best acquired prior to arrival.

COPÁN MAYA CAPITAL OF THE SOUTHEAST

TYPE: CITY • **ARCHITECTURAL STYLE:** TEMPLES, PALACES, AND BALLCOURTS
LOCATION: WESTERN HONDURAS • **CONSTRUCTION BEGUN:** FIFTH CENTURY C.E.

High-relief-carved stone monuments and sculptural facades epitomize the remains at Copán, one of the first Maya sites studied by archaeologists. Located in a fertile valley on the southeastern periphery of the Maya lowlands in western Honduras, the civic-ceremonial area was built along the west bank of the Copán River, from which the site takes its name.

Hieroglyphic inscriptions at Copán document a flourishing relationship with the ancient city of Teotihuacan in the early fifth century C.E. The site was already a prominent center well before that time, but its dynasty was not inaugurated until 426 C.E., when Yax K'uk' Mo' (First Quetzal Macaw) arrived—possibly from Tikal—to establish a dominion that lasted more than four hundred years.

The Great Plaza lies at the northern end of the monumental area, and contains seven remarkable three-dimensional portrait stelae of the city's thirteenth ruler and various altars. On the south side of the plaza, an elegant ballcourt with sculpted macaw imagery transitions to the magnificently restored Hieroglyphic Stairway of Temple 26. Carved with the longest known Maya inscription, the 2,200 glyphs on the stairway's sixty-three risers narrate the city's dynastic history up to the mid-eighth century.

Just beyond is the Acropolis, an elevated complex of pyramids, tombs, and courts dominated by Temple 16. Tunnels excavated into the platform supporting this temple documented a series of previous structures, including the spectacularly well-preserved Rosalia; all were built to memorialize the tomb of the founder, Yax K'uk' Mo', deep below. More than three hundred years later, in 776 C.E., Copán's sixteenth ruler dedicated Altar Q in the West Court at the base of Temple 16 to legitimize his right to the throne. This quadrangular monument displays the realm's sixteen rulers on its sides and a summary of Copán's dynastic history on its surface. Structure 22, in the East Court, is another striking building. Created in 715 C.E., to celebrate the twentieth anniversary of the thirteenth ruler's enthronement, it was designed to represent the sacred mountain where maize was born; in addition, the inner temple doorway is carved with an array of fantastic creatures from Maya cosmology that defines the chamber as the mountain's sacred cave.

A series of raised causeways connected other architectural assemblages to the Great Plaza. One of these, Las Sepulturas, was an upper-class residential

Opposite The inner doorway of the temple of Structure 22 in the East Court of the Acropolis.

Above, top West platform of Copán's principle ballcourt.

Above, bottom Altar Q commemorates Ruler 16's accession to the throne in 763 C.E.

neighborhood. Here, the House of the Bacabs, the palace of a royal courtier, provides an example of the finest Maya hieroglyphic writing. Its facade is embellished with two niches, each containing a scribe framed by the jaws of the underworld. Inside, finely sculpted full-figure glyphs inscribed on the 21.7 ft- (6.6 m-) long stone bench record its dedication in 773 C.E.

Copán declined quickly after its last monument, left unfinished, was fashioned in 822 C.E. Environmental degradation and power struggles may explain the kingdom's dynastic failure, but populations continued to live in and around Copán for another four centuries.

Any visit must include the Sculpture Museum, which has a magnificent replica of the Rosalia temple.

THE MAYA REALM OF **PALENQUE**

TYPE: CITY · **ARCHITECTURAL STYLE:** TEMPLES, PALACES, AND TOMBS
LOCATION: CHIAPAS, MEXICO · **CONSTRUCTION BEGUN:** FIFTH CENTURY C.E.

Long acknowledged as one of the most captivating Maya sites, Palenque is located on the northwestern frontier of the Maya lowlands in modern Mexico. From its vantage point on a limestone ridge leading into the Chiapas Highlands, it has a commanding view of the wide plains of the Gulf Coast. The city's original name, Lakamha (Great Waters), perhaps refers to the nine perennial streams that cascade down the three terraces upon which it was built. However, the name of the kingdom itself was B'aakal (Bone).

Palenque is famous in the annals of archaeology for two principal reasons. First, excavations in 1952 discovered a spectacular royal tomb beneath the Temple of the Inscriptions, confirming that many Maya pyramids were not just platforms to support temples but also were commemorative funerary buildings. Second, during the 1970s, its lengthy inscriptions played a key role in the decipherment of Maya hieroglyphic script.

The site was initially occupied around 250 B.C.E., but its first recorded dynasty was not founded until 431 C.E. by K'uk' Balam (Quetzal Jaguar; 397–435 C.E.). Significantly, this coincides with Teotihuacan's meddling in the royal lineages of Tikal and Copán and suggests that Palenque's dynasty may have been installed as part of this power play. In any event, by the end of the sixth century Palenque's kings had added the name of the sun god, K'inich, to their title as an explicit declaration of the divine source of their authority.

The late sixth century was a turbulent period in the city's history. With the death of King Kan B'alam (Snake Jaguar) in 583 C.E. without a male heir, his daughter Yohl Ik'nal (Heart of the Wind Place) became queen, one of the few Maya women to achieve that title; perhaps as an unforeseen consequence, during the next two decades

Palenque was pillaged on various occasions by rival Calakmul. Political problems persisted until 615 C.E., when K'inich Janaab' Pakal (Great Sun Shield), then a twelve-year-old boy, took the throne. His rule, and that of his sons and grandsons, marked Palenque's cultural climax in art and architecture.

One of Pakal's projects was the renovation of the Palace. The building, which rests upon a 33 ft- (10 m-) high platform with wide staircases and outer galleries on three sides, dominates the Central Plaza. Inside, a labyrinth of rooms and airy galleries opens onto sunken courtyards. Like other structures at the site, the Palace's exterior walls, mansard-like roofs, and roof combs bear the remains of naturalistic figures modeled in stucco that once were brightly painted. The four-story tower in the southwest patio is unique to Palenque and may have served as a watchtower or observatory.

Off the southwest corner of the Palace, the Temple of the Inscriptions commemorates Pakal's tomb. The vaulted burial chamber at the base of a long interior stairway contains a huge stone sarcophagus whose spectacular lid is carved with a scene of the king's rebirth as the maize

Left View of the civic-ceremonial core of Palenque.

Above The Temple of the Sun in the Cross Group. The piers of its wide doorways, its mansard-like roof, and its roof comb were all embellished with sculpted stucco figures.

Left A polychrome panel in Temple XIX, dedicated in 734 c.e., depicts the crown prince, Upakal K'inich, in ceremonial dress.

Above The lid of K'inich Janaab' Pakal's sarcophagus shows the rebirth of the king and his ascension into the heavens from the maw of the Underworld.

Opposite Seen from the Temple of the Inscriptions, Palenque's Palace consists of galleries and rooms arranged around sunken courts.

god after falling into the jaws of the Underworld; the sides of the coffin bear images of the king's ancestors shown sprouting from the earth like trees. Pakal's body was covered in toxic red cinnabar (mercuric oxide)—perhaps intended to preserve the royal remains—and richly adorned with jade jewelry. Directly to the west of his tomb, in Temple XIII, is the lavish cinnabar-rich burial of Tz'ak-b'u Ajaw (Lady of the Succession), Pakal's consort and mother of the two kings who succeeded their father.

East of the Palace, Pakal's eldest son, Kan B'alam II, constructed the temples of the Cross Group. Famous for their finely carved bas-relief limestone panels, the iconography and texts on these buildings deal with the birth of Palenque's gods, ancestral regeneration, agricultural fertility, and warfare, specifically Kan B'alam II's conquest of Toniná in 687 C.E. In recent years, more carved panels have been recovered from Palenque's temples XIX and XXI, enhancing our knowledge of the city and its rulers.

Palenque was one of the first Maya realms to fail. Its last known inscription dates to 799 C.E., and over the next two decades, as royals and nobles abandoned the city, its elegant residences and temples were occupied by squatters. Although the political authority of some other dynasties was undermined by a ninth-century drought, the abundance of water at Palenque suggests that its demise was different from that of its peers. Archaeologists have suggested that, in addition to the loss of forest habitat to agriculture, Palenque's stability may have been undermined by new maritime trade routes that shifted commerce to the coast.

Palenque's hot, humid jungle calls for insect repellent, long sleeves, and pants. It rains year round, so it is best to visit in the drier, cooler months of January and February.

THE MAYA KINGDOM OF **TONINÁ**

TYPE: CITY • **ARCHITECTURAL STYLE:** TEMPLES, PALACES, AND BALLCOURT
LOCATION: CHIAPAS, MEXICO • **CONSTRUCTION BEGUN:** FIFTH CENTURY C.E.

Nestled against the piedmont of the Ocosingo Valley, in the Mexican state of
Chiapas, where humid lowland jungles give way to the pine forests of the chilly
highlands, Toniná presides over the western Maya frontier. Although it is often
considered a minor center, archaeological and epigraphic evidence demonstrates
that Toniná was actively engaged in the trade networks and geopolitics of the
Maya lowlands between 550 and 900 C.E. The site is famous for the quality of its
three-dimensional sandstone sculptures of kings and captives, carved thrones
and panels, and the magnificent stucco friezes that still decorate some buildings.

The site's center has two main parts, the Great Plaza and the Acropolis; together they represent the flat primordial sea from which the sacred mountain of Mesoamerican cosmology rises. At the eastern edge of the plaza, a sunken ballcourt marks the entrance to the underworld. During the ballcourt's earliest construction phase, serpent heads carved in the Teotihuacan style decorated its sloping walls; later, after it and various temples were ritually destroyed in 687 C.E. by the rival kingdom of Palenque, these were replaced with sculptures of bound captives to commemorate the conquests of the city's third king, K'inich B'aaknal Chaak (Great-Sun Bone-place Rain God; 652–715 C.E.) in 699 and the realm's restoration. This ruler would go on to vanquish Palenque in 711, taking its king captive in revenge.

To the north of the Great Plaza, the Acropolis is a modified seven-tiered hill that towers 246 ft (73 m) over the valley floor, providing an impressive view of the surrounding countryside. The lower four levels have residential and administrative structures, while the upper three levels are dedicated to religious themes—burials on the fifth and temples on the sixth and seventh. The early-ninth-century stucco mural known as the Frieze of the Dream Lords on the platform wall of the sixth level segregates our world from that of the supernatural with a feathered lattice, punctuated with hanging decapitated human heads. This death imagery effectively divides the Acropolis into three vertical sections: the world of the living at its base, the transition to the land of the dead on the fifth level, and the celestial realm on the summit.

Toniná's place name (Popo) was first used in 568 C.E. Five years later, other communities begin to mention the city in their texts, primarily to commemorate the sacrifice of distinguished Toniná warriors. By the late seventh century, poignant sculptures of captive warriors and kings become common at the site, confirming the city's success in battles with other Maya kingdoms. Toniná's sculptures identify the emblem glyphs of its rivals on these monuments, but the name of Toniná is less frequent on those at other sites, suggesting that perhaps its dignitaries were rarely captured. Nonetheless, the absence of references might merely reflect its marginal frontier status. The last known Long Count date in the entire Maya area—January 15, 909—is recorded on Toniná's Monument 101 and it serves to mark the end of Classic period (250–900 C.E.) civilization.

Individual tours to the little-visited site of Toniná and its sculpture museum can be booked in either Palenque or San Cristóbal de las Casas.

Opposite The Frieze of the Dream Lords embellishes the platform wall of the sixth level of the Acropolis. It celebrates themes from Maya mythology about the Underworld.
Above View from the Acropolis of Toniná's main plaza.

CHICHÉN ITZÁ TOLTEC-MAYA CENTER

TYPE: CITY • **ARCHITECTURAL STYLE:** TEMPLES, BALLCOURTS, AND OBSERVATORIES
LOCATION: YUCATÁN, MEXICO • **CONSTRUCTION BEGUN:** FIFTH CENTURY C.E.

The forested yet dry plains of the northern Yucatán Peninsula have no rivers. For water, populations depend on sinkholes (cenotes) in the porous limestone bedrock to gain access to the underground aquifer. Chichén Itzá, which translates as "on the edge of the cenote of the Itzá," itself has four cenotes, the largest and most famous of which is the Cenote of Sacrifice. Here objects of gold, jade, wood, copal resin, rubber, shell, and pottery, in addition to humans, were offered to the rain god Chaak.

The site had a significant population by the seventh century C.E., but it was during the political turmoil that so adversely affected the Maya farther south during the ninth century that Chichén Itzá developed into a major center. While the site covers 5.8 sq mi (15 sq km), most of its monumental buildings are clustered in the 2 sq mi (5 sq km) core, which is divided into two sectors. The southern sector, with its extraordinary mosaic facades of the Puuc architectural style and hieroglyphic inscriptions dating from between 830 and 890 C.E., has the earliest buildings, although those of the northern sector—including the first rendering of the Castillo—were raised shortly thereafter. These latter buildings followed different architectural styles and used a foreign iconography linked to people from central Mexico who arrived in the mid-tenth century. Under the command of the leader K'uk'ulkan (Feathered Serpent or Quetzalcoatl), they introduced a new political order that rejected the conventional institution of kingship that had been central to earlier Maya realms. Some archaeologists interpret this distinctive cultural manifestation, usually referred to as Toltec, as evidence of a politico-religious movement associated with the cult of Quetzalcoatl, which sought to revitalize the Teotihuacan tradition at Chichén Itzá and at Tula in the central Mexican state of Hidalgo, 930 miles (1,500 km) to the west.

Opposite The recumbent Chacmool warrior statue guards the entrance to the Temple of the Warriors.

Above top An eagle and a jaguar, visual metaphors for warriors, devour human hearts on the Platform of the Eagles and Jaguars.

Above The early tenth-century Caracol had an interior spiral staircase that led to an upper story from which the rising of Venus at its northern and southern extremes could be observed.

Toltec–Maya Expression

Built in honor of Kukulkan, at the center of the Great Plaza the Castillo reflects two aspects of the solar calendar. First, its four staircases, one on each side, have ninety-one steps which, when added to a final plinth, total the 365 days of the solar year; and second, because its base is oriented twenty-two degrees east of north, the setting sun on both the March and September equinoxes projects the shadow of the stepped tiers of the pyramid's northwest corner onto the north balustrade. The balustrade terminates in a carved stone serpent's head, creating the illusion of an ophidian undulating to earth from the temple above. Farther south, the Caracol is another building of astronomical significance. Its two-story circular tower has a spiral staircase to the upper level where narrow windows allow the observation of specific celestial events, especially those related to the planet Venus.

The Temple of the Warriors stands at the eastern edge of the Great Plaza. A wide, once roofed colonnade along the western base of its platform is an intrinsic feature of Toltec architecture, as are the two upended, feathered serpent columns that frame the awkwardly recumbent warrior statue known as a Chacmool at the top of its staircase. Southeast of this building is a 4.4-acre (1.8-ha) plaza delimited by more colonnaded halls—the Group of the Thousand Columns—and which may have been the city's marketplace. A network of paved causeways connected Chichén's building complexes and cenotes.

The Great Ballcourt, and its associated skull rack, or *tzompantli*, occupies the west side of the Great Plaza; the interior court, measuring 489 × 118 ft (149 × 36 m), is the largest in Mesoamerica. Its four temples are embellished with murals and reliefs that display warrior imagery and battle scenes, and the lower sloping walls of the court are carved with processions of ballplayers who witness the decapitation of the defeated team captain at the center. All in all, the often metaphorical art of the Toltec period building facades is truly martial, teeming with uniformed soldiers, weaponry, battles led by figures associated with feathered serpents or solar disks, processions of captives, jaguars and eagles devouring human hearts, investiture rituals, episodes of bloodletting, and human sacrifice.

Despite its military might and command of coastal trade from its port at Isla Cerritos on the peninsula's north coast, Chichén Itzá may have succumbed to factional strife. By the end of the eleventh century, construction had ceased and much of the population had departed. However, in 1532, when the Spaniards tried to establish a capital at the cenote, there were still enough people to prevent the invaders from taking the pilgrimage center.

Chichén Itzá is best visited in the early morning or late afternoon to savor the beautiful play of light and shadow over the buildings and avoid the large tour groups.

Right The Casa de las Monjas (the Nunnery) was built in the ninth century baroque Puuc style that typifies the southern sector of Chichén Itzá.

Below The Castillo, built at the center of the Great Plaza, has two substructures; the final version was dedicated to K'uk'ulkan, the Feathered Serpent. In the background, the west facade of the Temple of the Warriors can be seen.

MITLA THE ZAPOTEC CITY OF THE DEAD

TYPE: RELIGIOUS CENTER • **ARCHITECTURAL STYLE:** PALACES AND TOMBS
LOCATION: OAXACA, MEXICO • **CONSTRUCTION BEGUN:** FIFTH CENTURY C.E.

The Zapotec city of Mitla in the Valley of Oaxaca, Mexico, rose to prominence around the ninth century C.E. Not only was it the seat of the oracular high priest, the Huijatoo, but its sanctuaries and tombs safeguarded the bundled remains of important lords, making it central to Zapotec religion after the decline of Monte Albán. Today the site is famous for the extraordinary mosaic facades of its palaces and cruciform tombs.

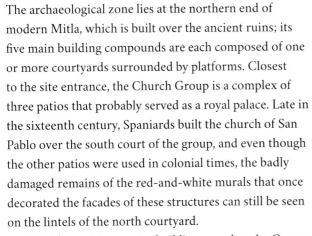

The archaeological zone lies at the northern end of modern Mitla, which is built over the ancient ruins; its five main building compounds are each composed of one or more courtyards surrounded by platforms. Closest to the site entrance, the Church Group is a complex of three patios that probably served as a royal palace. Late in the sixteenth century, Spaniards built the church of San Pablo over the south court of the group, and even though the other patios were used in colonial times, the badly damaged remains of the red-and-white murals that once decorated the facades of these structures can still be seen on the lintels of the north courtyard.

Mitla's most impressive building complex, the Group of the Columns, lies south of the church and consists of two courtyards. The north patio, dominated by the stunning Hall of the Columns on its north side, is thought to have been the residence of the high priest. Once painted red, the 125 ft- (38 m-) span of its outer walls displays mosaic panels made from volcanic ignimbrite that was mined from nearby quarries and then cut into standardized tesserae to create the building's textile-like, step-fret patterns. The entry to this building is an elongated room with six massive monolithic columns that, it is said, once housed statues of the Lord of the Underworld, Pitao Pezeelao, and his consort Xonaxi Quecuya, in addition to the bundled remains of important ancestors. A low

Opposite The main facade of the Hall of the Columns provides an extraordinary example of Zapotec stonework.

Above left The apartments of the Zapotec high priest have the only interior walls embellished with panels of stone fretwork.

Above right The six monolithic stone columns of the reception room of the Hall of the Columns once supported a wooden roof.

L-shaped passageway along the back wall leads to the elaborate apartments of the Huijatoo that, apart from the tombs, are the only buildings in Mitla with fretwork decorating their interior walls. The second plaza of this group, the Patio of the Tombs, is noteworthy for its two underground cruciform tombs, both carved into bedrock. These were used for funerary rituals associated with the veneration of noble ancestors. Significantly, the site's name, in both the Aztec (Mitla or Mictlan) and Zapotec (Liobaa) languages, refers to the land of the dead.

Mitla's position on the valley floor left it vulnerable to attack. A terraced hilltop settlement just west of the site was fortified late in pre-Hispanic history, perhaps to create a refuge in response to Aztec aggression that began during the fifteenth century. When the Spaniards arrived in 1521, Mitla was the principle religious city in Oaxaca, prompting the construction of the Church of San Pablo over its ruins.

Mitla is a short drive from the city of Oaxaca, and several other ruins, including Lambityeco and Yagul, can be visited along the way.

THE FORTIFIED HILLTOP CENTER OF **XOCHICALCO**

TYPE: CITY • **ARCHITECTURAL STYLE:** TEMPLES, PALACES, AND BALLCOURTS
LOCATION: MORELOS, MEXICO • **CONSTRUCTION BEGUN:** EIGHTH CENTURY C.E.

Xochicalco, or Place of the Flower House, is a fortified hilltop center that lies 24 miles (38 km) southwest of Cuernavaca in the Mexican state of Morelos. Guarded access points along the wide paved roads leading into the city and redoubts and lookouts perched on surrounding hills characterize its defensive location. Explorations at the site date back to 1777 and provide a wealth of data that document its key political and economic role in the region's unstable post-Teotihuacan period (650–900 C.E.).

The city's architects modified the rugged topography to hierarchically organize urban space. At the summit of the hill, the ruling family and its dependents lived in a protected two-story palace (the Acropolis), overlooking the main plaza where the site's most famous structure, the Temple of the Plumed Serpents, is located. Terraces with high retaining walls descend irregularly from this ample esplanade; many of these support important buildings, including three ballcourts. The center's 10,000–15,000 inhabitants lived in small residential compounds grouped into neighborhoods, each with at least one temple or administrative building.

Xochicalco's art meshes the styles and iconography of different regions. For example, the Temple of the Plumed Serpents uses a Teotihuacan-derived architectural profile,

but its imagery presents Maya-style bearded plumed serpents undulating around individuals portrayed in the manner of Maya kings, and calendrical glyphs that recall the Zapotec scribal tradition. Scholars have suggested that the personages enfolded by the structure's plumed serpents are the royal ancestors of the sovereign who commissioned the monument. On the panel above, a frieze of cartouches, each with a seated individual and place glyphs, might celebrate the tribute payments from subject towns. Little remains of the temple, but on the lower north wall a seated warrior bearing a shield, three darts, and a spear-thrower can still be seen.

Like so many Mesoamerican sites, Xochicalco has an astronomical observatory. It consists of an underground chamber with a 28.5 ft (8.7 m) shaft leading to the plaza floor above. Specialists have shown that the shaft could be used to observe the zenith passage in May and July as the sun transits to and from the Tropic of Cancer.

In the 1960s, archaeologists discovered three stelae that had been broken and buried beneath the floor of one of Xochicalco's temples (Building A). They are red-painted rectangular blocks, deeply carved on all four sides with images and glyphs that recall the Teotihuacan and Zapotec traditions. Some researchers believe that the face depicted on the front of each monument refers to a deity (Sun, Rain, and Earth), while others maintain that the place signs, dates, and other glyphs memorialize the victorious campaigns of three great rulers: 7 Reptile Eye, 7 Rain, and 4 Movement. These and other monuments provide some of the earliest uncontested evidence for a writing system in central Mexico.

Despite widespread political and trade connections that gave it an international flavor, Xochicalco's occupation, like that of other cities founded during these centuries, was short-lived, lasting from 700 to 900 C.E., when it was savagely sacked and burned. Xochicalco is easily reached from nearby Cuernavaca and is best visited in the early morning or late afternoon. The site museum is well worth a visit.

Opposite Detail of the carving on the sloping base of the Temple of the Plumed Serpents.
Above View across the site.

TENOCHTITLAN AZTEC CAPITAL

TYPE: ISLAND CITY • **ARCHITECTURAL STYLE:** TEMPLES AND MONUMENTS
LOCATION: MEXICO CITY, MEXICO • **CONSTRUCTION BEGUN:** FOURTEENTH CENTURY C.E.

In 1519 the Spanish conquistador Hernando Cortés described the Aztec capital of Tenochtitlan by comparing it to cities back home—in size it was like Seville or Córdoba, its main market twice the area of Salamanca's. It was a city of canals and canoes, with palaces, plazas, monumental sculptures, schools, ballcourts, an aqueduct to bring fresh water into the city center, imperial gardens, and a zoo. The four wide causeways that connected the island city to the mainland had wooden bridges that the islanders could remove during a siege. In a letter to the Spanish Crown, Cortés writes of a Great Temple, located within a walled precinct with seventy-seven other buildings, and taller than the belltower of Seville's Cathedral. Most of what he saw, however, was soon demolished as Spanish civilization steadily razed the pre-Columbian structures and used the stone to erect its own churches, administrative buildings, and residences.

Fragments of the Aztec city are sometimes uncovered by public works projects. For example, during the renovation of Mexico City's main square in 1790, several of the temple precinct's monuments were recovered; a few, considered monstrosities of the devil, were dynamited. Tunneling for the urban subway system, initiated in 1966, has produced many significant finds, including the small shrine preserved at the downtown Pino Suárez station. However, it was the 1978 discovery of a 10.5 ft (3.25 m) stone disk carved with the dismembered corpse of the goddess Coyolxauhqui that triggered large-scale excavations to salvage the remains of the Great Temple and surrounding buildings.

The Great Temple that Cortés visited in 1519 stood 148 ft (45 m) high while its sides measured 269 ft (82 m) on a side, but today only the foundations remain. It was designed to represent the sacred mountain of Aztec mythology and to reflect the two primary aspects of the imperial economy: agriculture and warfare. Thus the north staircase on its west facade leads to the temple of the rain god Tlaloc (agricultural fertility) while the south staircase rises to that of the solar

war god Huitzilopochtli (conquest). Huitzilopochtli was the patron god of the Aztecs, and his side of the four-tiered platform is embellished with allusions to his miraculous birth on Coatepec (Snake Mountain) and the dismemberment of his sister, Coyolxauhqui. Today, however, only the second of the Great Temple's seven building stages is entirely preserved, dated 1428 C.E.

Flanking the Great Temple on the north is the House of the Eagle Warriors, a ritual structure for Aztec military sodalities. Its stone benches are carved with soldiers marching beneath feathered serpents, and almost life-sized terracotta statues—two of eagle warriors and two of the eerie Lord of the Underworld—once flanked interior doorways. Recently, Mexico's Urban Archaeology Program discovered Tenochtitlan's Huey Tzompantli (Great Wall of Skulls) that once displayed the decapitated heads of captives sacrificed in front of Huitzilopochtli's temple. Next door, in the basement of the Spanish Cultural Center, remains of the school for young nobles (the Calmecac) can be viewed through "archaeological windows" open to the public.

The City's Treasures

As the seat of a great empire that spanned most of central Mexico, Tenochtitlan received tributes from faraway regions. Some items, including jaguars, swordfish, corals, sea stars, objects of jade, gold, and obsidian, pottery, and "animated" flint knives, were placed in stone offering boxes beneath the pavement surrounding the Great Temple. Many of these objects, and monumental sculptures, such as that of the clawed earth deity Tlaltecuhtli, are in the site museum. Like Rome and other ancient imperial capitals, Tenochtitlan was filled with statuary meant to impress and intimidate.

Tenochtitlan was founded in 1325 C.E. on an island in the middle of a brackish lake by a group of migrants from the north, the Mexica. For a century, the Mexica served as mercenaries for the city of Azcapotzalco, but in 1427 they allied themselves with other city-states to defeat their overlords and establish their independence. Twenty years later they began to conquer areas beyond the Valley of Mexico. By 1519, the empire's thirty-eight tributary provinces extended from the Gulf Coast to the Pacific Ocean. Although the Spanish conquest of the Aztec empire is often attributed to guns, horses, and infectious diseases, the invaders would not have been able to defeat the 200,000 inhabitants of Tenochtitlan in August 1521 without the help of their native allies, disaffected groups who had been overtaxed by the imperial system, and who saw this event as a victory over hated overlords, not a foreign conquest.

While the Great Temple and its site museum are core features of Aztec archaeology, many other monuments and building fragments can be found on walking tours of Mexico City's historic center.

Below Excavations in the heart of Mexico City have uncovered the foundations of Tenochtitlan's Great Temple and other buildings of the ritual precinct.

THE INCA CITADEL OF **MACHU PICCHU**

TYPE: CEREMONIAL AND RESIDENTIAL CENTER • **ARCHITECTURAL STYLE:** IMPERIAL INCA
LOCATION: CUZCO, SOUTHERN PERUVIAN HIGHLANDS • **CONSTRUCTION BEGUN:** FIFTEENTH CENTURY C.E.

Set within the high Andean landscape, the citadel of Machu Picchu is one of the greatest wonders of civilization. It epitomizes the skills of its builders, the Incas, in harmonizing the natural rugged landscape with their sophisticated stone-based architecture.

Machu Picchu is one of the most visited archaeological sites in Peru. The best known of the Inca sites, it was discovered by American explorer Hiram Bingham during an expedition to Cuzco sponsored by Yale University in 1911. Bingham was trying to find the last zone of resistance of the Incas during the Spanish conquest, the mythical site of Vilcabamba. Two years after his archaeological investigations here, the first article about Machu Picchu appeared in *National Geographic*.

A Rugged Landscape

The site is located in the Urubamba valley, 50 miles (80 km) northwest of the city of Cuzco, on a route that leads to the tropical forest. Built on top of a mountain some 7,970 ft (2,430 m) above sea level, the citadel covers an area of approximately 12.3 acres (5 ha) and, at its height, could have housed some 750 people.

According to archaeologists, the Incas founded Machu Picchu during the first half of the fifteenth century, possibly as a royal estate for their most famous emperor, Pachacutec. The construction of Machu Picchu in such a rugged area of high rainfall and dense vegetation required the Inca architects to stabilize the terrain. One of the main solutions was the construction of terraces, or platforms, on the mountain slopes, to provide level surfaces on which they could build.

This site is divided into two large areas: an agricultural area comprises a vast network of artificial terraces, while the urban area contains various constructions and plazas, including the Temple of the Sun, the Intihuatana Stone, and Temple of the Three Windows.

Left Temple of the Sun in Machu Picchu. In Inca architecture, the curved walls are related to religious functions.

Opposite Panoramic view of Machu Picchu. In the background rises the Huayna Picchu mountain.

The Site's Main Buildings

Machu Picchu has all the classic architectural components of an Inca city: squares, temples, palaces, astronomical observatories, residences for both the elite and their servants, and warehouses. In addition, there are unique buildings such as the Temple of the Sun. Standing on a large rocky outcrop, the temple's upper part features a semicircular wall that frames the upper part of the outcrop, the surface of which is marked with carvings. The walls have windows to allow observations and measurements of the movement of the sun. One window in particular lets in sunlight during the June solstice, to illuminate the carved rock inside. Below this structure, at the base of the outcrop of carved rock, is a cave. Its walls are carved and large trapezoidal niches hewn. At the entrance, the stone is carved to create a step. Even from inside this so-called mausoleum, it is possible to see mountain peaks. As such, Machu Picchu highlights the use of rocky outcrops, which the Incas carved to mimic certain natural forms of the surrounding landscape.

The Intihuatana Stone dominates the upper part of one of the most important sectors of the site. This stone, sculpted from a single piece of rock, sits atop a pyramidal rock platform. Archaeologists suggest that it was the sanctuary, or main huaca, of Machu Picchu, since its location provides an important view of the sacred mountains of the region, and an ideal spot from which to make astronomical observations for agricultural rituals.

Another impressive building at Machu Picchu is the Temple of the Three Windows, located in the sector of the Sacred Square. The three windows of this structure allow excellent views of the mountains and the Urubamba River, located to the east of the site. Excavations in this sector uncovered ceramic fragments, and it has been suggested that these may have been used in ceremonial rituals.

If you are in good physical shape, you can get to the site by trekking across the mountains. There is a museum in the nearby little town of Aguas Calientes.

Opposite, from top Urban sector of Machu Picchu. Terraces built to support plazas and architectural structures can be seen. The Temple of the Sun is located in the lower left corner. The Temple of the Condor in Machu Picchu combines carved stone outcrops with stone masonry.

Above, from top Temple of Three Windows. Temple of the Sun. Intihuatana Stone.

ANCIENT MUD CITY OF **CHAN CHAN**

TYPE: URBAN AND CEREMONIAL CENTER • **ARCHITECTURAL STYLE:** CHIMÚ
LOCATION: TRUJILLO, NORTHERN PERUVIAN COAST • **CONSTRUCTION BEGUN:** TWELFTH CENTURY C.E.

On the north bank of the Moche Valley in northern Peru lies the largest mud city in the Americas. Occupying an area of 7.7 sq mi (20 sq km), it is an impressive site that houses ten walled citadels (*ciudadelas*) built by the Chimú society (ca. 900–1470 C.E.), quite literally from a mixture of water and earth. The citadels are named Chayhuac, Uhle, Laberinto, Gran Chimú, Squier, Velarde, Bandelier, Tschudi, Rivero, and Tello. Together they constitute the city of Chan Chan, capital of the Chimor kingdom.

This city is located 3 miles (5 km) northwest of the city of Trujillo, in the Department of La Libertad, between the districts of Trujillo and Huanchaco. It is almost always sunny here, so it should come as no surprise that the name of Chan Chan translated as "shining sun."

The citadels were erected in a process that lasted, according to archaeological evidence, at least 300 years. During all this time, they underwent social, political, and economic change. Each citadel was a large rectangular enclosure with very high walls and restricted access.

These were the residences of the leaders of Chimú society, and served as their palaces, meeting and ritual areas, warehouses, and even mausoleums. High-relief decoration on the surface of the walls ranges from the depiction of coastal animals to geometric shapes. Since the citadels also included the mausoleums of the rulers, these buildings required a great investment in their construction. Eight of them had one or more mortuary platforms, all rendered in similar style and orientation. Members of the family maintained the mausoleums, highly restricted spaces in the

most intimate locations within the citadel. Human sacrifices were found in the main mausoleums of the citadels. It is estimated that around 300 young women could have been buried in secondary burial chambers surrounding the main chamber in the Huaca Las Avispas.

Beside the citadels, the site's architecture indicates a strong stratification of society, with different areas inhabited by people of differing status. For example, of the 140 wells supplying water to the city, 60 percent of them were located in the monumental zone and only 12 percent in the residential neighborhoods that were home to more than 90 percent of the population.

Due to its architecture and state of conservation, the city became a UNESCO World Heritage site in 1986. The site also features an important museum. A visit to the nearby beach town of Huanchaco is highly recommended.

Above left Decorations and walls with friezes made with mud in the Tschudi citadel.

Above Mud friezes depicting seabirds in the Tschudi citadel.

Below The front of the main plaza in the Tschudi citadel. Friezes decorate the main walls.

ANCIENT PILGRIMAGE CENTER OF
CHAVÍN DE HUÁNTAR

TYPE: CEREMONIAL AND RESIDENTIAL CENTER • **ARCHITECTURAL STYLE:** CHAVÍN
LOCATION: ANCASH, NORTHERN PERUVIAN HIGHLANDS • **CONSTRUCTION BEGUN:**
TWELFTH CENTURY B.C.E.

Nestling at the junction of the Mosna and Wacheqsa rivers at 10,335 ft (3,150 m)
above sea level, Chavín de Huántar is one of several important pilgrimage
and worship centers in the pre-Hispanic Andes. Located at the upper end of
the Conchucos Valley in the northern highlands of Peru, the site was built and
occupied mainly between 1200 and 500 B.C.E.

Listed as a World Heritage site by UNESCO, the Chavín de
Huántar archaeological site has impressive monumentality
and antiquity. Above all, its sculptural art in stone has
attracted attention since the nineteenth century, the
principal investigator being the Peruvian archaeologist
Julio C. Tello (1880–1947). The site was founded around
1200 B.C.E. and lasted almost a millennium, during which
time the architecture was extended. In addition, the
human settlement grew. At its peak, Chavín would have
had a population of 3,000 inhabitants.

The Temples
The monumental area of the site comprises a
concentration of buildings whose construction must have
required a great deal of work. They are built of stone and
mud, among which some large blocks of carved stone
stand out. Stone sculptures and lithic blocks with designs
in high and low relief depict hybrid beings that combine
humans, felines, birds of prey, and reptiles.

Right The monolithic Lanzón of Chavín de Huántar.
Opposite The sunken circular plaza in Chavín de
Huántar. The stairway leads to the Old Temple.

The most important architectural structures within the Chavín de Huántar complex are the so-called New Temple and the Old Temple. Both buildings are fronted by plazas and feature galleries inside and underground. On the back wall of the New Temple, one of the "tenon heads" is located in its original place. Over the years, archaeologists and inhabitants of the area have recovered more than a hundred of these heads that would originally have adorned the outer walls of the Chavín temples. Made of stone, they depict various anthropomorphic and zoomorphic beings, highlighting the presence of feline and raptor traits.

A number of structures here are reconstructions made in their original places. Among these, the Black and White Portal of the New Temple stands out—two large columns of stone, one dark and one light, on which low-relief designs depict anthropomorphic beings with raptor features. Both columns support stone blocks with carved designs.

Above Panoramic view of Chavín de Huántar. In the foreground are the quadrangular plaza and the New Temple is beyond it.

Below The Black and White Portal was made with lithic blocks, and is located in the front of the New Temple.

Opposite A tenon head in its original location. This lithic sculpture is located in the back wall of the New Temple.

on all four sides and depicts a pair of complex zoomorphic beings, difficult to interpret at first glance. Archaeologists believe it is a caiman, which would indicate the important influence of the Amazon region for Chavín leaders. In addition, if you look closely, you can see that it represents two different sexes adorned with iconographic elements inspired by botanical products and animals from different areas of the Andean world.

The Raimondi Stele represents an anthropomorphic being with feline characteristics and other attributes related to snakes. The figure holds a staff in each hand, a symbol of power. Because of its morphology and iconography, this stele must have decorated an important wall of a main building on the site, although the exact location has not been determined.

Chavín de Huántar was, at one time, the center of a pan-Andean religious cult that attracted many social groups, especially elites from other places. They came here seeking knowledge about nature and supernatural powers from the leaders of Chavín. Ritual practices were facilitated by the consumption of hallucinogenic plants, which induced altered states of consciousness. The intimidating architecture and sounds produced during the ceremony contributed to the experience.

The site's museum is in the modern town of Chavín.

Several other structures are worth seeing. In its original position within the main gallery of the Old Temple, the Lanzón is a monolith about 14.8 ft (4.5 m) high, sculpted in the form of a spearhead. This large stone depicts an anthropomorphic being with feline features.

Almost as impressive in size as the Lanzón, the Tello Obelisk measures 8.2 ft (2.52 m). Its surface is decorated

MOCHE HUACAS DEL SOL AND DE LA LUNA

TYPE: CEREMONIAL AND URBAN CENTER • **ARCHITECTURAL STYLE:** MOCHE
LOCATION: TRUJILLO, NORTHERN PERUVIAN COAST • **CONSTRUCTION BEGUN:** FIRST CENTURY C.E.

Rising up out of the arid desert landscape of northern Peru are the well-preserved remains of two pre-Hispanic monuments, the Huacas del Sol and La Luna. The site here was founded in the first century C.E. and abandoned in the ninth century. Its monumental architectural constructions, wealthy tombs, sculptured pottery, and metal artifacts represent one of the most important architectural complexes of sophisticated Moche society.

The two huacas are made from a huge number of rectangular adobe bricks, arranged in a series of monumental stepped platforms. During the whole period that Moche society lasted, people built and remodeled the huacas in several phases. It was this overlapping of new construction phases and remodeling of the structures over time that gave the huacas their final appearance.

The Huaca del Sol is the most imposing building and one of the most voluminous architectural works of South America. It is estimated that it would originally have been 1,130 ft (345 m) long by 525 ft (160 m) wide at its base, with a height of more than 131 ft (40 m). Archaeological investigations are relatively recent, but there is evidence that this huaca served as a political and administrative building.

The main platform of the Huaca de la Luna is about 950 ft (290 m) long by 690 ft (210 m) wide at its base, with a height of 66 ft (20 m). High-relief murals with depictions of human sacrifice suggest this structure served a religious purpose. Within, a series of enclosures and plazas characterize the Huaca de la Luna, with well-preserved polychrome murals depicting scenes relating to religion and the Moche political structure. Made from mud, in high relief, the figures in the friezes and the areas between them were painted in bright colors—mainly red, yellow,

white, and black. On the main facade it is possible to see a series of personages depicted at different levels, suggesting the existence of hierarchies in the Moche cosmovision. Friezes also exist in the interior of the Huaca de la Luna with more repetitive decorations that include the head of an anthropomorphic being with feline features inside diamond-shaped designs.

Opposite Detail of a polychrome frieze located in an inner enclosure of Huaca de la Luna.

Below View of the urban core of Huacas de Moche. In the background are Huaca de la Luna and Cerro Blanco.

At the base of Cerro Blanco, Plaza 3A revealed the remains of around a hundred male bodies. According to the archaeological and bioanthropological evidence, the Moche people sacrificed these men during a period associated with climatic crises related to El Niño, the warm phase of the El Niño–Southern Oscillation (ENSO), during the sixth century C.E.

Urban Core

In between Huaca del Sol and Huaca de la Luna, a series of architectural spaces coexisted with the main buildings. This was the urban area, home to permanent inhabitants of the city, principally specialist craftspeople who offered their products to the Moche elites. There is evidence here of workshops where ceramics, textiles, and metal and stone artifacts were produced. It is estimated that between 15,000 and 25,000 inhabitants would have lived at the site at its peak, and the city is generally accepted as the capital of this political entity.

Archaeologists believe that Moche society comprised at least two major regions: the Northern Moche and Southern Moche. Commonly referred to as the Huacas de Moche, the monuments here are the work of the Southern Moche, and are located in the lower Moche Valley on the outskirts of the modern city of Trujillo on the north coast of Peru. The site features a museum in which many of the site's remains are on display.

Left Polychrome friezes on walls and an enclosure located in a corner of the main plaza of Huaca de la Luna.

Above Panoramic view of Huaca del Sol. Behind this building, the Moche valley and Trujillo city can be seen.

THE PILGRIMAGE CENTER OF
PACHACAMAC

TYPE: RELIGIOUS AND POLITICAL CENTER • **ARCHITECTURAL STYLE:** LIMA, YCHMA AND INCA
LOCATION: LIMA, PERUVIAN CENTRAL COAST • **CONSTRUCTION BEGUN:** FIRST CENTURY C.E.

Taking advantage of the wealth of the land and its proximity to the sea,
the Pachacamac sanctuary occupies an area on the right bank of the Lurin
River, south of what is now Lima, the capital of Peru. It was one of the most
important of the pre-Hispanic ceremonial centers for more than a thousand
years, and the site was home to an important divinity that was believed to
"animate" the world.

Pachacamac dates from the Early Intermediate Period (ca. 200 B.C.E.–600 C.E.) to the Late Horizon (ca. 1450–1532 C.E.). Covering 1,150 acres (465 ha) today, it features a number of notable architectural structures that include the Old Temple, the Painted Temple, the Pyramids with Ramps, the Temple of the Sun, the Acllahuasi, the Palace of Tauri Chumpi, and the Pilgrims' Square.

Built from mudbricks on a rocky promontory, the Old Temple is Pachacamac's oldest building, and is currently very damaged. The Painted Temple is a stepped structure, built using adobe bricks and stone. Most noteworthy is its terraced facade with walls painted with colorful scenes representing anthropomorphic beings, plants, and fishes. Excavation work unearthed what has become known as the Idol of Pachacamac, a wooden pole that represents an anthropomorphic being with two faces. At the base of the Painted Temple in pre-Hispanic times was an important cemetery that was first systematically excavated at the end of the nineteenth century by the German researcher Max Uhle (1856–1944).

The so-called Pyramids with Ramps stand out— pyramidal buildings built of rough-cut stones and adobe bricks that had ramps leading to an upper platform. Although there is a debate about the date of these buildings, they were probably created by the Ychma society, although some were also expanded and continued to function during the Inca era.

Pachacamac in Inca Times

Although the cult of Pachacamac preceded the Incas, and this center of worship was already known and visited by people from all over the Andes, it was under the Incas

Opposite The Temple of the Sun. Built in the dominant area of Pachacamac, this shrine was dedicated to the sun by the Incas.

Right The Idol of Pachacamac was carved in wood and represents a bifrontal human personage.

that it became a main pilgrimage center, occupying a predominant place within the Inca road system or Qhapaq Ñan. The first Spaniards to arrive in Pachacamac in 1533 left important descriptions of the place and the religious practices developed there. We know from their accounts that, in order to enter the sanctuary, sanctuary pilgrims had to follow a strict diet for more than one month.

The Temple of the Sun remains the largest and best-preserved building on the site. Built on a rocky promontory, it stands about 130 ft (40 m) tall. The building is made up of five superimposed platforms that form a truncated pyramid. Although this temple belongs to the sanctuary of Pachacamac, in Inca times it was dedicated to the sun, a major divinity.

The Acllahuasi, or Mamaconas, was a place where the "chosen women" lived. This temple has many rooms with typical Inca architectural features that include niches and double-jambed trapezoidal doors. There are many examples of finely carved stone blocks, even in the base and low walls of the structure.

The Palace of Tauri Chumpi, according to Inca chronicles, would have been the residence of the *curaca*, or magistrate, of Pachacamac at the time of the Spanish conquest. Finally, the Pilgrims' Square is a leveled rectangular space that located just in front of the Temple of the Sun. Archaeologists suggest that, due to its proximity to the temple, this would have served as a waiting area for pilgrims. Many of the artifacts found at the site are on display in the site museum.

Above The upper level of the Temple of Sun from which there is a breathtaking view of the Pacific Ocean.

Opposite above Temple with Ramp. This construction followed the local architectural tradition of the central coast and was used up to Inca times.

Opposite The Acllahuasi. This was the "house of the chosen women" during the Inca times.

THE PRE-HISPANIC MONUMENTALITY OF **CARAL**

TYPE: RELIGIOUS AND POLITICAL CENTER • **ARCHITECTURAL STYLE:** CARAL **LOCATION:** DEPARTMENT OF LIMA, PERUVIAN CENTRAL COAST • **CONSTRUCTION BEGUN:** THIRD MILLENNIUM B.C.E.

A series of pyramidal platforms made of stone and mud dominate the pre-Hispanic Andean site of Caral. This ancient archaeological center occupies land in the North Chico region of Peru, an area that is particularly notable for containing an extraordinary accumulation of monumental archaeological sites built mainly during the Late Preceramic Period (3000–1800 B.C.E.). Caral is one of them and thought to represent one of the oldest civilizations in the world.

Discovered by the Peruvian archaeologist Ruth Shady (b. 1946), Caral has gained notoriety due to its monumentality and early complexity, and is a key site in our understanding of the development of the world's first complex societies. According to the published radiocarbon dates, Caral's buildings were constructed during the third millennium B.C.E., making them among the oldest expressions of monumental architecture in the Andean region. According to Shady, Caral was the capital of an early state, although opinions on this differ. Researchers do agree, however, that Caral was a site with a successful economy, and saw the development

of construction technologies, strategies for harnessing economic resources, and an extensive network of regional exchange. Its leadership lasted for more than 1,000 years.

The site was spread over 168 acres (68 ha). Shady and her team estimate that, at its peak, the settlement could have housed approximately 3,000 inhabitants. Among all the buildings that can be seen in here, the Templo Mayor is the most complex and voluminous. At its base, the building is 558 ft (170 m) long and 492 ft (150 m) wide. It was constructed in different architectural phases until it reached a height of 98 ft (30 m). It consists mainly of a series of overlapping platforms and a sunken circular court in the front of the building. The top of the temple is accessed by stairs located at the front.

Other large buildings at Caral include the Amphitheater Temple. In total there are thirty-two public architectural structures and an area of domestic occupation.

Of particular interest at Caral is the use of shicras in the construction of its buildings. Shicras are bags made of vegetable fiber cords, usually reeds. They were used to transport stones for building, and sometimes even placed as part of the fill in the construction work. This was a technique shared in much of the Norte Chico region.

Also among the finds were hundreds of human figurines. Made from unbaked clay, they stand out for the hairstyles and headdresses they wear. It is estimated that their function would have been related to propitiatory or fertility-related rituals.

Caral lies in the coastal valley of Supe, 110 miles (177 km) north of the city of Lima. In addition, it is an important tourist destination in Peru, a country already outstanding for its major ancient monumental sites. Caral is on UNESCO's World Heritage list.

Opposite Panoramic view of the Caral site.
Above The Templo Mayor in Caral.
Below Some of the unbaked clay figurines found at the site.

SIPÁN THE RICHEST MOCHE TOMB

TYPE: CEREMONIAL AND POLITICAL CENTER • **ARCHITECTURAL STYLE:** MOCHE
LOCATION: LAMBAYEQUE, NORTHERN PERUVIAN COAST • **CONSTRUCTION BEGUN:** FIRST CENTURY C.E.

Near the town of Sipán in the middle of the Lambayeque Valley, in the Zaña region of northern Peru, out among the fields of crops, stands Huaca Rajada, a mud pyramid eroded by rains, wind, and looting. In recent years, this unlikely structure has become one of the most emblematic archaeological sites of the South American Moche civilization.

It was here, in 1987, while investigating the site's funerary platform, that archaeologist Walter Alva (b. 1951) found the tomb of one of the most important rulers of Moche society—the Lord of Sipán. The site has gone on to yield the remains of a whole series of leaders since that time.

The funerary platform is built of adobe. Inside, a rectangular chamber had a roof supported by wooden beams. The platform grew in volume as new burial chambers were added during several stages of construction.

The main occupant of each tomb was male and lay inside a wooden coffin along with a large number of sumptuous objects. Offerings accompanying the Lord of Sipán included seashells, scepters, pectorals, ceramics, textiles, and other luxury items. The funerary chamber also revealed human sacrifices of children, women in ceremonial clothes, and men. The last, judging by the clothes and artifacts found, were warriors. Some of them had their feet amputated. Additional sacrifices included those of animals, such as

dogs and camelids. The supposition is that human sacrifices were made to accompany the leaders of Moche society on their journey to the afterlife. According to the iconography, the Lords of Sipán established intimate relationships with supernatural beings and forces.

The Sipán tombs—the first sites of royal burials to be found intact in South America—belong to a Peruvian civilization prior to the Incas. Many archaeologists consider the find to be one of the most important archaeological discoveries in South America of the last few decades.

Scientific analysis of the Lord of Sipán's skeleton indicate that this individual was about 5 ft 5 in (1.65 m) tall and around forty years old at the time of his death. The quality of his diet and his wealth of jewelry and ornaments made of gold, silver, and copper show that he was a high ranking person. As in Inca society, particular artifacts

made of precious metals symbolized a ruler's power. The scepters found in the tombs at Huaca Rajada bear designs relating to the main personage. Semi-lunar headdresses are also emblematic of power among the Moche elite.

Huaca Rajada lies some 20 miles (32 km) east of the city of Chiclayo in the middle of Peru's coastal Lambayeque Valley, a place of great beauty. The site also features a superb museum, which should not be missed. However, the most important pieces of the Sipán tombs, even the human remains, are in the Museum of Royal Tombs of Sipán located in Lambayeque city.

Opposite A view of platforms in Huaca Rajada. In this archaeological complex was built the funerary platform where Sipán leaders were buried.

Above Replica of the Tomb of the Lord of Sipán, located in the same place where the original tomb was found by archaeologists.

THE NAZCA LINES DESERT GEOGLYPHS

TYPE: GEOGLYPHS • **ARCHITECTURAL STYLE:** N/A
LOCATION: NAZCA, SOUTHERN PERUVIAN COAST • **CONSTRUCTION BEGUN:** FIRST CENTURY C.E.

Etched into desert rock, 1,312 ft (400 m) above sea level, and some 250 miles (400 km) south of Lima, in Peru, is one of the world's most astounding collections of ancient geoglyphs. Many of them are long lines that must have served as ritual paths, but the most famous are those that take on zoomorphic, botanical, and anthropomorphic shapes. Totaling more than 1,000 straight lines of varying length and more than 800 animal figures, these are the Nazca Lines, created during the height of the Nazca society, around 1–650 C.E.

Spanning the valleys of Palpa and Nazca in Peru's Ica region, this remarkable site covers an area of around 111,000 acres (45,000 ha). The wonderful figures etched here represent a wealth of coastal and jungle birds that include hummingbirds, condors, herons, cranes, pelicans, seagulls, and parrots. There are other animals, too—a monkey, a spider, a snail, a whale, a dog, llamas, iguanas, and lizards. A number of anthropomorphic figures feature also.

Given that some of the figures extend up to 985 ft (300 m) in size, it begs the question as to how the ancient Nazquenses made them—and why. As to the former, research indicates that they used cords and stakes to align the paths, and followed small-scale drawings as models for etching the lines on the desert surface. As to the latter, since their discovery in the first half of the twentieth century, the meaning of the Nazca Lines has been a matter of debate: archaeologists such as Julio C. Tello and Toribio Mejía Xesspe believed them to be sacred roads; American historian Paul Kosok argued that Nazca's lines formed a great astronomical book; and the pioneering researcher María Reiche believed that the site served as a gigantic solar and lunar calendar, which the ancient Nasquenses used to forecast the best harvest seasons. More recently, Japanese archaeologist Masato Sakai has suggested that

some lines served ritual or ceremonial purposes while others functioned as markers or road guides that indicated the path and the distance from one town to another.

Whatever the reasons for their creation, the tradition of making geoglyphs in this region predates the Nazca Lines, and is known to have continued well into the Inca era. None can match these, however, in terms of volume and size.

Easily accessible to visitors today—the Pan-American Highway crosses the region—the Nazca Lines became a UNESCO Cultural Heritage of Humanity site in 1994.

Below Geoglyph of a spider (150 ft / 46 m long).
Opposite top Geoglyph of a hummingbird (312 ft / 95 m long).
Opposite bottom Geoglyph of a monkey (262 x 246 ft / 80 x 75 m).

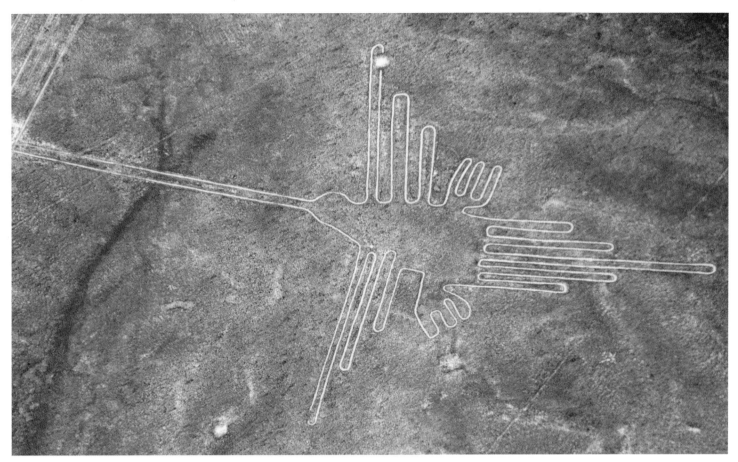

THE MEGALITHIC CITY OF **TIWANAKU**

TYPE: CEREMONIAL AND URBAN CENTER • **ARCHITECTURAL STYLE:** TIWANAKU
LOCATION: DEPARTMENT OF LA PAZ, BOLIVIA • **CONSTRUCTION BEGUN:** FOURTH CENTURY C.E.

About an hour's drive from Bolivia's capital, La Paz, a series of impressive megalithic constructions make Tiwanaku one of the most attractive and mysterious archaeological sites in South America.

According to researchers, Tiwanaku society originally existed as a theocracy, with a priestly elite using religion as its primary strategy for maintaining control. After the seventh century, however, a warrior class took over.

This archaeological site is located 9.3 miles (15 km) southeast of the immense Lake Titicaca in Bolivia, at 1,265 ft (3,855 m) above sea level. Tiwanaku is also the name of the main religious and urban center of a society that developed here between the sixth and eleventh centuries C.E. Members of Tiwanaku society settled not only in what is modern Bolivia, but also in regions that make up parts of modern Peru and Chile.

Monumental Architecture

The archaeological site at Tiwanaku is characterized mainly by its monumental stone-block architecture, much of it decorated in high relief and with incised decoration. The complex comprises an urban center built around a megalithic ceremonial core occupying an area of between 900 and 1,480 acres (400–600 ha). Architectural constructions include the Kalasasaya, the Akapana, the Putuni, and the Puma Punku, all centered around two main avenues and astronomically aligned with amazing precision.

The Kalasasaya is a ceremonial structure with an area of 5 acres (2 ha). It is most noteworthy for its imposing staircase and walls of stone blocks (many of the stone walls were rebuilt in the twentieth century). At the top of the

Above The Gate of Kalasasaya was reconstructed in the twentieth century. It frames the Ponce Monolith.

Opposite above Walls and tenon heads of the Semisubterranean Temple.

Opposite below Huge stone blocks on top of the Puma Punku platform.

platform is the 9.9 ft (3 m) Ponce monolith, named in honor of its discoverer, the archaeologist Carlos Ponce Sanginés. At the west end of this platform is the famous Puerta del Sol, a gate made in a huge lithic block, with the main character known as the "staff god" depicted in the central place.

The dominant building is the Akapana, a pyramidal structure made mainly of mud, with stone-block walls. Pottery and copper fragments, camelid bones, and human burials have been discovered here, in the first and second levels of the pyramid. The first level yielded evidence of human sacrifices—dismembered children and males with their skulls absent—accompanied by dismembered camelids and pottery. On the second level was a completely disjointed human torso. According to archaeologists, these finds represent sacrifices made for the construction of the building.

American archaeologist Wendell C. Bennett (1905–1953). Standing an impressive 24 ft (7.3 m) tall, the monolith represents an anthropomorphic personage in elegant dress. The surface of the character's outfit is profusely decorated with classic Tiwanaku designs.

Beside the impressive architecture at Tiwanaku are a number of ceramic and metal artifacts. However, due to conservation problems, there is little evidence of textiles or woodwork, though such artifacts have been found in Tiwanaku sites elsewhere. The site also features an important museum with many archaeological finds from Tiwanaku itself (included the Bennett monolith) and surrounding prehispanic sites. The nearby town of Tiwanaku was founded in Spanish colonial times and its main plaza and church (with two Tiwanaku stone sculptures in front) are worth visiting.

Left The Kalasasaya platform viewed from the top of Akapana. On the right, the Semisubterranean Temple can be seen.

Below The Ponce monolith depicts a human figure, probably a Tiwanaku leader.

The Putuni, a rectangular platform with a height of 4 ft (1.2 m) high, was the burial site of the society's elites. The Puma Punku is a monumental complex with walls and architectural features built of with megalithic stones. What stands out in this complex is the dedication and effort with which the stones were carved, since their surfaces and angles are perfect.

Among the sculptures found at Tiwanaku, the best known is the Bennett Monolith, named for its discoverer,

3

EUROPE AND NORTHERN ASIA

Europe inevitably forms the largest section of this book, because it was here that the discipline of archaeology was really developed, and because its countless sites span a colossal period from our early ancestors at Atapuerca through Ice Age art to prehistoric megalithic monuments and tombs, Bronze and Iron Age sites, and on into medieval times. But of course, a crucial component encompasses the prehistoric sites of the Aegean and those of the classical world, primarily in Greece and Italy. To many people, archaeology itself is exemplified by places such as Pompeii and the ruins of Athens and Rome.

Left The milecastle at Castle Nick, to the west of Housesteads Roman fort, provided a gateway through Hadrian's Wall in England.

EUROPE AND NORTHERN ASIA
LOCATIONS

TANUM BRONZE AGE ROCK ART

TYPE: ROCK ART • **ARCHITECTURAL STYLE:** N/A
LOCATION: COASTAL SOUTHWEST SWEDEN • **CONSTRUCTION BEGUN:** CA. 1500 B.C.E.

On the west coast of Sweden facing the North Sea, in a region known as Bohuslän, granite outcrops scraped by retreating glaciers protrude from the wooded landscape. After the Ice Age, they lay close to the shoreline, but today they are found 80–100 ft (25–30 m) above sea level and some distance inland due to the rebound of the land from the weight of the ice. During the Bronze Age, about 1500 B.C.E., the inhabitants of southern Scandinavia used these outcrops as "canvases" on which to engrave hundreds of thousands of images.

Bohuslän contains the densest concentration of Bronze Age rock art in Scandinavia, and the Tanum World Heritage site is the "capital" of rock art in Bohuslän. Several hundred distinct outcrops with engravings are known around Tanum, while many more certainly lie buried under soil and moss. Although many engravings are now filled with red or white paint to make them more visible they originally did not have any color to set them off from the surrounding rock.

Bronze Age rock artists made their carvings by pecking and grinding the rock surfaces with stone hammers and points. Even the simplest image required hours of work. The resulting complex compositions depict the Bronze Age world of their makers. Several thousand engravings of ships have been identified, reflecting the maritime life of these societies. The most common are ships with upward-curving prows and sterns. Many carry people—perhaps on expeditions. Engravings of humans are often conspicuously male. They carry weapons, pull plows, ride chariots, and play trumpets. Cattle, horses, deer, birds, and canines also appear. Beside these identifiable figures are abstract designs such as suns (or wheels) and spirals. Engravings of hands and feet appear frequently, as do cupmarks, or small pecked pits.

Archaeologists puzzle over whether the rock artists planned their images on the stone canvasses in one single

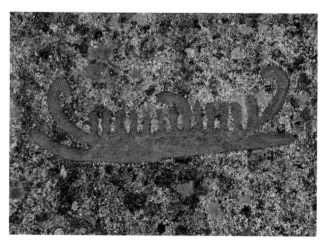

episode or added them sequentially to existing displays. Were these outcrops already special in some way, or did the engravings make them significant? It is clear that many depict scenes from everyday life, such as plowing, herding, hunting, and traveling by ship and wagon. Others appear to show rituals and processions, while images of fighting with spears and battleaxes reflect the institutionalized status of warriors in Bronze Age society.

Various interpretations of the Scandinavian rock art have been advanced, but no single theory accounts for everything. One possibility is that they formed backdrops to rituals such as initiations. Another is that they represented the creation of memories for future generations by commemorating life events, or to express a relationship between the worlds

of the living and of deities or myths. Whatever it is trying to communicate, the Bronze Age rock art at Tanum, and elsewhere, provides modern-day visitors with a glimpse of the worldview and cosmology of a complex stratified society.

The 500 engravings on an outcrop at Vitlycke show the full portfolio of the Bronze Age artists. A short walk away, the Vitlycke Museum offers guided tours of nearby engraved outcrops. Other rock art panels can be reached from the museum by car or on hiking trails.

Opposite Rock carvings of warriors and a ship.

Above Composite images, such as warriors merged with ships, were perhaps intended to impart desirable qualities to individuals.

GAMLA UPPSALA
A LANDSCAPE OF POWER

TYPE: BURIAL MOUNDS AND ROYAL MANOR • **ARCHITECTURAL STYLE:** EARTHEN MOUNDS
LOCATION: EASTERN SWEDEN • **CONSTRUCTION BEGUN:** CA. 600 C.E.

Just over a mile (2 km) north of the modern city of Uppsala in eastern Sweden lies the ancient site of Gamla Uppsala (Old Uppsala). On a low ridge bounded on either side by farmland and pastures, several immense mounds dominate the site. Gamla Uppsala offers more than these great tumuli, however. The complex also includes smaller mounds, boat burials, flat burials, workshops, and settlements in use at various times during most of the first millennium of the Common Era.

The No. 2 bus from the Old Market in Uppsala brings the visitor to its final stop: Kungshögarna, the Royal Mounds. Three mounds—Västhögen, Mellanhögen, and Östhögen—dominate the landscape, surrounded by about 250 surviving smaller mounds. Östhögen, or East Mound, is the largest, currently about 30 ft (9 m) high and with an oval plan 180 ft (55 m) wide and 250 ft (75 m) long. In 1846–1847, the Swedish National Antiquary, Bror Emil Hildebrand (1806–1884), dug a tunnel 80 ft (25 m) into East Mound but found only burned bones and fragments of grave goods. Three decades later, he returned to dig an immense trench into Västhögen, or West Mound, where he found a similar array of fragmented artifacts and bones. At the time, Hildebrand was not impressed.

Although the artifacts and bones did not seem impressive in the mid-nineteenth century, their significance has since been realized. It is now thought that the mounds were built during the late sixth or early seventh century C.E. (previously they had been dated somewhat earlier). Fragments of ornamented bronze sheet in East Mound were probably decorations on a helmet. The individual in West Mound was an adult man buried with markers of high status, including a sword made in Western Europe with a handle ornamented by garnets set in gold. His ivory gaming pieces were possibly of late Roman origin. Although the artifacts were highly fragmented and burned, close examination reveals their artisanship and distant origins.

While mounds were built at Gamla Uppsala, the practice of burying nobility in complete boats with

lavish unburned grave goods began a tradition of boat burial that continued into Viking times. Two spectacular boat cemeteries lie a short distance north of Gamla Uppsala. At Välsgarde, fifteen boat burials are known. At Vendel, with fourteen boat burials, helmets have been found that have parallels with one found in the celebrated boat burial at Sutton Hoo in England.

Gamla Uppsala developed from a necropolis into a royal manor on a terraced area adjacent to the mounds. This complex included a great timber hall 165 ft (50 m) long and up to 40 ft (12 m) wide, and a workshop area yielding hundreds of garnets. Gamla Uppsala became a seat of both royal and religious power, mentioned in sagas and legends; it subsequently turned into a monumental national symbol in the nascent Swedish state, and today is a major tourist attraction. The Gamla Uppsala Museum sets the history of the site in its wider context, and visitors can walk along the ridge and around the mounds.

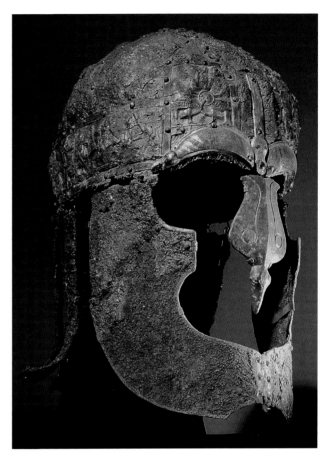

Right One of the helmets from the boat cemetery at Vendel.
Below Panorama, with the sun just visible, of Royal Mounds in Gamla Uppsala.

KING HARALD BLUETOOTH'S **FORTRESSES**

TYPE: FORTIFIED STRONGHOLD • **ARCHITECTURAL STYLE:** TIMBER RAMPARTS AND LONGHOUSES
LOCATION: ZEALAND, DENMARK • **CONSTRUCTION BEGUN:** 980 C.E.

About an hour's drive southwest from Copenhagen near Slagelse, not far from the west coast of the Danish island of Zealand, lies Trelleborg. This circular rampart is one of several fortresses that King Harald Bluetooth ordered to be constructed between 975 and 981 C.E. to consolidate his rule over Denmark and the adjacent part of southern Sweden. Others include Aggersborg and Fyrkat in northern Jutland, Nonnebakken on the island of Fyn, and Borgeby in southern Sweden.

Trelleborg is the best-studied of Harald's strongholds. It was first excavated in the 1930s, after a local motorbike club had rented the site and planned to turn it into a motocross track. What had been envisioned as a small rescue excavation turned into an archaeological project lasting many years.

Fortresses of the Trelleborg type are remarkably similar, indicating that they were built to a preordained plan using a fixed unit of measurement. Their earth and stone ramparts are perfectly round and surrounded by a moat. Aggersborg is the largest, nearly 800 ft (240 m) across, while Fyrkat and Nonnebakken are about 400 ft (120 m) in diameter. Trelleborg is slightly larger at 440 ft (134 m), with ramparts 15 ft (5 m) high. Inside the walls, they have symmetrical layouts. Starting with gates at the four points of the compass, main streets cross the interior, dividing it in four. Within each of these precincts, bow-sided longhouses are arranged to form quadrangles around interior courtyards.

Trelleborg was built on a peninsula by a swamp, which drained into a lake connected to the sea. Viking ships could navigate right up to the fortress. Dendrochronology (tree-ring dating) of wood from its moat indicates that it was cut in the winter of 980 C.E., so it is likely the rampart was built in the spring of 981. Trelleborg differs from the other ring fortresses in that it has a precinct outside the circular rampart with additional longhouses and a cemetery. A secondary rampart and ditch protect this external area and also block the peninsula on which the complex is located. It is thought this was added after the original fortress was built.

The function of these Viking fortresses is uncertain. A likely explanation is that they served as garrisons to control the local populations. Strangely, there is no mention of Trelleborg or the other fortresses in any documentary account, so it is believed that they were in use for a short time, perhaps ten to fifteen years. Today visitors can tour Trelleborg's rebuilt ramparts, where outlines of the longhouses have been marked with concrete posts and one has been reconstructed. Finds from the excavations are on display in a museum at Trelleborg and in the National Museum in Copenhagen. Fyrkat, north of Århus, has offers similar attractions for visitors.

Meanwhile, the memory of King Harald Bluetooth, who connected the small kingdoms of Denmark, lives on as the name for a wireless communication technology.

Opposite, clockwise from top left Aerial view of Trelleborg. Reconstructed gate. Reconstructed bow-sided longhouse. Outlines of the excavated houses.

A MONUMENTAL LANDSCAPE IN
THE BOYNE VALLEY

TYPE: BURIAL MOUNDS, TIMBER AND DITCH ENCLOSURES • **ARCHITECTURAL STYLE:** MOUNDED EARTH
WITH ENGRAVED STONES • **LOCATION:** EASTERN IRELAND • **CONSTRUCTION BEGUN:** CA. 3500 B.C.E.

At dawn on the winter solstice (and on a couple of days before and after), the rising sun
shines down a passage into the burial chamber of Newgrange at the Bend of the Boyne in
the Republic of Ireland. Two more passage tombs are located nearby. Along with Newgrange,
they represent three of the most significant passage tombs in Western Europe.

The Bend of the Boyne, or Brú na Bóinne in Irish, is a
broad loop of the Boyne River, which flows languidly
through the countryside north of Dublin before reaching
the Irish Sea east of Drogheda. Just west of the M1
motorway, the bend gives its name to the surrounding
area. In recent years, as well as being celebrated as the
location of these three passage tombs, it has been shown
to contain a vast ceremonial landscape that also features
timber circles and ditched enclosures.

Ancient peoples constructed passage tombs from large
slabs of stone set upright and roofed over with even larger
blocks, to form a tunnel-like corridor leading into a central
burial chamber in which they placed cremated bones.
Originally, they covered passages and chambers with mounds
of earth and stones, but over the millennia the mounds have
become eroded or material has been carried off for other
uses. In Ireland, four major passage tomb cemeteries form a
chain across the island, from Carrowmore and Carrowkeel in

the west to Loughcrew and the Bend of the Boyne in the east. All date from the second half of the fourth millennium B.C.E.

At the Bend of the Boyne, the passage tombs of Knowth, Dowth, and Newgrange lie a short distance apart, each on a high spot in the landscape. Newgrange is the most famous, an immense mound about 280 ft (85 m) in diameter outlined by ninety-seven oblong blocks of stone, many carved with curvilinear designs. After excavations in the 1960s and 1970s, Newgrange was controversially reconstructed. Bright quartz pieces lying beside the mound were interpreted, probably implausably, as having originally formed a wall, so the gleaming reconstructed facade of Newgrange looks like no other passage tomb.

The burial complex at Knowth has also been reconstructed, but much less fancifully than Newgrange. The main mound, 227 ft (67 m) across, contains two independent passages leading to separate chambers, one from the east side, and the other from the west. The stones of Knowth, including 127 curbstones averaging about 6 ft (2 m) in length, abound with engravings of spirals, sunbursts, and other abstract motifs. Seventeen smaller tombs surround the main mound, along with later prehistoric features that include a timber circle from the third millennium B.C.E.

Dowth is the least studied of the Boyne passage graves. It is not reconstructed, and a crater caused by nineteenth-century excavation has never been filled. Dowth also contains two separate passages and burial chambers, each entering at the west side of the mound. Near the Dowth mound, renovations at the eighteenth-century manor house of Dowth Hall have since revealed an additional small passage tomb about half the diameter of Newgrange, but also with decorated curbstones.

Opposite Newgrange's circular facade.

Right, from top Iconic engraving on stone in the Newgrange passage. Newgrange entrance. Roof of the burial chamber at Newgrange.

Farther Afield

The summer of 2018 was extremely dry in Ireland. Anthony Murphy, a journalist and photographer from Drogheda, brought his camera drone out to the Brú na Bóinne to shoot aerial photos of some of the monuments. In a field not far from Newgrange, Murphy spotted the cropmarks of a hitherto-unknown monument, consisting of a double circle of short-ditch segments about 500 ft (154 m) in diameter, surrounded by a double outer circle of posts. Rapidly nicknamed "Dronehenge," this new monument appears to be the remains of bedding trenches for timber posts that formed two concentric rings.

Aerial and geophysical surveys have revealed many other timber circles or ditched enclosures on the Bend of the Boyne. Most date to the same period as the passage tombs, while some are slightly earlier or later.

Far from being simply a megalithic cemetery, it now appears that the Bend of the Boyne was a vast ritual landscape with both tombs and enclosures, joining comparable complexes at Stonehenge, Carnac, and Orkney in reflecting the spiritual and social lives of the inhabitants of northwestern Europe between 3500 and 2000 B.C.E.

Today, visitors can enter this world through the Brú na Bóinne Visitor Centre, from which shuttle buses depart for Newgrange and Knowth. Here they can also see exhibits that explain the sites in detail, as well as enter a lottery to be one of the few individuals allowed to enter the Newgrange chamber on the winter solstice.

Above Knowth and its satellite tombs.

Left Engraved curbstone at Newgrange.

BUILDING **HADRIAN'S WALL**

TYPE: MILITARY • **ARCHITECTURAL STYLE:** ROMAN
LOCATION: NORTHUMBERLAND AND CUMBRIA, ENGLAND • **CONSTRUCTION BEGUN:** 122 C.E.

The extensive frontier system established by the Roman Emperor Hadrian (76–138 C.E.) in 122 C.E. cuts across some of the most rugged landscapes in Britain. The most dramatic sections were built along the crags of the Whin Sill. Hadrian's Wall runs 80 Roman miles (73 miles/117 km) from Wallsend on the river Tyne on the east to Bowness-on-Solway on the broad estuary on the west.

The original plan seems to have been for a wall with small garrisons placed in so-called milecastles and two turrets placed in the intervening sections. This pattern continued, without a wall, along the Cumbrian coast in the west. One of the best preserved milecastles in this coastal section remains at Swarthy Hill, to the north of Maryport; it sits on a small hill and provides clear views across the Solway Firth to Scotland.

The main part of the frontier consisted of a ditch to the north, a wall, and then a flat-bottomed ditch with two raised mounds on either side (known as the vallum) to the south. One of the crossing points of the vallum, complete with the foundations of a monumental gateway, has been preserved to the south of the fort at Benwell in the western suburbs of the city of Newcastle. The western sections of the wall were originally constructed in turf. Some sections, running in parallel with the later stone wall, can still be detected just to the west of where the frontier crossed the Irthing River near the fort of Birdoswald (west of the modern village of Gilsland).

It was only after work started on the wall that the decision was made to bring the major garrisons for the frontier onto the line of the wall. One of the best-excavated forts lies at Chesters, 5 miles (8 km) north of Hexham. The cavalry unit based here protected the crossing of the North Tyne River—remains of the bridge

Above Milecastles like this at Cawfields Crag housed small numbers of men to secure the frontier.

Opposite Larger military garrisons were placed in forts such as this one found at Housesteads.

that formed the frontier are still visible. A well-preserved bathhouse is located near the river on the east side of the fort, as is the house for the commanding officer of the unit.

Some of the most challenging sections of the wall were in its central section, along the craggy Whin Sill. One of the most visible remaining infantry forts lies at Housesteads, about 5 miles (8 km) north of Bardon Mill, at the eastern end of this section, with commanding views to the north. Two well-preserved milecastles also remain in this section, at Castle Nick and Cawfields.

The path of the original frontier was based on that of a road, later known as the Stanegate, which ran to the south of the wall. This was guarded by a series of forts. One of the best preserved is at Vindolanda (southwest of Housesteads). Parts of the fort have yielded important organic materials, as well as some of the archive of the Roman unit (and the commanding officer's archive) that provide insights into garrison life in northern Britain.

At Carrawburgh, an infantry fort in the eastern central section of the wall, 3.7 miles (6 km) west of Chesters, excavations have revealed a small temple dedicated to the eastern god Mithras. This deity was popular on the Roman frontiers.

The best way to see the wall is to walk (boots are sensible). The AD 122 bus service runs from Easter to September on the road immediately behind the wall. This connects with the Tyne Valley railway at Hexham. Visitors should go to the Great North Museum, an easy walk from the Haymarket station on the Newcastle Metro, or the Tullie House Museum in Carlisle.

STONEHENGE
AND ITS RITUAL LANDSCAPE

TYPE: ALIGNMENTS OF STANDNG STONES • **ARCHITECTURAL STYLE:** MEGALITHIC
LOCATION: SOUTHWEST ENGLAND • **CONSTRUCTION BEGUN:** AROUND 3000 B.C.E

Standing tall and enigmatic, some 85 miles (136 km) west of London, the standing stones of Stonehenge on Salisbury Plain are among the world's most iconic archaeological monuments. Rivaled only by the Pyramids at Giza, the Acropolis in Athens, and the Cliff Palace at Mesa Verde, they have been a subject of fascination for centuries. Recently, however, archaeologists have realized that this stone circle is just one part of a huge ritual precinct where people congregated during the third millennium B.C.E.

The story of Stonehenge is one of increasing complexity, paralleled by other ceremonial landscapes such as those at the Boyne Valley, Carnac, and Orkney. It seems the stones visible today represent only the final construction phase of a monument that was reconfigured repeatedly over several centuries.

The story of Stonehenge has long concentrated on the famous stone circle itself: how it was built and for what purpose. Beginning around 3000 B.C.E., the first project at Stonehenge involved digging a circular ditch about 330

ft (100 m) across and piling up a bank outside the circle. (The term "–henge" derives from an ancient Saxon word meaning "hanging," perhaps due to a resemblance to gallows. Now the term refers to ditched enclosures with the bank outside the ditch.) Around the interior, upright bluestones were placed into fifty-six holes called Aubrey Holes. Transporting the bluestones may have been a ritual

Below Cloudy sunrise over Stonehenge.
Opposite Overhead view showing ditch and bank.

in itself. Quarried in the Preseli Mountains in southern Wales, about 125 miles (200 km) away, they journeyed along trails to the Welsh coast, across the Severn Estuary by boat, and then overland to the Salisbury Plain. From the beginning, Stonehenge was a cemetery, with the total number of cremation graves estimated at between 150 and 250 over several centuries.

The first configuration of Stonehenge lasted nearly 500 years, until the middle of the third millennium B.C.E. Between 2600 and 2400 B.C.E., it assumed the form that would be recognizable today, with the erection of the major upright stones and lintels. The stones used for these are called sarsens, common sandstone boulders from the Marlborough Downs about 20 miles (30 km) away. Their sheer size required immense effort by people and animals

as well as sophisticated engineering techniques to drag them across the landscape and put them in position.

Starting from the center, a horseshoe configuration of pairs of immense vertical sarsens connected by horizontal lintels was erected. Five such "trilithons" were built. This operation is even more impressive because the lintels have sockets in the underside that needed to be located precisely over posts on the tops of the uprights before being lowered into place. Bluestones pulled out of the Aubrey Holes were arranged in arcs around the trilithons. Finally, a circle of upright sarsens with continuous lintels was erected to enclose the trilithons and bluestones. At the same time, several other bluestones were set in place along the ditch and beyond. The most important of these is the Heel Stone, located outside the enclosure.

Over the next several centuries, the bluestones were rearranged several times and the ditch recut. More circles of holes were dug outside the sarsen circle, but stones apparently were not placed in them. Ritual activity finally stopped around 1600 B.C.E. Stonehenge sat silent for several millennia, although it remained conspicuous in the landscape.

Beyond the Stone Circle

What was the purpose of Stonehenge? The question has challenged archaeologists for centuries. It was certainly a place of burial, but who could be buried there? The standing stones have astronomical alignments, including the celebrated summer solstice sunrise over the Heel Stone and the lesser-known midwinter solstice sunset. Theories advanced in the 1960s, that Stonehenge was some sort of calendar or observatory, are now considered overblown. Prehistoric people often aligned their monuments on significant annual celestial events.

More clues to Stonehenge's function come from the surrounding countryside. The area around Stonehenge had already seen considerable prehistoric activity by Mesolithic hunter-gatherers and Neolithic farmers. Modification of the surrounding landscape began several centuries before the first stones were installed at Stonehenge itself.

Beneath an immense henge with timber circles at Durrington Walls, 2 miles (3.2 km) northeast of Stonehenge by the Avon River, traces of a large settlement contemporaneous with the major construction phase at Stonehenge have been found. Vast quantities of cattle and pig bones suggest that feasting took place. The settlement at Durrington Walls has been interpreted as an encampment of pilgrims, perhaps even the builders of Stonehenge, who made a spiritual journey to the ceremonial precinct.

Today's pilgrims to Stonehenge arrive by car via the A303 road or by bus departing from Salisbury, about 10 miles (16 km) to the south. From the visitor center, a bus can be taken to the henge itself. At Durrington Walls, about 10 minutes away, a signposted walking trail leads visitors through a section of the Stonehenge landscape.

Opposite Reconstruction showing the settlement at Durrington Walls near Stonehenge in about 2500 B.C.E.
Below Stonehenge sarsens with their lintels.

THE EVOCATIVE STONES OF **CARNAC**

TYPE: ALIGNMENTS OF STANDNG STONES • **ARCHITECTURAL STYLE:** MEGALITHIC
LOCATION: SOUTHERN BRITTANY, FRANCE • **CONSTRUCTION BEGUN:** BEFORE 3000 B.C.E.

When the cyclists riding in the Tour de France visit southern Brittany and its picturesque seascapes, they often pass close to one of the most remarkable concentrations of prehistoric monuments in Europe: Carnac. The area around this small seaside resort was the focus of intense activity more than 5,000 years ago, with dozens of ancient sites in an area measuring 116 sq mi (300 sq km). Many of these sites are tombs, both long mounds and passage graves, but Carnac itself is best known for several sets of parallel standing stones, called menhirs, that extend over half a mile (0.8 km) in places.

The word "menhir" is drawn from an ancient Breton word meaning "long stone," set upright into a hole and often reaching several feet in height. Such standing stones are found throughout Atlantic Europe dating from the Neolithic period and into the Bronze Age. Their true significance is a mystery, although archaeologists presume some sort of ritual activities occurred in association with them.

Of the eleven or more alignments in the Carnac area, the four most important are called Kerzerho, Kermario, Le Ménec, and Kerlescan. The last three are very close to the town of Carnac, while Kerzerho is about 5 miles (8 km) to the northwest near Erdeven. Of these, Kerzerho is the longest, with ten rows of more than 1,100 stones stretching over 1.25 miles (2 km), although many have disappeared in the last 150 years. Among them is a row of immense menhirs, the Giants of Kerzerho, which stand up nearly 20 ft (6 m) tall.

Kermario, Le Ménec, and Kerlescan are better known, but each one is complicated in its own way. Kermario has between seven and ten rows at any one point, running up to 0.7 miles (1.2 km) long with 1,029 surviving stones, while Le Ménec consists of ten to twelve slightly converging rows about 0.62 mile (1 km) long, containing 1,069 stones. More compact at 1,165 ft (355 m) long and 456 ft (139 m) wide, Kerlescan has 555 menhirs in twelve to thirteen rows. Le Ménec and Kermario, along with Kerzerho, are oriented west–southwest to east–northeast, although the irregularity of the alignments and their angled rows means that this should not be taken to indicate an interest in astronomical events other than, perhaps, sunrise or sunset.

The exact purpose of the Carnac alignments is unknown. There were clearly intentional choices in the sizes of certain menhirs, such as the Giants of Kerzerho, and in their siting. For example, at Kerlescan, larger stones are concentrated at one end of the rows and gradually get smaller toward the other end. The alignments at Le Ménec and Kerlescan terminate in enclosures defined by additional standing stones. One popular interpretation is that the Carnac alignments were processional paths that led to stone enclosures in which rituals occurred.

The Carnac alignments were the final element in a vast ritual landscape that began at least a millennium earlier, incorporating immense earthen mounds, tall single menhirs, and chambered tombs. Like the Boyne Valley in Ireland, Orkney at the northern tip

of the British Isles, and the Stonehenge environs, the constructed landscape around Carnac is another example of the deep, long-term engagement by Neolithic peoples in ceremony and symbolism.

Carnac lies about five hours by car from Paris and under two hours from Nantes. Route D196, "Route of the Alignments," brings the visitor to Maison des Mégalithes (House of the Megaliths) and the visitor center. Be sure to visit other megalithic monuments in the Morbihan region, which are spectacular in their own right.

Above View of the Carnac stones.

COVALANAS CAVE ART

TYPE: DECORATED CAVE • **ARCHITECTURAL STYLE:** N/A
LOCATION: RAMALES, CANTABRIA, SPAIN • **CONSTRUCTION BEGUN:** AROUND 22,000 YEARS AGO

Around fifty of the decorated caves of the last Ice Age are open to the public. Of these, one of the most moving and rewarding to visit is Covalanas, in northern Spain, near the town of Ramales. Reaching the cave involves a steep climb up a track about half a mile (600 m) long, but the journey is well worth the effort. The cave is small, dry, and pristine, with no staircases or electric light. Visitors see it as it would have been seen in the Ice Age, and can get extremely close to the art.

This art was discovered on September 11, 1903, making it the second decorated cave to be discovered in Spain after Altamira. Excavations in its entrance chamber found virtually nothing—this was not a cave that was ever occupied, but a cave visited for artistic purposes only. The large El Mirón Cave, directly below it, was the major occupation site of this area, and presumably it was one of the inhabitants of that site who made his or her way up the cliff to this small cavity and decided to decorate it.

The details of technique, content, and style make it highly probable that all of the figures in Covalanas Cave were made by a single person in one artistic episode, thought to have taken place in the Solutrean period (ca. 20,000–22,000 years ago). The animal figures are all drawn using the same technique—rendered in outline with dots of iron oxide (red ocher or hematite). Some dots were clearly applied with fingers, others with the more flexible thumb; some are very separate, others juxtaposed. Using this deceptively simple technique the artist managed to express tremendous variety in posture, perspective, and movement.

For a long time, historians considered this technique to be the work of a single artist or perhaps a school.

However, since the discovery of the same technique in other caves, it has become clear that this was a regional and chronological phenomenon, and that it was widespread in northern Spain at one time.

The artist clearly studied Covalanas Cave carefully before drawing the figures; there are signs of planning and symmetry. The images begin some way into the cave, after a point where you are walking on the original floor level. It is noticeable that they occur in the part that is narrowest and highest.

Almost all the animals drawn on both walls are female red deer (seventeen in all), although one larger deer on the right wall is thought to be a male, which has shed its antlers, because of its musculature. A large animal on the left wall, probably an aurochs, displays a masterly use of the rock shape for its body. The best group of females on the right wall displays twisted perspective (the bodies in profile, but both ears visible) and superimposition, while one animal is looking back over its shoulder. Toward the end of the gallery is a large horse, with a flowing mane and a long tail.

Opposite The horse and two of the female deer in Covalanas.

HUMAN FOSSILS AT
SIERRA DE ATAPUERCA

TYPE: NATURAL CAVES AND ROCK SHELTERS • **ARCHITECTURAL STYLE:** N/A
LOCATION: BURGOS, SPAIN • **CONSTRUCTION BEGUN:** N/A

The mountains 5.4 miles (14 km) east of the Spanish city of Burgos have yielded some of the richest and most informative collections of human fossils in the world. Although today a dry upland, during the Pleistocene (Ice Age) the limestone supported a verdant landscape, well watered by rivers and springs, with an abundant fauna that formed rich hunting and scavenging for early humans in the Lower, Middle, and Upper Pleistocene.

A series of caves, shafts, and rock shelters formed, exposed and filled by river action over this period, their sediments revealing human and animal bones and stone tools spanning the Palaeolithic to the Bronze Age. The oldest deposits belong to the Trinchera del Ferrocarril (Trench), the wide railway cutting that exposed deep sections through the karst and brought to light its sedimentary fills, now excavated in several locations. Of those that are visible from the path, the oldest are the Gran Dolina and Sima del Elefante, two deep shafts that together span the period from 1.2–0.1 million years ago (mya). The remains of at least eleven humans from these shafts form the definitive fossils for the archaic *Homo antecessor*, and stone-tool cutmarks on their bones show that some were cannibalized. Simple stone tools and butchered animal bones show that this tall, muscular human was exploiting the rich opportunities of the area, including the carcasses of large red deer- and bisonlike animals, although the presence of carnivores such as large panthers and hyenas shows that competition for carcasses was intense. A third visible sequence is in the Galería, dating to 0.5–0.2 mya, the oldest levels of which overlap with the youngest at the Dolina and Elefante sites. Early Neanderthals—probably the descendants of

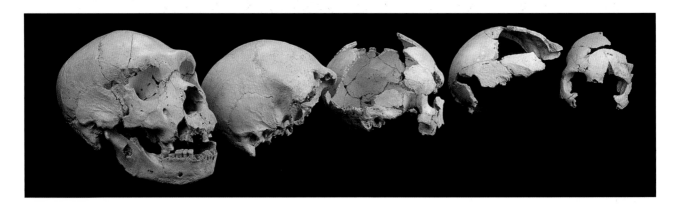

the earlier populations—used this cave repeatedly as a shelter in which to butcher the carcasses of animals that had fallen down into this natural trap. In its oldest levels they used the Acheulean hand-ax toolkit, evolving over time to the flake-based tools of its uppermost levels, which are more characteristic of classic Neanderthals.

Although inaccessible to the public, 0.5 mya deposits in the Sima de los Huesos (Pit of the Bones) have yielded one of the richest collections of human fossil remains in the world. These are best explored in the museum in Burgos. The pit's sediments include the remains of at least twenty-eight individuals of the archaic human *Homo heidelbergensis*, perhaps deliberately placed around what was originally a deep shaft opening into daylight.

Atapuerca continues to yield up its secrets, with human remains coming to light in the Cueva del Fantasma, probably intermediate in age between the Gran Dolina and Sima de los Huesos, and the Cueva del Mirador, so far the youngest of the sequence.

A walking route through the Trench takes the visitor past several of the sites. The Museum of Human Evolution in the city of Burgos contains extensive displays of the main stone and bone finds from Atapuerca's sites.

Opposite Some of the skulls extracted from the Sima de los Huesos.
Above, left and right The Galeria and the Sima del Elefante in the trench.

ICE AGE ROCK ART IN THE **CÔA VALLEY**

TYPE: OPEN-AIR ROCK ART • **ARCHITECTURAL STYLE:** N/A
LOCATION: VILA NOVA DE FOZ CÔA, PORTUGAL • **CONSTRUCTION BEGUN:** AROUND 30,000 YEARS AGO

Numerous pecked animal images and fine incisions populate the fractured
vertical schist rocks flanking this tributary of the Douro River in northeast Portugal.
Collectively, they represent the biggest known display of open-air Ice Age art in the world.

In 1989, preparations began on the construction of a huge dam along the Côa River, set to raise the river's water level by about 330 ft (100 m). It was during the ensuing archaeological survey of the region that these Ice Age rock carvings were first noticed. By 1994, news of the growing number of discoveries had reached the outside world, and specialists from around the globe, together with many local people—not least the schoolchildren of Vila Nova de Foz Côa—began a campaign to try and preserve this unique resource. This seemed an impossible task, since work on the dam was already well underway, and millions had already been spent. Nevertheless, thanks to the campaign, and to a change of government, the dam was indeed halted at the end of 1995. The area subsequently became an archaeological park and gained UNESCO World Heritage site status in 1998.

Today work continues on discovering and studying the valley's art, which is scattered over a distance of 10.6 miles (17 km). Three important concentrations of petroglyphs are open to the public here, providing an excellent sample of this remarkable art.

At Canada do Inferno, it is known that many figures are already beneath the water, the Pocinho Dam, constructed in the 1980s, having raised the river's level by several feet. But many remain visible to the visitor, both on the riverbank and up the rocky slope—primarily aurochs, horses, and ibex, the three most common species depicted in the Côa Valley.

Left A petroglyph panel at Penascosa, seen at night, comprising mostly aurochs.

Opposite Another panel at Penascosa, showing two horses and two ibex.

At Penascosa, on a rock above the parking area, stands a large stag figure, abraded onto the rock rather than pecked. Farther on is a splendid panel of aurochs, horses, and ibex, while several other major collections of similar animal figures are visible farther on still, at different levels. These include a large horse figure, facing left. Below it is a fish depiction. Nearby is a horse with three heads in different positions—a characteristic feature of Côa art.

Nighttime visits to Penascosa are recommended, as the figures are far easier to see under artificial light.

At Ribeira de Piscos is a wonderful composition of two horses facing each other and with overlapping heads. Farther on, rocks bear fine figures of two aurochs as well as a remarkable ithyphallic human figure. Huge aurochs figures dominate the river at the confluence and must originally have been visible from quite a distance.

On stylistic grounds, the Côa art has been attributed to a period from the Gravettian (ca. 30,000 years ago) to the Magdalenian (ca. 12,000 years ago). Excavations of occupation sites in the area have fully confirmed this attribution.

In 2010 a magnificent new museum opened just outside Vila Nova de Foz Côa, dedicated to the region's rock art. It also houses a shop and restaurant. All visits to the sites leave from the museum in official vehicles.

HOCHDORF'S IRON AGE CHIEF

TYPE: BURIAL MOUND WITH TIMBER CHAMBER • **ARCHITECTURAL STYLE:** MOUNDED EARTH
LOCATION: SOUTHWEST GERMANY, NEAR STUTTGART • **CONSTRUCTION BEGUN:** CA. 530 B.C.E.

Just before 500 B.C.E., tremendous wealth poured into the area of today's southwest Germany and eastern France. Iron Age elites had established contact with Greek trading colonies on the Mediterranean coast, specifically at Massalia (modern Marseille). In exchange for luxury goods from workshops in Italy and wine, they supplied food, furs, and slaves to the Greeks. Their accumulated wealth was buried with them.

In 1977, archaeologists excavated a burial mound just outside the town of Hochdorf an der Enz, northwest of Stuttgart. Originally measuring some 20 ft (6 m) high and around 200 ft (60 m) across, it had been reduced in height by plowing and was barely visible. Most important, it had not been robbed in antiquity, as was the fate of so many contemporaneous burial mounds.

Excavations revealed a pit extending about 8 ft (2.5 m) below the original ground surface, measuring about 36 sq ft (11 sq m). Within this pit were two nested timber boxes with wooden roofs. The outer box measured 25 sq ft (7.5 sq m) and 5 ft (1.5 m) deep, and the inner box measured 15 sq ft (5.7 sq m) and contained the burial and grave goods. The space between the boxes was filled with stones, while more rocks were piled over the roof. Unfortunately, the builders misjudged the ability of the roof to bear the load, and it collapsed into the burial chamber. This misfortune was beneficial in that it caused perishable items to become waterlogged and thus preserved. In addition, if looters had managed to dig through the earthen mound, the jumble of rocks over the occupant of the tomb and his sumptuous grave goods would have deterred them.

A man about forty years old lay on a bronze couch decorated in repoussé dimples with scenes of wagons and dancers. The eight legs of the couch were figures of women with upraised arms, and casters under their feet permitted the couch to be rolled. The man's clothing and leather shoes were decorated with gold bands, and he wore a gold neckring and bracelets, about 21 oz (600 g) of gold in all.

By the foot of the couch sat a large bronze cauldron, probably made in a workshop in southern Italy. Figures of lions adorned its rim and it held around 130 gallons (500 litres). Inside was a small gold bowl. The cauldron contained residue from mead, made from fermented honey. Perhaps the nine drinking horns that hung on

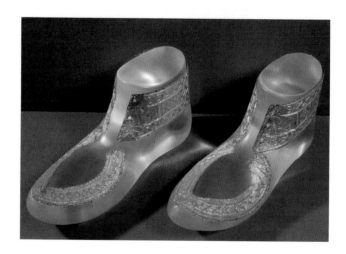

the fabric-draped walls of the burial chamber were filled from this cauldron. Across the chamber from the couch a four-wheeled wagon served as a platform for additional grave goods, including nine sets of bronze dishes, all wrapped in cloth.

Down the street from the Hochdorf mound, the Keltenmuseum houses a reconstruction of the burial chamber and its finds. A metal arch gives visitors to the site an impression of the original dimensions of the mound. Next to the museum is a replica of an Iron Age farmstead based on excavations in nearby fields. Hochdorf is about a half-hour by car from Stuttgart via route B10. You can also get there by bus from the train station at Vaihingen an der Enz. A short walk from the museum past the cemetery brings the visitor to the rebuilt mound.

Opposite Gold trim originally on Hochdorf shoes.
Above The restored Hochdorf mound.

GERMANY'S NEANDERTHAL REMAINS

TYPE: NATURAL CAVES AND ROCK SHELTERS • **ARCHITECTURAL STYLE:** N/A
LOCATION: METTMANN, NEAR DÜSSELDORF, GERMANY • **CONSTRUCTION BEGUN:** N/A

Since the discovery in August 1856 of the skeleton of the Neanderthal type specimen near Düsseldorf, Germany's Neander Valley (*Thal*) has been synonymous with our biological sister group: *Homo neanderthalensis*—the Neanderthal.

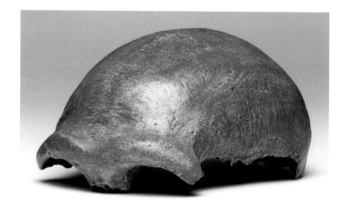

The steep-sided little valley, pocked with caves and rock shelters, was a celebrated beauty spot, but was progressively destroyed throughout the 1850s to satisfy the demands for limestone for Prussian construction. By the mid-decade, quarrymen had reached the Kleine Feldhoffer Grotte, a very small cave close to the valley top. Fortunately they would clear sediments from the caves by hand prior to dynamiting the rock, and as they worked, part of a skull and several bones of the body of an adult were dislodged and fell downslope, coming to rest in the rubble below. The quarry directors spotted them. Thinking they were of a cave bear, they set aside the remains to show to a local schoolteacher, Johann Carl Fuhlrott, who collected the more interesting of the valley's bones for discussion in natural history classes with his schoolchildren. To his everlasting credit, Fuhlrott realized the bones belonged not to a cave bear, but to an anatomically primitive human, of the sort that scientists like Charles Darwin were beginning to predict should be found in Ice Age deposits. In fact, several had been unearthed already: a jaw from Engis Cave in Belgium and a cranium from Gibraltar had come to light several decades beforehand, but natural scientists were not then ready to understand that humans had evolved and had once been incredibly diverse.

By 1856 science was ready. Fuhlrott contacted a professor of anatomy at Bonn University, Hermann Schaaffhausen (1816–1893), who confirmed that the bones belonged to an adult with a distinct anatomy, and the two published details of the remains in 1857. In 1862 an Irish anatomist, William King (1809–1886), gave the remains their formal name, *Homo neanderthalensis*. The cave's location, now quarried away, was forgotten, and the smaller fragments of bones remained where they lay, covered in quarrying rubble. Originally buried by his group, his head facing the 10-ft-wide (3 m) cave mouth, Neanderthal 1, as he became known to science, is one of the most pathological Neanderthals known, attesting to the hard life they lived. Before he died, at around the age of forty, he had fractured his arm, which had healed with a deformity; fractured his head in a fall; suffered with bad sinuses; and had an unknown bone-eating disease.

Radiocarbon dating has established he lived to adulthood around 40,000 years ago, shortly before the Neanderthals became extinct. Later re-excavation of the cave's spoil recovered many bone fragments, deriving from at least three Neanderthals, as well as stone tools that show it was also used as a campsite. Remarkably, Neanderthal 1's humerus preserved DNA, ensuring a double significance as the first Neanderthal remains to be recognized and one of the few used to sequence ancient DNA from a distinct human biological group.

The valley remains a pleasant spot, and the site of the Feldhoffer cave is marked. In the vicinity, the Neanderthal Museum presents the history of the site and the relevance of its finds for human evolution. Both are near Mettmann, but the original bones from the site are housed in the LVR-Landesmuseum in Bonn.

Opposite The original skullcap from Neanderthal 1, now in the Landesmuseum, Bonn.
Below An aerial view of the Neander Valley.

SALT AND WEALTH AT **HALLSTATT**

TYPE: SALT MINES AND CEMETERY • **ARCHITECTURAL STYLE:** N/A
LOCATION: AUSTRIAN ALPS • **CONSTRUCTION BEGUN:** CA. 1300 B.C.E.

Since the middle of the nineteenth century, a series of excavations at the Hallstatt cemetery, high up in the Austrian Alps, have yielded evidence of an ancient mining community made rich on the proceeds of salt.

Prehistoric miners at Hallstatt and other locations among the Austrian Alps south of Salzburg extracted vast quantities of rock salt that could be traded throughout central Europe. Salt was an essential commodity for preserving meat and fish. People and lactating cattle also crave salt in their diets. By the beginning of the first millennium B.C.E., demand for salt had reached such a level that communities that could produce it in pure form could become very wealthy. In the Alps, some mountains sat atop immense quantities of crystalline salt deposited when an ocean covered the area millions of years ago. In some places, these deposits could be reached by tunneling from the surface.

At Hallstatt, a high Alpine valley overlooks a deep lake. Under the adjacent mountains, immense quantities of crystalline salt were deposited when an ocean covered the area millions of years ago. During the second millennium B.C.E., Bronze Age miners began tunneling into the mountainside to follow veins of salt. In doing so, they left behind traces of their presence. The veins are up to 16 ft (5 m) thick, so miners used notched logs as ladders to reach their tops, while a remarkable wooden staircase was built about 1343 B.C.E. to move between levels. Cloth, leather, and wood artifacts were preserved in the salt and rediscovered by later miners.

Right Halstatt, Austria.
Opposite Example of Ramsauer's burial documentation.

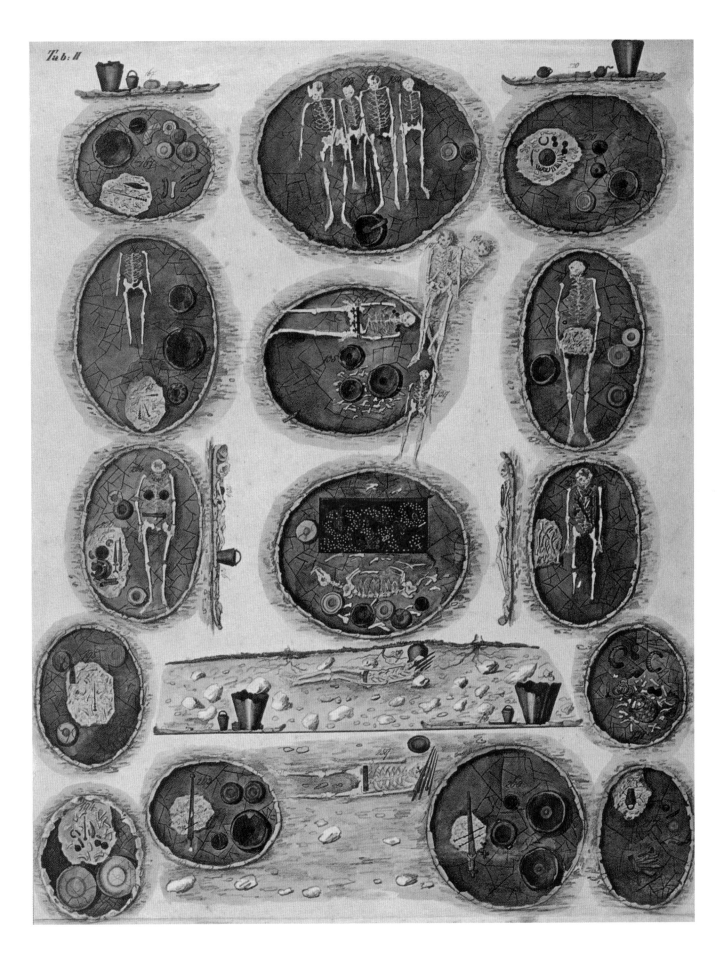

The peak of prehistoric mining activity occurred during the early Iron Age in the eighth century B.C.E., when tons of salt were extracted from the Hallstatt mines and exported throughout central Europe. Entire families, including children, were engaged in breaking salt loose using metal and antler tools and carrying it to the surface in leather backpacks and woolen sacks. No contemporaneous settlements have yet been found, so the details of their daily lives are unknown, but much of their time was spent inside the mountain working by torchlight. Some died in cave-ins. The corpse of one victim entombed in salt was found in 1734 and reburied in the village below.

Tremendous wealth flowed back into the Hallstatt community from its trading partners, reflected in the luxury items found in a cemetery just below the entrance to the modern mines. In 1846, the mine manager, Johann Georg Ramsauer (1795–1874), began to excavate human burials that had begun coming to light during digging

for gravel. By 1863, he had excavated 980 graves, which he recorded with watercolor paintings made by Isidor Engel. Since then, additional excavations, such as those by Marie, Duchess of Mecklenburg-Schwerin (1854–1920) in 1907, Friedrich Morton (1890–1969) in 1937–39, and the Natural History Museum in Vienna since 1993 have brought the total to about 1,500. Many more remain to be discovered, for archaeologists estimate that there were probably over 5,000 burials originally.

Both cremation and skeleton burials have been found in the cemetery, with the cremations being relatively "richer" in their grave furnishings. They can be dated to between 800 and 400 B.C.E., a time known as the Hallstatt Period in the archaeology of central Europe, which reflects the significance of the site. The graves contained all sorts of luxury items, including iron and bronze swords and daggers and bronze bowls, buckets, helmets, and cauldrons. Exotic materials in the graves reflect long-distance contacts and access to talented artisans, many

south of the Alps. For example, a sword handle carved from ivory (either African or Asian) was inlaid with Baltic amber, while glass vessels can be traced to the upper Adriatic area.

Recent excavations have shown that Ramsauer largely ignored (and discarded) highly fragmented pottery found in the burials in favor of the spectacular weapons, ornaments, metal bowls, and a small number of intact pottery vessels. Techniques have been developed to reconstruct the crushed pottery found in recent excavations, so it is now possible to study these important burial goods. It is clear that the ceramic vessels display a high degree of technical expertise.

Since the beginning of the twenty-first century, picturesque Hallstatt town has been overrun with tourists seeking an authentic Alpine village amid spectacular scenery. A belief propagated in social media that the town of Hallstatt provided the visual inspiration for the setting of Disney's *Frozen* movies also draws visitors. Those interested in archaeology can escape the crowds by taking a funicular railway to the base of the high valley and walking up to the salt mines and the Iron Age cemetery. Tours of the mines make it possible to imagine the world of the miners.

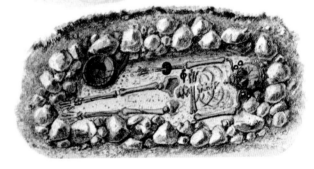

Opposite The remains of a 3,000-year-old prehistoric wooden staircase at the salt mine in Hallstatt.

Above top Overall view of the valley, with the cemetery leading up to the salt mine.

Above Example of Ramsauer's burial documentation.

THE IRON AGE SETTLEMENT AT **BISKUPIN**

TYPE: FORTIFIED SETTLEMENT • **ARCHITECTURAL STYLE:** TIMBER DWELLINGS AND RAMPARTS
LOCATION: NORTHWEST POLAND • **CONSTRUCTION BEGUN:** 738 B.C.E.

North of Gniezno in northwest Poland, Route 5 runs across the Polish plain, past fields and pastures, occasionally skirting lakes connected by streams. Prehistoric people were drawn to these lakes from the Stone Age onward. During the millennia that followed, they established many settlements among them. South of Żnin, a road turns off east toward Gąsawa, where signs direct the visitor to Biskupin. Here, in 1933, a waterlogged Iron Age settlement was discovered on a peninsula in one of the lakes.

Rising waters had inundated the site, preserving the timbers, which were then exposed when the water level dropped. A local schoolteacher notified archaeologists, who began excavations the following year to remove the peat and soil in which the timbers were embedded. Gradually, outlines of structures emerged from the tangle of logs, and photographs from an observation balloon revealed the plan of the settlement.

Multipurpose buildings serving as dwellings, workshops, stables, and storerooms ran in parallel rows, sharing common walls. Each unit was about 26 ft (8 m) by 30 ft (9 m), with a stone hearth in the center. If they were all occupied at the same time, several hundred people probably lived very close together. Log streets separated the rows of houses—eleven streets in all—with another road surrounding the inhabited area. Encircling the whole, a rampart of wooden cribs filled with earth and stone enclosed an area approximately 525 ft (160 m) wide by 660 ft (200 m) long. Pointed posts at the outer base of the rampart served as a breakwater and deterred attackers from getting close.

Through dendrochronology (tree-ring dating), we know almost exactly when Biskupin dates from. Most of the trees used in the houses, streets, and the rampart were felled between 747 and 722 B.C.E. More than half were cut during the winter of 738–737 B.C.E. That year must have been a busy time on the Biskupin peninsula. First, the inhabitants laid out the streets and houses, since their regularity could not have been accomplished without planning. They then cut timbers to exact lengths to build the houses in uniform dimensions and to pave the streets. Finally, they constructed and filled the timber cribs for the ramparts.

The inhabitants went out to fields and pastures through a single gate to cultivate wheat and millet and to tend herds of livestock. Back within the ramparts, they made iron and bronze implements, pottery, and wove woolen cloth. Archaeologists have recovered many wooden artifacts from the waterlogged deposits, including wheels and plows. After several decades, rising lake water levels appear to have doomed the settlement.

The Biskupin Iron Age settlement has been reconstructed as an archaeological park, comprising a replica of the wooden buildings, streets, and ramparts, along with a museum displaying the finds. A recent addition to the complex is the reconstruction of a nearby Neolithic settlement from about 4500 B.C.E., where a longhouse and burials were discovered in the 1950s.

Opposite Various views of the reconstructed settlement with its wooden buildings, streets, and ramparts.

THE ANCIENT CITY OF **ROME**

TYPE: CITY • **ARCHITECTURAL STYLE:** CLASSICAL
LOCATION: ITALY • **CONSTRUCTION BEGUN:** 447 B.C.E.

The majestic remains of imperial Rome form part of the cityscape of this historic city. The temples and triumphal arches of the forum are reminders of the expanse of the empire, and the Colosseum represents the cruelty of public spectacle.

Augustus (63 B.C.E.–14 C.E.), the first Roman emperor, claimed to have transformed the city of Rome from a city of brick to a city of marble. One of the most significant of his monuments is the Ara Pacis (Altar of Peace) that lay next to the Tiber to the north of the Ponte Cavour. The architectural reliefs have been reconstructed in a purpose-built structure that suggests the nature of the altar. It was decorated with a continuous frieze, reminiscent of those from the Parthenon at Athens and on the Great Altar of Zeus at Pergamon. Among the scenes are members of the family of the emperor Augustus coming to make a sacrifice and thus expressing their piety for the traditional Roman gods. This was a reminder of the new order in the Roman world as it moved away from the Republic and the civil wars. The frieze includes a scene showing the mythical origins of the city of Rome with Romulus and Remus. Other reliefs provide a reminder of the bounty enjoyed by the city of Rome, reflecting the benefits of peace that were to be enjoyed under Augustus.

Adjacent to the Ara Pacis was the Mausoleum of Augustus. The achievements, the Res Gestae, of the emperor were displayed on now-lost bronze plaques outside; copies on marble were displayed on the temple to the imperial cult in Ancyra (modern Ankara) in Turkey. The very name of the structure alluded to the burial place of Mausolus in Halikarnassos (modern Bodrum) in western Turkey, one of the wonders of the ancient world.

The choice of placing this burial place for Augustus' family in the heart of Rome placed a new emphasis on the city.

Augustus erected a sundial to the southeast of the altar. Although this can no longer be seen, the Egyptian obelisk, originally made for the sixth-century B.C.E. pharaoh Psammetichus II at Heliopolis, was re-erected in the Piazza di Montecitorio and bears a Latin inscription recording Augustus' role. It dates to 10 B.C.E.

The Roman Forum

The political heart of the city of Rome lay in the forum, where the senate met in the curia. The area developed over time. Its limits are marked by two dominant victory monuments: the arch of Titus, recording the capture of the city of Jerusalem in 70 C.E. (and showing some of the trophies from the sack of the temple) in the reliefs; and the arch of Septimius Severus, recording his spectacular victories in the eastern empire against the Parthians and the creation of a new province of Mesopotamia in 199 C.E.

To the north of the main forum was the forum of Augustus, which contained the great temple of Mars Ultor (the Avenger) that had been promised by the emperor before the battle of Philippi in northern Greece in 42 B.C.E. Behind

Opposite, from top The interior of the Colosseum. The Corinthian columns of the temple of Vespasian and Titus, and the temple of Saturn looking toward the Palatine.

it stands the wall, some 98 ft (30 m high), constructed to protect these public spaces from the risk of fire in the densely populated areas of the city.

One of the other public areas was the forum of Trajan, northwest of that of Augustus, which commemorated the expansion of the empire in Dacia (modern Romania) in 106 C.E. This contained a new market cut into the slopes of the Quirinal hill. At the western end of the forum, behind the Basilica Ulpia, Trajan placed his burial in a large base supporting a column decorated with a spiral frieze showing scenes from his conquest of Dacia. A large bronze statue of the emperor originally stood on the top, although this has now been replaced by one of St. Peter. Adjacent to the column was a library with two wings, each containing works in Latin or in Greek.

Palaces

Adjacent to the Roman forum was the Palatine hill, the location of the imperial palace. Some first-century B.C.E. houses have been popularly linked to the emperor Augustus and his wife Livia. Remains of Domitian's palace dating to the late first century C.E. are visible. The complex includes an extensive banqueting hall, as well as an audience chamber where citizens could approach the emperor.

On the slope of the Esquiline hill are the remains of part of Nero's Golden House, which was decorated with wall paintings and sculptures. It was hidden under the platform created for the construction of the baths of the Emperor Trajan after the death of Nero in 69 C.E. The grounds of the Golden House included a lake, and the emperor Vespasian turned this space into the Colosseum, a major amphitheater for hosting gladiatorial shows. This structure was funded by booty from the sack of Jerusalem.

Above One of the Dacian captives from the forum of Trajan, reused on the Arch of Constantine.

Opposite The Arch of Titus commemorates the sack of the city of Jerusalem during the Jewish revolt.

Victory Monuments

A range of monuments celebrated Rome's victories across its expanding empire. The second-century C.E. philosopher-emperor Marcus Aurelius marked his victories over the northern tribes who were threatening the empire. His column, still standing in the Piazza Colonna, was reminiscent of that created by Trajan.

Panels from the dismantled triumphal arch of Marcus Aurelius were reused in the arch of Constantine that stands next to the Colosseum. Constantine's monument celebrated not the defeat of Rome's enemies, but that of his rivals for imperial power, specifically Maxentius, who was defeated at the battle of the Milvian Bridge in 312 C.E. The arch incorporates defeated Dacians who appear to have been removed from Trajan's forum, as well as roundels from an unknown Hadrianic building.

The main archaeological sites such as the Roman forum, the Colosseum, and Trajan's column are within easy walking distance of each other. The Colosseo Metro station is conveniently situated for this area. Sturdy shoes are a must for Rome's streets.

THE BURIED CITIES OF
POMPEII AND **HERCULANEUM**

TYPE: URBAN • **ARCHITECTURAL STYLE:** CLASSICAL
LOCATION: BAY OF NAPLES, ITALY • **CONSTRUCTION BEGUN:** SIXTH CENTURY B.C.E.

The brooding presence of Mount Vesuvius dominates the cities of Pompeii and Herculaneum, destroyed and buried during the volcano's eruption in 79 C.E. A vivid eyewitness account of the eruption survives in the works of the younger Pliny, and provides a compelling background to the dramatic end of these communities. The wall paintings and objects preserved by the destruction bring these ancient cities back to life.

The ancient city of Pompeii lies 16 miles (26 km) southeast of the modern city of Naples. Excavations have provided an insight into the range of domestic, social, and economic activities in the city. The main public area, the forum, is located in the west, and a temple of Jupiter on a high podium dominates the north end of the city. At the southwest corner is the basilica used for legal cases; it contained an internal colonnade, though only the brick bases have survived the eruption and early trophy hunters. On the east side, adjacent to the temple of Jupiter, is the macellum, or meat and fish market, constructed in the second century B.C.E. At the southeast corner is the major building donated by a prominent woman named as Eumachia in the inscription. Her husband held public office in 3 C.E. Eumachia's portrait was found inside the building, and she is known to have been a public priestess. The actual purpose of this building is undetermined, although the dedication made clear her loyalty to the emperor Augustus. Eumachia's monumental tomb has been located outside the Nuceria gate on the southeast side of the city.

Five sets of public baths have been identified at Pompeii. The forum baths lie immediately to the north of the forum and were built ca. 80 B.C.E. An inscription

shows that they were constructed at public expense. The Stabian baths were remodeled in the Augustan period and contained an open exercise area.

The amphitheater is located in the southeast corner of the city. It was designed to hold up to 15,000 spectators. The structure was the gift of two magistrates whose benefaction is recorded in two inscriptions. The amphitheater was the scene of a riot in 59 C.E. between the people of Pompeii and the town of Nuceria; an image of the riot has survived in a wall painting from one of the private houses at Pompeii. The gladiatorial barracks were found near the Stabiae Gate on the south side of the city. The rooms were found to contain gladiatorial equipment, including ornate Thracian helmets.

Some of the most intimate spaces in Pompeii are the public bars and inns. Wine amphorae were found stacked in the Bar of Asellina. Decoration in the Bar of Salvius shows a pair of men gambling at a board game.

Several cemeteries outside the main gates of Pompeii have been excavated. Those outside the Herculaneum Gate on the northwest side included a number of those individuals who held high public office and who were buried in monumental and ostentatious tombs.

Opposite The bronze statue of Apollo from the sanctuary of Apollo.

Below The temple of Jupiter at the north end of the forum at Pompeii, with Vesuvius in the background.

Private Houses

One of the largest private houses found at Pompeii is the House of the Faun. It contained a number of high-quality mosaics, including one depicting the victory of Alexander the Great over Persian King Darius at the battle of Issos. This may now be seen in the Archaeological Museum in Naples (though a replica has been installed in the house). Careful excavation of gardens, and the taking of casts of the roots, has allowed the reconstruction of plantings within these private spaces. In the House of the Vettii there is a blend of small-scale classical sculpture as well as fountains, all sitting within the colonnade. In the House of the Golden Bracelet a series of wall paintings with birds in the shrubs forms the backdrop to the actual plantings.

One of the finest residences outside the walls of Pompeii to the northwest is the Villa of the Mysteries. The name derives from the paintings, set against a vivid red background, that show part of a mystery cult. Although the figures are linked to the god of wine, Bacchus, the event seems to be related to the admission of women into some type of ritual.

Above The peristyle and garden in the House of Venus in a Shell.

Below The amphitheater at Pompeii was the site of a riot in 59 C.E.

Right The former sea front of Herculaneum with the Suburban Baths and the terrace of Marcus Nonius Balbus.

Herculaneum

Herculaneum lies 11 miles (18 km) to the northwest of Pompeii at the foot of Vesuvius. The city was buried under as much as 75 ft (23 m) of volcanic debris, presenting a more complicated situation than at Pompeii. The high temperatures of the series of pyroclastic flows that struck the city means that organic materials, including bodies, were carbonized. Thus wooden features including doors and furniture have survived. A baby's cradle was found in the House of Marcus Pilius Primigenius Granianus. It is also possible to see mezzanine floors in some of the structures.

Two sets of baths have been excavated: the Central baths, and the Suburban baths (in the southwest of the city). The Suburban baths were in the process of refurbishment at the time of the eruption, and building materials were found inside the rooms.

Both sites are reached by Circumvesuviana from Naples, alighting at Pompeii Scavi or Ercolano Scavi. In both cases there is a short walk to the archaeological site. These train services can be packed. The site of Pompeii is extensive, and sensible shoes are a must. The Archaeological Museum in Naples is well worth a visit.

THE ANCIENT CITY OF **ATHENS**

TYPE: TEMPLE, CIVIC • **ARCHITECTURAL STYLE:** CLASSICAL, ROMAN
LOCATION: ATHENS, GREECE • **CONSTRUCTION BEGUN:** 447 B.C.E.

The sunset view of the Parthenon and the Athenian Acropolis from the Philopappos Hill in Athens presents an enduring reminder of the power of classical architecture on western Europe. Looking westward you can see the line of the Long Walls, constructed to allow the city to function in time of siege, that connected the city with the fortified harbor of the Piraeus.

The Periclean City

The Archaic city of Athens was effectively destroyed in the Persian invasion of mainland Greece in 480 B.C.E. The newly constructed temple of Athena on the Acropolis was left in ruins. Athens' relationship with other city-states changed in the years following the Persian Wars. A league formed to resist Persian encroachments soon became an empire with its members paying tribute to Athens. This income helped to fund a major building program in Athens from the middle of the fifth century B.C.E. Visitors could follow the different projects via a series of publicly displayed accounts cut onto marble stelae that map the spending and progress. Many of the fragments are displayed in the Epigraphic Museum in Athens.

At the heart of the building program was the monumental temple of Athena, known as the Parthenon. This new temple contained the colossal chryselephantine statue of the goddess designed by the sculptor Pheidias. Although the statue has not survived, there is a detailed description by the second century C.E. Roman travel writer Pausanias, and a number of small marble replicas are known. The temple was heavily decorated with architectural sculptures. The west pediment, which faced anyone approaching the temple, depicted the battle for the control of Athens. At the east end, above the main entrance to the temple, a pediment showed the birth of Athena, framed in the two corners by the chariots of Helios and Selene. Square reliefs, or metopes, gracing the exterior of the temple above the columns showed the mythical conflict between the Greeks and the forces of barbarism: centaurs, Amazons, and giants. On the upper wall of the interior building, and inside the columns, a continuous frieze started at the west end and processed separately along the north and south sides. It showed a grand procession with riders, chariots, and then sacrificial animals. The two processions met above the east door, where the Olympian gods viewed the folding of the sacred peplos.

The main entrance to the Acropolis was monumentalized by a grand gateway with multiple doors known as the Propylaia. The structure contained a large dining room on its north side. The Propylaia was left unfinished when war with Sparta broke out at the end of the 430s B.C.E. However, victories in the early stages of the war were commemorated in the construction of the Ionic temple of Athena Nike that stood on the south bastion,

Opposite The Acropolis of Athens, an ancient citadel that sits on a rocky outcrop above the city.

and was accessed from the Propylaia. The Athenians constructed the Erechtheion in the final stages of the Peloponnesian War. One of its striking features was a porch supported by architectural women, or caryatids, overlying the earlier Archaic temple. The temple contained a number of features, including the sacred olive tree that Athena had given to the city. The theater of Dionysus was cut into the south slope of the Acropolis. This was the setting for the plays that were written during the fifth century B.C.E. by Sophocles, Euripides, and Aristophanes.

The political heart of the city of Athens lay in the agora, to the north of the Acropolis. The earliest democratic structures can be dated to the sixth century B.C.E., although the Persians destroyed them. A great drain running along the west side determined the orientation of buildings in the agora. At the southern end was the circular tholos, where the tribe that held office for the month was based. Immediately to the north was the bouleuterion, where the council consisting of fifty members from each of the ten tribes met. To the east of the bouleuterion was a long statue base representing the ten eponymous heroes of Athens, where notices relating to the tribes were displayed. The Athenians built the temple of Hephaistos on the low hill behind the bouleuterion, probably in the 440s.

Cemeteries were located outside the walls of the city, alongside the roads leading out into Attica. One of the best explored is in the Kerameikos to the northwest. This area was used from the Archaic period, and some of the sixth-century stelae and monuments were reused in the walls that were constructed after the Persian destruction of the city.

The Roman City

The Arch of Hadrian to the east of the Acropolis, constructed in 132 C.E., marks the distinction between the Classical city and the later Roman expansion. There are two inscriptions on each side of the arch: "This is Athens, the former City of Theseus" and "This is the City of Hadrian not of Theseus."

Athens underwent transformation from the reign of Augustus (63 B.C.E.–14 C.E.). A round Ionic structure linked to the cult of Roma and Augustus was placed to east of the Parthenon, probably shortly after 27 B.C.E. In 15 B.C.E. Agrippa, the son-in-law of Augustus, visited Athens and placed an odeion, or concert hall, in the open space of the agora. This replaced the fifth-century Odeion of Pericles, adjacent to the theater of Dionysus, that had been destroyed during the siege of Sulla in 86 B.C.E. Adjacent to the odeion was a temple of Zeus. Mason marks indicate that, during the early Roman period, this fifth-century B.C.E. building was dismantled and re-erected in the agora, probably for use in the Roman imperial cult.

The Romans constructed a new market to the east of the agora. The western entrance, built in Doric style and echoing Periclean Athens, carried an inscription, dated to 11–9 B.C.E., which showed it was a benefaction of Caesar and Augustus. The structure consisted of an open area surrounded by a colonnade, with shops behind. Immediately to the east of this new market was the Hellenistic Tower of the Winds.

At the end of the first century C.E., during the reign of the emperor Trajan (53–117 C.E.), an Athenian benefactor,

Opposite The Odeion of Herodes Atticus on the south slope of the Athenian Acropolis.
Above left The reliefs of the Wind Gods, Notos (south) and Euros (southeast), on the Tower of the Winds.
Above right The Olympieion in the early morning light.

Titus Flavius Pantainos, presented the city with a new library that was constructed to the southeast of the agora beside the Panathenaic way. It was under Trajan's successor, Hadrian (76–138 C.E.), that the city was reformed. He built a major library to the north of the Roman market that contained lecture rooms. It used imported marble from as far afield as western Asia Minor; the inner colonnade contained 100 columns quarried in Phrygia. The most important structure built during Hadrian's reign was the monumental Olympieion, probably dedicated during his visit to Athens in 131–32 C.E. The building had been started in the late sixth century B.C.E. but had never been completed. The structure is over 360 ft (110 m) in length, and was surrounded by 104 Corinthian columns.

The archaeological sites of the Kerameikos, the Agora, the Acropolis, and the Olympieion are easily reached from the Athens Metro stations (Kerameikos, Thissio, and Akropolis). There are site museums at the Kerameikos, the Agora (in the Stoa of Attalos), and adjacent to the Akropolis Metro station; some stations have small displays of finds made during their construction. The National Archaeological Museum contains artifacts from Athens as well as the rest of Greece.

THE SANCTUARY OF ZEUS AT **OLYMPIA**

TYPE: SANCTUARY • **ARCHITECTURAL STYLE:** CLASSICAL
LOCATION: PELOPONNESE, GREECE • **CONSTRUCTION BEGUN:** 776 B.C.E.

Olympia is the home of the original Olympic Games, traditionally founded in 776 B.C.E. and continuing into the Roman period. The remains of the running track lie adjacent to the sanctuary of Zeus, which contains the foundations of the god's temple that once housed a colossal gold and ivory cult statue.

The ancient Greek site of Olympia, lies in Elis in the western Peloponnese, 186 miles (300 km) by road west of Athens. The site is located at the confluence of the Alphaios and the smaller Kladeos rivers. At the heart of the sanctuary was the temple of Zeus, constructed in the Doric order between 470 and 456 B.C.E. It was made from local limestone with a stucco finish; the foundations of

the temple and several fallen sections of column remain. The building contained the now-lost gold and ivory statue of the seated god, which was created by the sculptor

Opposite The colonnade in the third century B.C.E. gymnasium used for training athletes.
Below The fallen columns from the temple of Zeus, the focal point of the sanctuary.

Pheidias in the mid-fifth century B.C.E. The second-century C.E. Roman travel writer Pausanias described the statue—it seems to have been removed to the Palace of Lausus in Constantinople (modern Istanbul) in late antiquity. A German team excavating the ancient workshop to the west of the temple of Zeus, in which the statue was made, revealed remains of materials and molds used in its creation; the building was later converted into a Christian basilica. The temple of Zeus featured marble architectural sculptures. At each end, square metopes showed the labors of Herakles, such as the cleaning of the Augean stables and the capture of the Cretan bull. Freestanding statues filled the triangular pediments at each end of the building: at the east end, facing the stadium, was a scene depicting the mythical founding of the games with the race between Oenomaos and Pelops, and Zeus presiding at the center. At the west end was the mythical battle between the Lapiths and the Centaurs with Apollo at the center. Close to Apollo is the Athenian hero Theseus, who is about to bring an axe down on the head of a centaur. The use of the centauromachy may have been used to allude to the clash between the Greeks and barbarians, and specifically to the Persian wars that had concluded with the Greek victories at Salamis and Plataia in 480 and 479 B.C.E. The sculptures themselves are on display in the on-site archaeological museum.

To the north of the temple of Zeus stood the much older temple of Hera, also constructed in the Doric style, and probably dating to around 600 B.C.E. Excavations have yielded a limestone female head that probably represented the goddess. A fourth-century B.C.E. marble statue of Hermes holding a young Dionysus by the Athenian sculptor Praxiteles was also found inside the temple.

Immediately to the west of the temple of Hera was a round structure in the Ionic style, the Philippeion, constructed by Philip II of Macedon (382–336 B.C.E.) after his victory over the Greek alliance led by Athens and Thebes at the battle of Chaironeia in 338 B.C.E. Philip II's son, Alexander the Great (356–323 B.C.E.), completed the temple, and gold and ivory portraits of members of the Macedonian family were displayed inside, probably deliberately hinting at their semidivine status. The benefactor Herodes Atticus added a monumental fountain house on the north side of the Altis in the second century C.E. (Herodes Atticus's odeion can be seen on the south side of the Athenian Acropolis).

Below left The circular Philippeion served as a sanctuary for the deified members of the Macedonian royal family.
Below right The stadium, looking northwest from the sanctuary.
Opposite The archaic temple of Hera on the north side of the Altis.

The Stadium Area

Immediately to the east of the sanctuary, but connected to it by a tunnel, was the stadium where the athletic events took place. At the west end was the grooved starting line. The stadium has a length of 600 Olympic feet (630.8 ft/ 192.27 m). A special area for the judges was located at the midpoint. The hillside slope of the Kronion to the north of the stadium provided space for viewers to watch the festival. It has been estimated that the stadium could hold some 45,000 viewers. On a terrace on the north side of the sanctuary stood a line of treasuries established by the different urban communities of the Greek world; their foundations are clearly visible. The group here mainly represented some of the Greek colonies in southern Italy and Sicily, including Metapontum and Syracuse. The purpose of these structures was to store and display the civic dedications to Zeus.

The precinct contains numerous bases for inscribed monuments celebrating victorious athletes, although the statues themselves, originally in bronze, are now lost. A tall pedestal surmounted by a statue of Victory (Nike) stood to the southeast of the temple of Zeus. The inscription records that it was the work of Paeonius of Mende (in northern Greece), and the monument celebrated the victory of the Messenians (the subjected region in the southwest Peloponnese) over the Spartans in the 420s B.C.E., during the early stages of the Peloponnesian War. The Nike itself was over 9.8 ft (3 m) tall and showed her descending into the sanctuary; it is displayed in the site museum.

Olympia is reached by train from Pyrgos (about 30 minutes), and the archaeological park is about a 15-minute walk from the station. There is a major archaeological museum at Olympia displaying the architectural sculptures from the temple of Zeus. Two other museums explore the history of the excavations and the history of the Olympic games.

THE ROMAN COLONY AT **CORINTH**

TYPE: CITY • **ARCHITECTURAL STYLE:** CLASSICAL, ROMAN
LOCATION: PELOPONNESE • **CONSTRUCTION BEGUN:** EIGHTH CENTURY B.C.E.

The ancient city of Corinth is dominated by the Acrocorinth that rises to a height of 1886 ft (575 m) behind the city, welcoming travelers to the Peloponnese. It was orginally the site of a small temple of Aphrodite, or Venus, regarded as the ancestor of Julius Caesar (100–44 B.C.E.), who founded the Roman colony here. The lower city provides some of the most important Roman remains in Greece, as well as two well-preserved harbor complexes.

Corinth itself was established in the eighth century B.C.E., and continued as a city until 146 B.C.E., when the Romans destroyed it and left the site abandoned for nearly a century. Few substantial remains survive from this earlier period, except for the Archaic temple of Apollo constructed in the Doric style in the mid-sixth century B.C.E.; seven columns are still standing. The Romans later adapted the building by removing the interior columns in order to allow for different cult practices.

Julius Caesar refounded the city as a colony in 44 B.C.E. It became the seat of the Roman governor of the province of Achaia. The architecture of the city was deliberately Italian, as opposed to Greek, with temples constructed on raised podia (contrasting with the earlier Doric temple above the forum). Latin was the language of choice for public inscriptions, at least for the first two centuries of the colony's life.

The heart of the Roman colony was the forum, lying to the south of the hill dominated by the earlier Doric temple. It contained the legal center of the community, with a basilica at the eastern end that was found to contain portrait statues of the Julio-Claudian family. At the western end, raised on a terrace above the open space, was a monumental temple (temple E), possibly linked to the Roman imperial cult. The original building was constructed in the Doric

Above The temple of Apollo, viewed from the peribolos of Apollo across the Lechaeum Road.

Opposite The Lechaeum Road, looking to the south toward the forum. The Acrocorinth dominates the city.

style, probably in the early first century C.E. It was rebuilt at the end of the century in the Corinthian style, and placed on a podium 11 ft (3.4 m) high.

Remains of the sloping auditorium of an ancient Greek theater have been excavated to the west of the Doric temple. The theater probably dates from the fifth century B.C.E., but was adapted in the early years of the Roman colony, when a substantial stage building was constructed. Adjacent to the theater is a square. Cut into large slabs laid along the edge is a Latin inscription, originally in bronze lettering, that records the benefaction of Erastus, who gave this facility to the colony from his own money as part of his election promise after he had taken up the office of aedile (an elected official in charge of public buildings).

Several bathhouses have been excavated in the city. A set on the Lechaeum Road, immediately outside the archaeological park, was constructed around 200 C.E. They may have been a gift of Eurykles of Sparta.

In the Archaic period, a trackway or *diolkos* crossed the Isthmus of Corinth, allowing small vessels to traverse the narrow piece of land; remains can still be seen adjacent to the nineteenth-century Corinth Canal. The emperor Nero (37–68 C.E.) had a plan to cut a canal to turn the Peloponnese into a true island, but never completed the project. Two major harbors developed here in the Roman period. Cenchreae was established on the Saronic Gulf and provided access to the eastern Mediterranean. Lechaeum was placed on the Gulf of Corinth, allowing access to the Adriatic and Italy. These facilities were intended to enable the movement of goods to avoid the dangerous route around the south coast of the Peloponnese.

Corinth is easily reached from Athens by means of suburban train as well as by intercity coach. There are buses from the town center to the archaeological park, where there is a museum displaying finds from the city and local area.

THE SANCTUARY OF **DELPHI**

TYPE: SANCTUARY • **ARCHITECTURAL STYLE:** CLASSICAL
LOCATION: CENTRAL GREECE • **CONSTRUCTION BEGUN:** EIGHTH CENTURY B.C.E.

High in the mountains of central Greece, a sacred path snakes its way up a steeply sloping site toward a famous temple dedicated to the Greek god of prophecy, Apollo. Close to Mount Parnassus, which stands at just under 8,200 ft (2,500 m), this is Delphi, home to the Pythian games. The site lies 6 miles (10 km) from Itea on the Gulf of Corinth, and 118 miles (190 km) northwest of Athens.

Just inside the entrance to the sanctuary is a lavish monument constructed by the Spartans to mark their naval defeat of the Athenians at the battle of Aigospatamoi in 405 B.C.E., right at the end of the Peloponnesian war. It originally contained a portrait of the Spartan commander Lysander and faced an Athenian monument that marked the victory over the Persians at Marathon in 490 B.C.E.

Different cities of the Greek world kept valuable dedications in treasuries that lined the path leading up to the temple of Apollo, and a number of them have been reconstructed. The treasury of the island of Siphnos is decorated in the Ionian style with a continuous architectural relief that records the battle between the Olympian gods and the giants. It contains one of the earliest uses of a caryatid, a female figure acting as a column. The point at which the path turns—a choice location on this route—is dominated by the treasury of the Athenians, decorated with architectural panels presenting the parallel deeds of Herakles and the Athenian hero Theseus. A tradition recorded in the Roman period suggested that the treasury had been constructed using the booty won from the Persians at the battle of Marathon.

The temple of Apollo is supported on a massive terrace. A new temple was constructed following the destruction by fire of an earlier building in 548 B.C.E. The pediments at each end of the building featured sculptures: the battle with the giants in the west, and the appearance of Apollo in the east. There was a tradition that the exiled Alcmaeonid family from Athens paid for the marble sculptures in 505 B.C.E.

To the east of the temple is a large altar where the ancient Greeks made sacrifices to Apollo. Adjacent to this is the base of a bronze cauldron erected by the different Greek cities to mark the defeat of the Persian army at the battle of Plataia in 479 B.C.E. Bronze twisted snakes supported the cauldron, each bearing inscriptions of the names of the cities. The cauldron was removed in late antiquity to Byzantium (modern Istanbul), where it remains on display in the hippodrome.

At the top of this site lies the stadium that hosted athletic events for the Pythian games. French excavations revealed the remains of a bronze charioteer, dedicated as a victory monument by one of the rulers of Gela in southern Sicily. The statue is displayed in the site's archaeological museum.

There are daily public buses to Delphi from Athens as well as coach tours. An overnight stay would be advised. There is a major archaeological museum at the site displaying architectural sculptures as well as small finds.

Opposite, from top The temple of Apollo, the location of the Delphic oracle. The theater, with the temple of Apollo and the Treasury of the Athenians beyond.

WELL-PRESERVED **AKROTIRI**

TYPE: TOWN • **ARCHITECTURAL STYLE:** CYCLADIC LATE BRONZE AGE
LOCATION: SANTORINI, GREECE • **CONSTRUCTION BEGUN:** CA. 1650 B.C.E.

Present-day visitors to the Cycladic island of Santorini are greeted by the sight of picture-postcard Greek villages atop high cliffs. On closer inspection, it will be found that the cliffs are formed of many layers of pumice, surrounding a caldera, evidence of the major volcanic eruption which changed the appearance of the island forever. In the middle of the second millennium B.C.E., this eruption buried the town of Akrotiri.

Also known as Santorini, the island of Thera lies in the Aegean Sea, approximately 60 miles (100 km) north of Crete. Its present-day appearance reveals its volcanic heritage, since the archipelago to which Santorini now belongs was originally a single island. There has been ongoing discussion regarding the date of the volcanic eruption the destroyed the island. The traditional date, derived from archaeological comparison with objects

from sites elsewhere, is around 1500 B.C.E. However, recent scientific studies suggest that it may have occurred approximately a century earlier. The debate continues.

Archaeological investigations at Akrotiri have revealed that it was a prosperous and highly developed Bronze Age settlement, aided by a location that enabled it to take advantage of trade routes in the Aegean. In particular, contact with the Minoan society on Crete is demonstrated by some of the subjects of wall paintings, particularly those showing monkeys, and a few objects inscribed with Linear A script, as used in Minoan palace administrations, including at Knossos.

Given the preservation of the settlement, archaeologists have been able to visualize objects that would not normally have survived. For example, they found evidence of the use of wooden furniture. Pouring plaster of Paris into cavities in the ash revealed the shapes of tables and beds, their form preserved even though the wood from which they were made had rotted. Unlike the Roman sites of Pompeii and Herculaneum, no traces of people or animals exist, suggesting that the population had made its escape.

In private houses, the ground floor was primarily used for the storage and preparation of food. Evidence includes large storage vessels, known in Greek as *pithoi*, some of which were made locally, with others imported from elsewhere in the Cyclades or from Crete.

Surviving Art

Wall paintings are a particular feature of Akrotiri. Found in their original locations, they are much better preserved than examples at other Aegean sites. This has enabled archaeologists to reconstruct the decorative schemes of individual rooms and groups of rooms.

One wall painting ran around the top part of a room in the West House. Known as the Flotilla Fresco or Ship Procession Fresco, it shows a fleet of eight large and elaborately decorated ships, accompanied by three smaller vessels, seemingly traveling between two ports. In addition to valuable information on ship construction, the Flotilla

Opposite Ground floor rooms in Building Complex Alpha at Akrotiri, showing large storage vessels.

Above, from top Gold figurine of an ibex, found near Xeste 3 during construction of the new shelter over the site. A section of the Flotilla Fresco from the West House.

Fresco also gives an insight into the appearance of the island's buildings. Other wall paintings in the West House include a depiction of two young fishermen, shown life-sized, carrying their catch. Another, on the doorjamb of an adjoining room shows a young woman, identified as a priestess from her distinctive clothing and the object she carries, which may be

an incense burner. The wall paintings from the West House, and others from the site, aid our understanding of clothing from this time, as there is very limited evidence of actual textiles from this period in the Aegean.

Several wall paintings are interpreted as showing religious scenes, often with women as the main participants, which can be seen in the decoration of the large building known as Xeste 3. This structure was likely to have hosted community, official, and religious functions. With a footprint of around 3,230 sq ft (300 sq m) and extending up to three stories tall, its wall paintings provide the most complete picture of cult activity at Akrotiri.

The fragile nature of the archaeological remains at Akrotiri requires protection from the elements, and there has been a shelter over the site since it opened to the public. To ensure the long-term protection of the site and to enhance the visitor experience, a new shelter opened in 2012 covering 16 acres (6.5 ha). In order to achieve the most favorable temperature inside the building, the architects incorporated features that take account of environmental conditions. This has not only succeeded in creating an unforgettable experience for present-day visitors, but also has contributed to the preservation of this unique site for years to come.

While there is no museum at the site, finds from the excavations at Akrotiri are on display at the Museum of Prehistoric Thera in Fira, the main town on the island.

Above Remains of buildings at Akrotiri protected by the modern shelter.
Opposite Wall painting from Building Complex Beta showing blue monkeys.

THE FORTIFIED CITADEL OF **MYCENAE**

TYPE: PALACE AND TOMBS • **ARCHITECTURAL STYLE:** MYCENAEAN
LOCATION: PELOPONNESE, GREECE • **CONSTRUCTION BEGUN:** CA. 1600 B.C.E.

Mycenae was built on a limestone outcrop, in a commanding position in the landscape, its location is as impressive today as it was in antiquity. The archaeological site is about 1.2 miles (2 km) from the modern-day village of the same name, situated in the northeast of the Peloponnese, Greece.

Mycenae is immortalized in legend; in Homer's epic poem *The Iliad*, the citadel was the home of King Agamemnon, leader of the Achaean forces against the Trojans. The palace on the summit of the citadel is also the setting for the murder of Agamemnon by his wife Clytemnestra and her subsequent murder by her son Orestes, as dramatized in the *Oresteia* by Aeschylus. There is evidence of occupation at Mycenae from the seventh millennium B.C.E. onward, although the visible archaeological remains date from the late seventeenth to the thirteenth centuries B.C.E., a time when Mycenae was the leading center of Bronze Age society on the Greek mainland.

Visitors to the site are immediately reminded of the Homeric epithet "Well-Built Mycenae." The citadel is still surrounded by impressive walls built in the technique known as "Cyclopean," as it was believed by the ancient Greeks that the stones were so large they must have been moved by the Cyclopes, a race of one-eyed giants. No less impressive to the modern-day visitor is the Lion Gate, set within the fortification walls, so-named because of the sculpture in the gate's relieving triangle, which depicts a pair of lionesses. Other impressive evidence of ancient engineering skill is a secret cistern, which ensured that the inhabitants of Mycenae would not be without water in the event of a siege.

Above left The citadel of Mycenae in the middle distance with "houses" in the foreground.
Above right The Lion Gate set into "Cyclopean walls," leading into the citadel at Mycenae.
Opposite Interior of the tholos tomb known as the Treasury of Atreus.

Mycenae's Graves

Two funerary enclosures, Grave Circles A and B, each contain more than twenty burials and were in use from the end of the seventeenth until the sixteenth century B.C.E. The majority of tombs are of a type known as a "shaft grave," which could contain multiple burials over time. The grave offerings and complexity of construction suggest that the deceased were the early rulers of Mycenae.

Grave Circle B is the earlier of the two, with the first burials dating from the end of the seventeenth century B.C.E. Situated outside the fortification wall, it was an unexpected discovery in 1951, found during excavations of a later Mycenaean tomb. Grave Circle A had been discovered much earlier, in 1876 by the German businessman-turned-archaeologist Heinrich Schliemann. Although over half

of the burials in Grave Circle B were shaft graves, others were simpler in their construction. The most lavish burials contained bronze weapons, gold jewelry, and well-crafted items such as a tiny seal-stone made from amethyst and a bowl made from rock crystal in the shape of a duck. The most unusual discovery, however, was a face mask made of electrum, an alloy of gold and silver. The finds in Grave Circle A were even more elaborate, with large quantities of bronze weapons and gold jewelry, some probably worn in life. Other gold items were made for the funeral, such as five spectacular gold masks and disks from burial shrouds. A number of items indicate that the deceased had links with Minoan Crete, such as elaborate daggers with decoration made from inlays of precious metals and metal vessels made in shapes typical of Minoan design.

Cult Practices

The part of the site now known as the Cult Center was situated on the west slope of the citadel hill. It consists of a group of five structures, now covered with a roof to protect the archaeology. The finds, which include wall paintings depicting various aspects of Mycenaean cult practice, suggest this area was used for religious purposes.

The archaeological remains extend outside the citadel, and much of the settlement lay on the southern and eastern slopes of the hill. Also outside the citadel is the tomb known as the Treasury of Atreus, built around 1250 B.C.E., which had already been plundered when it was visited by the Roman traveler Pausanias in the second century C.E. It was once believed that tombs of this type were storehouses for valuables. Consisting of a round chamber, known as the tholos, it is approached by an unroofed passage with sides of dressed stone. The chamber is built of thirty-three courses of dressed stone, fitted so that each course slightly overlaps the one below it. The elaborate decoration of the tomb's exterior suggests that the original appearance of the tomb would have been stunning.

The site is just over a mile (about 2 km) from the modern village bearing the same name, which is close to the main road between Corinth and Argos. There is a small museum at the site, although the most famous finds from Mycenae are displayed at the National Archaeological Museum in Athens.

Above Grave Circle A, showing the shaft graves and perimeter wall added in the Mycenaean palace period.

Right One of the gold masks from Shaft Grave IV, Grave Circle A.

GOURNIA A BRONZE AGE TOWN

TYPE: TOWN • **ARCHITECTURAL STYLE:** MINOAN
LOCATION: CRETE, GREECE • **CONSTRUCTION BEGUN:** CA. 1800 B.C.E.

Walking along the narrow paved streets of Gournia and looking into the remains of its houses, the modern-day visitor is rewarded with arguably the best impression of life in an Aegean Bronze Age town that this region has to offer.

The site lies in eastern Crete, on a low ridge close to a natural harbor. The ancient name of the settlement is not recorded, and the modern name of Gournia derives from the Greek term for the many stone basins that were visible on the site before excavation and still remain inside its ancient buildings.

There is evidence of occupation at Gournia from the third millennium B.C.E., known as the Final Neolithic period. However, the archaeological remains seen today date mainly from 1800–1500 B.C.E., contemporary with the second phase of the Minoan palaces, named after Minos, the mythical king of Crete. The most characteristic features of the settlement are small, simple houses, the largest of which occupied an area of around 16.5 sq ft (5 sq m). The majority of architectural remains are the stone foundations of the buildings, of which the mudbrick and timber superstructures have not survived. The lower floors would have been used for storage, reached by trapdoors and ladders from above. However, a few houses have large, more imposing, entrances leading from the street.

The largest, most ambitious, architecture at Gournia is a structure known as the "palace." Although occupying an area of approximately 98 x 131 ft (30 x 40 m), it is neither as complex nor as monumental as the Minoan palace at Knossos. However, the discovery of several objects inscribed with Linear A script support the idea that the palace at Gournia was an administrative center.

In addition, the palace appears to have been the focus for cult ceremonies, including feasting.

Life at Gournia came to a sudden end in the middle of the second millennium B.C.E., when, in common with the other major sites on Crete, the town and its palace were destroyed by fire. Evidence of some reoccupation in the Minoan post-palatial period is demonstrated by the presence of a small, single-roomed shrine, around 9 x 13 ft (3 x 4 m). The room's function was identified by the presence of terracotta female figurines with upraised arms and several examples of cult vessels known as "snake tubes," which would have been displayed on the stone bench at one end of the room.

The settlement was initially excavated in the early years of the twentieth century by a team under American archaeologist Harriet Boyd, later Harriet Boyd Hawes, the first woman to direct a major archaeological excavation on Crete.

Gournia is in east Crete, easily accessible just off the coastal road, and a journey along the road provides splendid panoramic views of the site. The majority of the finds from Gournia are exhibited at the Archaeological Museum of Heraklion.

Opposite, from top A paved street at Gournia, alongside the stone foundations of houses. The town and palace of Gournia, close to a natural harbor on the Aegean Sea.

THE MINOAN PALACE AT **KNOSSOS**

TYPE: PALACE • **ARCHITECTURAL STYLE:** MINOAN
LOCATION: CRETE, GREECE • **CONSTRUCTION BEGUN:** CA. 2000 B.C.E.

The attractive and highly distinctive Bronze Age material culture on the island of Crete is named "Minoan" after its mythical king. The site at Knossos, a short drive from the modern city of Heraklion, is the largest and most significant of the Minoan palaces. The considerable reconstructions of the palace by the British archaeologist Sir Arthur Evans, following his excavations in the early part of the twentieth century, give a striking impression of the extent and opulence of the Minoan buildings. In addition, Knossos had a long, and frequently prosperous, history both before and after the Minoan era.

Although there is evidence of a pre-Neolithic presence on Crete, the first settlers did not arrive at Knossos until around 7000 B.C.E., when they established their homes on the site of what was to become the later Minoan palace. The use of the term "palace" is somewhat misleading; in addition to being a residence, archaeology suggests that the palaces were the economic, religious, creative, and administrative focus of a series of states, similar to Greek cities of the Classical period. In addition to having extensive archives of clay tablets, the palaces supported a large number of specialist artisans, best known for their production of a remarkable series of wall paintings, now fragmentary. This era came to a violent and abrupt end in the middle of the second millennium B.C.E.,

when many of the major sites on Crete, including the palace at Knossos, were destroyed by fire.

Shortly afterward, the palace was rebuilt and reoccupied, seemingly by Mycenaean invaders from the Greek mainland, and many of the remains that can be seen at Knossos today date from this period. The area continued to be inhabited until the fourteenth century B.C.E., when the palace was destroyed by fire, and not

Opposite Loggia at the North Entrance of the palace, with a restored fresco of a charging bull.

Above Throne Room with original gypsum throne and restored wall paintings depicting griffins.

rebuilt. Although the surrounding area flourished for another 2,000 years, the palace site was never reinhabited, possibly because of its supposed associations with the myth of the Minotaur, a creature that was part man, part bull. In the late first century B.C.E. the Roman emperor Augustus (63 B.C.E.–14 C.E.) established a colony named Colonia Julia Nobilis Cnossus to the north of the palace site, which became one of the main Roman cities on Crete.

The Palace Layout

The plan of the palace is complex, reflecting its size and its multifunctional nature. Architecturally, it appears to

have been designed from the central court outward. The central court would have served as a focus for the many ceremonial activities of the palace.

There were several entrances to the palace, none of which was especially grand or spectacular. The approach from the west is that used by today's visitors and, indeed, may have been the norm in the past. In the west court, a bust of Sir Arthur Evans (1851–1941) greets visitors—he began archaeological work at Knossos in 1900.

The west court was paved, crossed by raised causeways, and gives a good view of the west facade of the palace, which had a lower course of large blocks of gypsum. Quarried locally, they would have appeared startlingly white when freshly cut.

The western magazines were among the first parts of the palace to be excavated, in the late nineteenth century, by Minos Kalokairinos (1843–1907), an antiquarian who lived in Heraklion. In 1878 Kalokairinos uncovered a section of the west part of the palace and produced a sketch of the throne room. Facing the throne is a sunken area around 3 ft (1 m) below the main floor level, which Evans termed a "lustral basin," suggesting the area was used for cult practice. Also off the west side of the central court of the palace was a shrine with two stone-lined sunken pits, named by Evans the Temple Repositories due to the religious characteristics of their contents. At the northwest corner of the palace, the Royal Road led from the complex to the west toward the town.

Following the excavations at Knossos, Evans wished visitors to appreciate the magnificence of the Minoan buildings. Accordingly, he arranged for extensive reconstructions to be made to the architectural remains, based on images in the Minoan wall paintings found at Knossos. In addition, Evans commissioned restorations of wall paintings from the site, which were instrumental in popularizing Minoan society. The wall paintings depicted men and women undertaking various activities, including cult ceremonies and the sport of bull leaping.

The Palace is 3 miles (5 km) south of Heraklion, the administrative capital of the island. The Archaeological Museum of Heraklion has the majority of finds from Knossos, and it is possible to visit both site and museum on the same day.

Opposite General view of the northern part of the Palace of Minos at Knossos.

Right, from top The restored Grand Staircase linking the several floors of the east side of the palace. The West Magazines with large vessels (pithoi) and pits used for the storage of agricultural produce. Faience figurines, known as the Snake Goddesses from the Temple Repositories off the Central Court.

THE **PERGAMON** ACROPOLIS

TYPE: ROYAL CITY • **ARCHITECTURAL STYLE:** CLASSICAL
LOCATION: WESTERN TURKEY • **CONSTRUCTION BEGUN:** THIRD CENTURY B.C.E.

Perched atop a steep mountain in Mysia, northwestern Turkey, Pergamon (modern Bergama) was the royal capital of Philetairos (343–263 B.C.E.), founder of the Attalid dynasty in 282 B.C.E. Some 19 miles (30 km) from the sea, the site is one of great drama, its design following the countours of the mountain so that the upper city pivots around the city's steeply stepped theater.

This Hellenistic city was transformed after Attalos I (241–197 B.C.E.) defeated the Gauls (who had settled in Galatia in what is now central Turkey). The victory was commemorated in the sanctuary of Athena that was located, with a Doric temple (the foundations are clearly visible), on a terrace above the theater. Within its precinct were a number of monuments commemorating the Attalid victory. Although these are now lost, one of the likely candidates was the "Trumpeter," better known as the Dying Gaul; a later copy is on display in the Capitoline Museum, Rome. Attalos' son and successor Eumenes II (197–158 B.C.E.) enhanced this space with the construction of colonnades (stoas) and a monumental gateway (propylon) that bears the inscription, "King Eumenes to the victory-bearing Athena."

Carved trophies of war decorate the gateway. On the north side of the sanctuary stood the celebrated library of Pergamon. Access was via the upper story of the sanctuary's stoa. The library contained a reading room that held 15–20,000 works. Inside this space was a 11.5 ft- (3.5 m-) high marble statue of the Athena Parthenos, a copy of Pheidias' colossal gold and ivory statue dating to the 440s B.C.E. that once stood in the Parthenon on the Athenian acropolis.

Dominating the skyline of the Pergamon acropolis, to the southwest of the sanctuary of Athena, was the monumental stepped altar of Zeus, constructed by Eumenes II. This structure uses the battle between the Greek gods and the giants to evoke the Attalid victory over the Gauls, just as the Parthenon's decoration celebrated Greek

victories over the Persians in the early fifth century B.C.E. Inscriptions identified some of the figures. Parts of the continuous relief deliberately quote elements from the architectural sculpture of the Parthenon on the Athenian acropolis. The altar itself was reached via twenty steps; those approaching the altar were flanked by colossal figures in the reliefs. This central area was surrounded by the myth of Telephos from whom the Attalids claimed their descent.

Royal palaces occupied the east side of the Pergamon acropolis, adjacent to the sanctuary of Athena and the library. They contained a central courtyard (peristyle).

Attalos III bequeathed the city to Rome in 133 B.C.E. Under the Roman Emperor Hadrian (76–138 C.E.) a massive temple to the divine Emperor Trajan

(53–117 C.E.) was constructed to the northwest of the sanctuary of Athena and immediately above the theater.

The major sanctuary of the healing-god Asklepios was constructed in the lower city. It contained a temple of the god, dedicated by a Roman consul in ca. 150 C.E., that was a smaller version of the Pantheon at Rome.

There are buses to the town of Bergama where there is a museum containing finds from the ancient city. There is a steep climb to the royal city or you can take a taxi (and enjoy walking down). Stout shoes are recommended.

Opposite Parts of the Temple of Trajan have been reconstructed. This area overlies part of the Attalid city.
Above The steeply sloping Hellenistic theater with the platform for the Temple of Trajan above it.

NOVGOROD THE GREAT

TYPE: MEDIEVAL CITY · **ARCHITECTURAL STYLE:** OLD-RUSSIAN ARCHITECTURE
LOCATION: NOVGOROD OBLAST, NORTHWEST RUSSIA
CONSTRUCTION BEGUN: TURN OF THE NINTH AND TENTH CENTURIES C.E.

Novgorod (which means New Town in Russian) is one of the country's oldest cities, known as a cradle of Russian statehood and famed for its thousand-year history and incredibly rich archaeology. It has for centuries been the largest trade hub of Eastern Europe, with links to Scandinavia and Germany, as well as to the Black Sea and Muslim centers of the East. It happily escaped the Mongol invasion that reduced the other large cities of Russia to ashes. The modern city, which stands on top of many cultural layers of the medieval town, bears the name of Veliky Novgorod (Novgorod the Great). It lies on the Volkhov River, 3.7 miles (6 km) from Lake Ilmen, 340 miles (550 km) northwest of Moscow and 90 miles (145 km) southeast of St. Petersburg. Since 1992 the historic monuments of Novgorod and its surroundings have been on the UNESCO World Heritage List.

Excavations and finds

The first attempts at archaeological investigation in the city took place in the early nineteenth century, but serious excavations in Novgorod began in the 1920s and 1930s and continue to this day. The systematic research carried out by V. Artsikhovsky, M. Karger, V. Yanin, V. Sedov, and other famous archaeologists was unequalled in Russia, or even Europe, in terms of the scale of the work, the number of discovered artifacts, and scholarly achievements. Nevertheless, only about two percent of the ancient city has been studied so far.

From an archaeological point of view Novgorod is unique. The extremely damp soil with its anaerobic effects ensured amazing preservation of organic materials such as wood, leather, bone, birchbark, fabrics, and grain. Occupation layers up to 23–25 ft (7–8 m) thick preserved stacks of wooden pavements and house walls. In fact 800-year-old logs are so hard that they could be re-used for construction and trucks could easily drive over the ancient pavements. A thin layer of corrosion formed quickly on metal objects buried in the damp clay, protecting them from further destruction. Also, because of this great humidity, the citizens avoided building foundations beneath their houses, cellars, and utility pits, so later layers have not disturbed earlier ones.

Excavations have revealed entire quarters of the medieval city with buildings, streets, and an infrastructure system, as well as an extensive collection of artifacts— at least 150,000 individual finds. Among the artifacts are tools and manufacturing implements, household utensils, means of transportation, tableware and food remains, shoes and clothing, warriors' weapons and riders' equipment, jewelry and musical instruments, adult games and children's toys, coins and stamps, birchbark manuscripts, fragments of frescoes, architectural details of houses and remains of furniture, residues of raw materials and of various crafts, and more.

Opposite The great St. Sophia's Cathedral built in 1045–50 C.E., the oldest surviving stone church in Russia.

The main focus of archaeological investigation has been the city's households. These were large complexes. Each included a two- or three-story house, servants' cabins, outbuildings, and almost always some kind of craft workshop. With all its political and commercial importance, Novgorod was primarily a town of craftsmen, the largest center of handicraft production in northeast Europe. Excavations have revealed about 150 handicraft workshops from the eleventh to fifteenth centuries: leatherworkers, jewelers, blacksmiths, coopers, potters, casters, turners, bone cutters, glassmakers, shoemakers, brewers, weavers, dyers, and bakers among them.

Novgorod is also considered to be one of the major centers of Russian culture and spirituality—one of the oldest schools of icon painting and the birthplace of national stone architecture. The town's citadel (*kremlin*) was built in the tenth century from wood, and was destroyed many times by fire. In the fifteenth century it was rebuilt of stone and brick in the shape of an oval wall with twelve towers and two gates. But the church—St. Sophia's Cathedral—had already been built of stone and brick inside the wooden kremlin in the eleventh century. After that, more than fifty churches were built in Novgorod and its vicinity, and some of them still survive. They were decorated with beautiful frescoes and icons. Among the excavated workshops there is one in which a whole group of painters worked with their apprentices, and even the name of the master—Olisey Grechin—has been established. In 2000 the oldest dated Slavonic book was discovered in Novgorod. It consists of wooden plaques covered with wax, on which the texts could be scratched and erased many times; it dates to the turn of the eleventh century. The excavations have also yielded a major collection of medieval musical instruments.

Below The Novgorod Kremlin—one of the two cylindrical towers, built in the fifteenth century, in the process of reconstruction.
Opposite Birchbark manuscript N 35, dating back to 1320—1340.

Chronology

Novgorod is a unique example of a productive combination of historical, archaeological, and scientific methods of dating. The earliest mention of its name has been found in a chronicle of 859 C.E., and the town was first called Novgorod the Great in a chronicle from 1169. Many other written sources provide rich information on the city's later history. Archaeological dating in Novgorod is extraordinarily accurate, because the streets were paved with wood, and most of the houses were constructed from wood, which makes it possible to use dendrochronology (tree-ring dating). Dates can be calculated accurately to within one year of a tree's cutting. Hence any wooden structure in Novgorod can be precisely dated, as can the artifacts contained within it. The first pavements were laid in the 930s C.E. and had to be replaced every ten to twenty years. Stacks of up to thirty timber floorings exist, dating from the tenth century (lowermost) to the fifteenth (uppermost), grew on the ancient streets of Novgorod. Finds made between those layers have been dated with an accuracy of ten to twenty years. Radiocarbon dating has also been used here, and confirms that the earliest dates for the citadel and for the bridge over the Volkhov River are of the mid-tenth century. However, there is a problem with dating a thin mixed layer that lies beneath the first pavement.

Birchbark manuscripts

One of the greatest successes of Russian archaeology in the last century is the discovery in Novgorod of an absolutely new kind of historical source—manuscripts, scratched on birchbark. The first example was found in 1951, but more than 1,100 have now been unearthed in the city, as well as several at other sites. The manuscripts are found in all the stratigraphic layers of Novgorod from the first half of the eleventh to the second half of the fifteenth centuries. Tools for writing on birchbark have also found in the layers of 953–989 C.E.

Most of the birchbarks are private letters of a business nature (debt collection, trade and household instructions), but there are also drafts of official acts (wills, receipts, bills of sale, court records, and so on). Rarer, but of particular interest, are church texts (prayers, memorial lists, orders for icons, morals), literary and folklore subjects (jokes, riddles, homework instructions), love letters and records of an educational nature (alphabet, school exercises, children's drawings, and scribbles). The last, created by a six- to seven-year-old boy Onfim are especially famous.

The discovery of birchbarks significantly changed our understanding of the city's culture, showing that literacy in medieval Novgorod extended to all segments of society—including villains! Ordinary people wrote letters to each other, and women were no exception. These manuscripts shed light on many obscure aspects of Novgorod's history, and contain priceless evidence about written and spoken language, households, everyday life, and the personal relationships of the city's medieval people.

Visitors to the city can expect to see beautiful wooden and stone architecture, numerous medieval churches and monasteries (including the great St. Sophia's cathedral built in 1045–50, the oldest stone church in Russia), archaeological digs in several parts of the city, and rich collections of artifacts in the city museum.

THE KURGANS AND MEGALITHS OF **KHAKASIA**

TYPE: ARCHAEOLOGICAL MONUMENTS • **ARCHITECTURAL STYLE:** N/A **LOCATION:** REPUBLIC OF KHAKASIA, SOUTH SIBERIA, RUSSIA • **CONSTRUCTION BEGUN:** THIRD MILLENNIUM B.C.E.

The Republic of Khakasia in southern Siberia is one of Russia's richest in terms of archaeology, its landscape defined by a high concentration of megalithic funerary and memorial constructions. The most visible and most famous of these features a collection of extraordinary stone statues and kurgans (burial mounds) surrounded by a perimeter made of stone slabs and megaliths, some of which are decorated with petroglyphs.

Steppe idols

Only a century ago, megalithic statues were as characteristic a feature of the historical landscape of Khakasia as the kurgans. Today, almost all of them are in museums. These beautiful, mysterious monuments, dubbed "steppe idols" by eighteenth-century travelers and scholars, are usually 6.5–16.5 ft (2–5 m) tall, made of sandstone or granite. They were carved by the skillful artists of the Okunev culture, which existed in the region during the Early Bronze Age (2600–1800 B.C.E.). The statues usually have an effigy in the middle or lower part. Realistic human faces are very rare: anthropomorphous face masks with three eyes are typical, decorated with intricate lines and curves, sometimes with bull horns and ears, and often with very complicated headdresses. Figures with large stomachs and breasts probably represent pregnant females. The statues are marked with solar symbols and solar rays sometimes surround a face mask. These amazing objects were not funerary monuments, but erected for ritual purposes, and remained objects of cult and reverence long after. The Khakas people, four millennia later, honored ancient statues, worshipped them, and made offerings to them. Even today traces of fat and butter remain on the mouths of stone idols, believed to help people have more children, better health, and greater wealth.

The Cemetery Steppe

Surrounded and protected by mountains and taiga, the Khakasia steppe has a gentle continental climate, and an abundance of animals appropriate for farming and pastoralism. The region has always attracted different tribes and peoples, many of whom have left burial sites. From the Eneolithic onward, all cultures used stone slabs for building graves and kurgans; some of them were distinguished by huge megalithic funerary constructions. When, in 1721, the German scholar Daniel Gottlieb Messerschmidt came here to investigate Siberia at the behest of Peter the Great, he was so amazed by the abundance of kurgans with stone slabs that he considered the whole area to be a huge cemetery with the deceased having been brought from all over Asia. Even in the nineteenth century, the central part of Khakasia was still known as the Cemetery Steppe.

Opposite Decorated stone stelae in the perimeter of a burial mound in the Safronov cemetery.

The great kurgans of Salbyk and Barsuchy Log

Especially numerous among the kurgans are those of the Tagar culture, a people who inhabited the region in the ninth to third centuries B.C.E., and who covered all of Khakasia with their cemeteries, some containing hundreds of kurgans. The Tagar kurgans consisted of pyramidal mounds made of turf and clay, within a perimeter built of stone slabs with tall menhirs in the corners and on the sides. Early examples were intended for one person and had several feet of perimeter and four corner stones. As the culture developed, kurgans began to vary in size. Larger examples with bigger megaliths—and more of them— were constructed for collective burials, with especially grandiose structures erected for nobles. The most famous concentration of "royal" kurgans lies in the Salbyk valley, 37 miles (60 km) north of Abakan, where several kurgans are known whose diameter exceeds 164 ft (50 m) amid a hundred of normal size. One of them, the biggest kurgan and megalithic structure in the whole of Siberia, is the so-called Great Salbyk, excavated in the 1950s. Today all that remains is its impressive stone construction, a square with sides measuring 230 ft (70 m), made of gigantic blocks of Devonian sandstone. At the corners, along the sides, and beside the entrance, are twenty-three huge vertical stone slabs, some weighing up to fifty tons. The mound, which before excavation looked like an average hill, was originally pyramidal in shape, 82–98 ft (25-30 m) high. The tomb had been ravaged, unfortunately, and the only finds were a bronze knife dating to the fourth or fifth century B.C.E. and a big clay vessel. The person buried in Great Salbyk was clearly a great chief and leader of a union of tribes, or even a powerful "tsar" of the whole region.

In 2004–2005 another "royal" kurgan, Barsuchy Log, was excavated in the Salbyk Steppe and dates to the fifth century B.C.E. Originally the mound had been a pyramid more than 33 ft (10 m) high, with a square stone wall measuring 177 × 177 ft (54 × 54 m), and a stone perimeter of twenty-nine decorated slabs. The wall consisted of vertical slabs with corner and intermediate megaliths, but it also had an internal masonry of horizontally laid slabs, which is unusual for the Tagar culture. This tomb had also been robbed in antiquity, but its complicated structure of logs was well preserved due to many protective layers of birchbark.

Decorated stelae

The slabs and megaliths used in the construction of kurgans are often decorated with pecked and engraved images. Sometimes the builders reused statues and stelae taken from sanctuaries or cemeteries of earlier periods. In other cases images were created specifically for a given burial. Most often, however, people of later cultures made the depictions on surfaces exposed aboveground. Most of the kurgans in Khakasia belong to the Tagar culture, and the great majority of the kurgan rock art dates from the Xiongny-Xianbei period that followed (last centuries B.C.E. to first centuries C.E.), and is associated with migrants from North China and Mongolia. These petroglyphs most probably reflect afterlife transition rituals; they depict animals, humans and flying birds, as well as concentric circles, spirals, labyrinths, and other abstract motifs. Such open-air "galleries" can be seen everywhere in Khakasia, but the most impressive is that of the Safronov cemetery, which has the biggest decorated kurgan slabs—the tallest megalith is about 16.5 ft (5 m tall)—and many of them are literally covered with interwoven and intersecting images.

Excursions to the kurgans with megaliths are organized by many tour agencies in Abakan, the Republic's capital, while rich collections of decorated megaliths exist in Abakan and Minusinsk museums, as well as in an open-air museum in the village of Poltakov.

Opposite, clockwise from left Archival photo showing a Khakas man next to a stone statue of the Okunev culture. Perimeter stone structure of the Barsuchy Log kurgan. A fantastic monster of the Okunev culture depicted on a stone slab. A typical Khakassian steppe landscape with kurgan stone slabs.

SIBERIA'S **OGLAKHTY MOUNTAINS**

TYPE: NATURAL AND CULTURAL LANDSCAPE • **ARCHITECTURAL STYLE:** N/A
LOCATION: REPUBLIC OF KHAKASIA, SOUTH SIBERIA, RUSSIA • **CONSTRUCTION BEGUN:** N/A

The Oglakhty mountainous massif in south Siberia is a remarkable example of the interweaving of culture with nature. This picturesque territory presents a unique combination of mountain, forest, steppe, and coastal landscape, inhabited by a range of rare and endangered plant and animal species. The region is literally saturated with evidence of its cultural transformation through the millennia. It's a rich archaeological heritage that features all kind of monuments, among them numerous visually attractive rock art sites.

Settlements, burial mounds, and burial grounds

The Oglakhty and adjacent steppe areas have been inhabited for millennia. During the Upper Palaeolithic people hunted big mammals here, some species of which became extinct, while others changed their habitats. In the northern foothills of the range, a major site from this period has rich collections of stone tools and palaeontological remains. It has not been excavated, but was exposed by the activity of the Krasnoyarsk reservoir. The camps of Neolithic hunters have been excavated in the southern foothills of Oglakhty. From the Eneolithic up to modern times, increasing numbers of people came here, each of their cultures influencing the next—hunters and fishers, settled farmers and metalworkers, nomadic and seminomadic pastoralists, warriors and civilians, for example. These periods are represented by various funerary constructions, most of which feature slabs of the Devonian red sandstone from the Oglakhty mountains.

Numerous cemeteries with hundreds of graves are concentrated in the steppe foothills and intermontane valleys. The most notable are the stone-and-earth mounds of the Tagar and Tes cultures (ninth century B.C.E. to second century C.E.). They have rectangular stone perimeters with high intermediate and corner slabs, and a mound inside. The graves were also made of stone slabs. Early burial sites were small and intended for one individual, but as the culture developed the mounds grew higher, the perimeters became bigger with increased numbers of intermediate stones, and the burials became collective. These complicated funerary constructions with highly visible slabs are an essential feature of the historical landscape of the Minusinsk basin in general, and Oglakhty in particular. Unfortunately almost all of these burials were looted in antiquity.

The opposite applies to the burial grounds. Thanks to their less conspicuous presence in the landscape, many

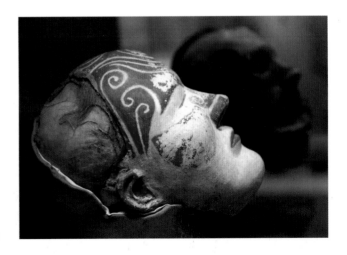

of these preserve rich burial assemblages. Oglakhty is especially famous for a huge cemetery of the third to fourth century C.E., which belongs to the Tashtyk culture. The first grave was discovered by chance and excavated in 1903, with further excavations taking place in the 1960s. Some burials had exceptionally well preserved organic material due to natural factors and the funerary constructions. The funerary practices are very unusual: in the same grave were found not only buried bodies (mummies), but also leather imitations of bodies containing the remains of cremations. Both types are dressed in fur clothes, and have distinctive hairstyles, and painted funeral masks on their faces. Unique materials from the Oglakhty Tashtyk cemetery are now on display in the Historical Museum in Moscow and the Hermitage Museum in St Petersburg.

The stone wall

Oglakhty is famous for its so-called fortress—an enormous stone structure, consisting of horizontally laid sandstone slabs, which surrounds the mountainous massif as a wall. It runs for almost 15.5 miles (25 km) along the steep edge of the mountains, and blocks the passage to seven valleys between them. In some places a ditch is visible in front of the wall; there are also bastions and some zigzag-shaped sections. The wall is up to 6.6 ft (2 m) wide, and now only 3.3 ft (1 m) high because, in the mid-twentieth century, the slabs were dismantled for construction. The records of early travelers mention that it was about 6.6 ft (2 m) high. This grandiose construction was presumably erected during the tenth to twelfth centuries C.E. to protect local people against Uighur invasions.

Opposite A painted gypsum mask on a female skull from the Oglakhty cemetery (Tashtyk culture).

Above Images of Tashtyk archers pecked into rock, with a view of the Yenisei River.

Rock art

Rock art is undoubtedly the most important cultural feature of the Oglakhty range. The peculiarities of the terrain provided a huge number of convenient "canvases" to ancient artists. There are numerous Devonian red sandstone outcrops and, wherever they exist, there are images on the rocks. They have been made using all known techniques—pecking, engraving, abrading, and painting—and represent all the cultural and chronological periods identified in the archaeology of south Siberia from at least the Neolithic up to the ethnographic present. Most of the images feature on vertical rock surfaces, but others exist on stone blocks lying on the slopes, as well as on slabs used for mound construction. Rock art sites are scattered across the entire range. The richest concentrations are on the riverside cliffs (most of them now beneath the waters of the

Krasnoyarsk reservoir, recorded before the flooding) and on the southwestern slopes of Sorok Zubiev (Forty Teeth) mountain. Together, the known rock art sites—fourteen in total—form the largest rock art complex of the Minusinsk Basin, acknowledged as one of the world's richest rock art areas. The complex is of exceptional value in terms of its coverage of chronological periods, diversity of styles, high artistic qualities, and repertoire of images and subjects.

The most interesting images are the earliest, made with great realism and artistic skill: wild horses, aurochs, wild boars, bears, elks and deer, as well as enigmatic anthropomorphic figures and boats with "passengers." Their date is unknown. They may be Neolithic, but cannot be less than five or six millennia old. In the past, all the coastal cliffs were entirely covered with such figures. Of later rock art, the most noteworthy include images of

daggers and chariots from the Late Bronze Age, beautiful decorated deer and horse figures in the Scythian style, a cauldron and a yurt, numerous shamanic scenes, and many other subjects, styles, and images from various epochs and peoples, reflecting Oglakhty's turbulent past.

The Oglakhty mountain range extends for 9 miles (15 km) and is located on the left bank of the Yenisei River (now the Krasnoyarsk reservoir), 37 miles (60 km) downstream of Abakan, the capital of the Republic of Khakassia. The territory is on the UNESCO Tentative List and is partially protected by the State Natural Reserve, which organizes excursions to the sites of Oglakhty.

Above The southwestern slopes of the Oglakhty Range.

Right Petroglyphs on a kurgan slab, in the Tagar culture cemetery in the northern part of the range.

THE PETROGLYPHS OF
TOMSKAYA PISANITSA

TYPE: ROCK ART SITE • **ARCHITECTURAL STYLE:** N/A **LOCATION:** KEMEROVO OBLAST, SOUTHWESTERN SIBERIA, RUSSIA • **CONSTRUCTION BEGUN:** THIRD MILLENNIUM B.C.E.

Sited in a most picturesque location, 37 miles (60 km) downstream from the city of Kemerovo in Siberia, Tomskaya Pisanitsa is a tremendous riverside cliff covered with petroglyphs, carved 4,000–5,000 years ago, with a natural rocky platform in front of it. This rare peculiarity—the rocky platform—made the place appropriate for a sanctuary in antiquity and for a museum today. Tomskaya Pisanitsa, which in modern Russian means "rock art site on the Tom River," is one of the most interesting rock-art sites in Russia, famous for its very long history of investigation.

The cliff holds the largest concentration of images among many other decorated rocks occurring for 30 miles (50 km) on the right bank of the Tom River, and is the center of the Historical, Cultural and Natural Museum-Reserve Tomskaya Pisanitsa.

The Russians who came to Siberia in the sixteenth and seventeenth centuries were particularly impressed with the abundant ancient imagery on the rocks along many Siberian rivers. They called them Pisanitsas, from the Russian word *pisanyi*, which means "decorated, covered with drawings or inscriptions." One such scenic rock, facing the Tom River in southwest Siberia and surrounded by beautiful pine forests, already attracted the attention of the first explorers in the seventeenth century, and a remarkable description of it survives in a chronicle from around 1645. P. J. von Strahlenberg published the first scholarly description of the site, along with a drawing in 1730, in Stockholm. He based his work on data obtained by D. G. Messerschmidt (1685–1735), a German scholar who led the very first academic expedition to Siberia (sent there by order of Peter the Great), and who had actually discovered this rock art site for science in July 1721. Subsequently many famous

travelers and scholars, from both Europe and Russia, visited the rock on the Tom River and published their descriptions, thoughts, drawings, tracings, and photographs. As a result, this site has the richest historiography and iconography of all Asian rock art sites.

Several vertical siltstone panels on the cliff bear more than 300 images and many fragments of destroyed figures. About half of the imagery is concentrated on one huge panel, the so-called Upper Frieze, which is more than 16.5 ft (5 m) long and 6.5 ft (2 m) high. It is situated above human height, above another panel—the Lower Frieze—which is badly damaged because of its greater accessibility. A narrow layer separates the two friezes and it is a mystery quite how the depictions on the inaccessible Upper Frieze were made. Nevertheless, its vast flat surface was once filled with an elaborate multifigured composition, which was then continuously added to and renewed.

Opposite, clockwise from top Some fragments of the Upper Frieze of Tomskaya Pisanitsa: images of elks and a human figure; an elk's head in profile and an owl; a bear; a bear and human figures with rays around their heads and ambiguous motifs in their hands.

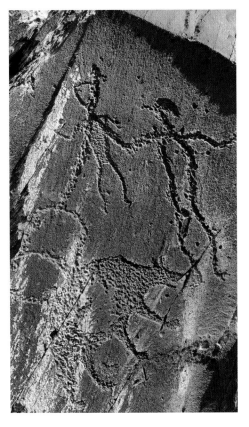

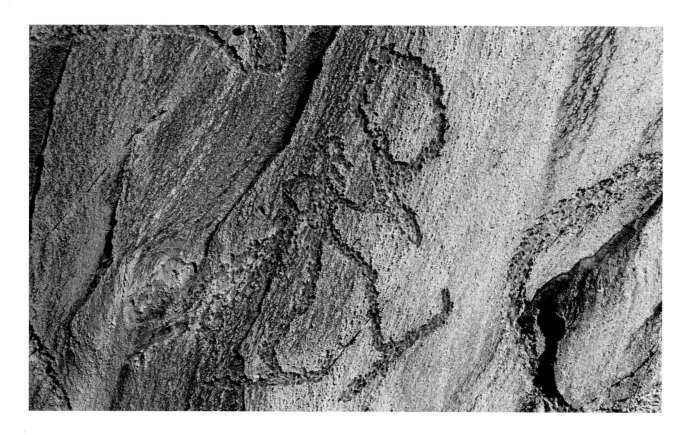

A Wealth of Diverse Imagery

The dominant image here is undoubtedly the elk. The depictions of this beautiful animal are made with great skill and are very expressive: elks are represented in motion, their long double-hoofed legs fully stretched out, or sometimes with front and hind legs crossed beneath the strongly humped torso. Their heads are particularly naturalistic with almond-shaped eyes, a typical elk muzzle with a big nostril, and a characteristic dewlap hanging down below the jaw. In some figures the heart and aorta are also shown; others are simply represented as contours with vertical arched stripes on the necks, the significance of which remains unknown. Elks still inhabit the forests around the museum reserve, and it is believed that the site is located precisely at a point where elks used to cross the river.

Besides elks there are images of a bear, a fox, and a doe, as well as several bird species, such as an owl, a crane, a heron, and a duck. The most famous of the bird images is that of the owl, which has become the "logo" of the museum reserve.

Anthropomorphous images at Tomskaya Pisanitsa are quite numerous and diverse in their iconography. Only a few of them are ordinary human figures, while the others are depicted in unusual poses, with various attributes (horns, halos, and rays around the head, incomprehensible objects in the hands, skis, bows, and so on), and sometimes with features of birds and animals, or wearing masks. Unlike the realistic images of animals, the anthropomorphous figures are emphatically unreal, most likely depicting mythological characters. There are also images of face masks (some are intricate, while others are just three dots representing the eyes and mouth), depictions of boats, and numerous complex symbols and signs.

The images are rendered using known rock-art techniques: pecking, engraving, abrading, and painting. The best preserved are the pecked figures, especially those that have been renewed and deepened over the centuries. The original scenes on these riverside rocks have seen much reworking over the millennia, their figures, subjects, and compositions supplemented, transformed, rethought, and renewed by subsequent generations of rock artists. This makes the task of dating and interpreting them even more difficult than usual. However, it has been established that the earliest images at Tomskaya Pisanitsa were created at least in the Early Bronze Age (late third to early second millennium B.C.E.), as some figures bear strong similarities in their style and iconography to the monumental and portable art from dated sites of adjacent areas. In order to make the dating of the rock art more precise, the museum reserve has carried out excavations near the rocks. Some recent discoveries show that the area was inhabited in the Neolithic. There are also layers of the Early Bronze Age and later. Interestingly, bronze artworks of much later periods were found in sediments above the Upper Frieze during conservation activities, which means that this place continued to be a sanctuary long after the creation of its imagery.

There are many other archaeological, ethnographic, and natural features in the reserve, including a special museum on the rock art of Asia within the Museum-reserve. The site is open to visitors year-round and excursions by boat to other sites can be organized in the summer.

Opposite A human figure on skis with a bow. This is the oldest rock art image of a skier in Siberia.

Above An aerial view of the cliff with petroglyphs on the Tom River, the sanctuary of Tomskaya Pisanitsa.

4

AFRICA

To many people, Egypt represents archaeology, and certainly its wealth of spectacular sites—especially the pyramids, Sphinx, temples and tombs—are among the most popular destinations in the world for archaeological tourism. Any TV documentaries on Egyptian sites or mummies are guaranteed a huge audience! But Africa is a vast continent, and there are many other varied treasures to be found far from Egypt: from the traces of our earliest ancestors to the rock art of the Drakensberg, from the impressive and mysterious ruins of Great Zimbabwe to the great monoliths of Aksum and the astonishing rock-cut churches of Lalibela.

Left Interior of the richly carved and decorated Biete Maryam church in Lalibela, Ethiopia.

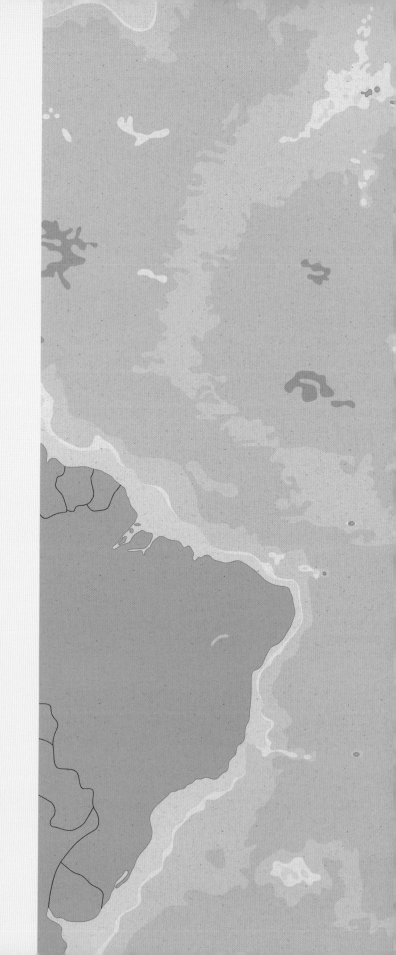

AFRICA
LOCATIONS

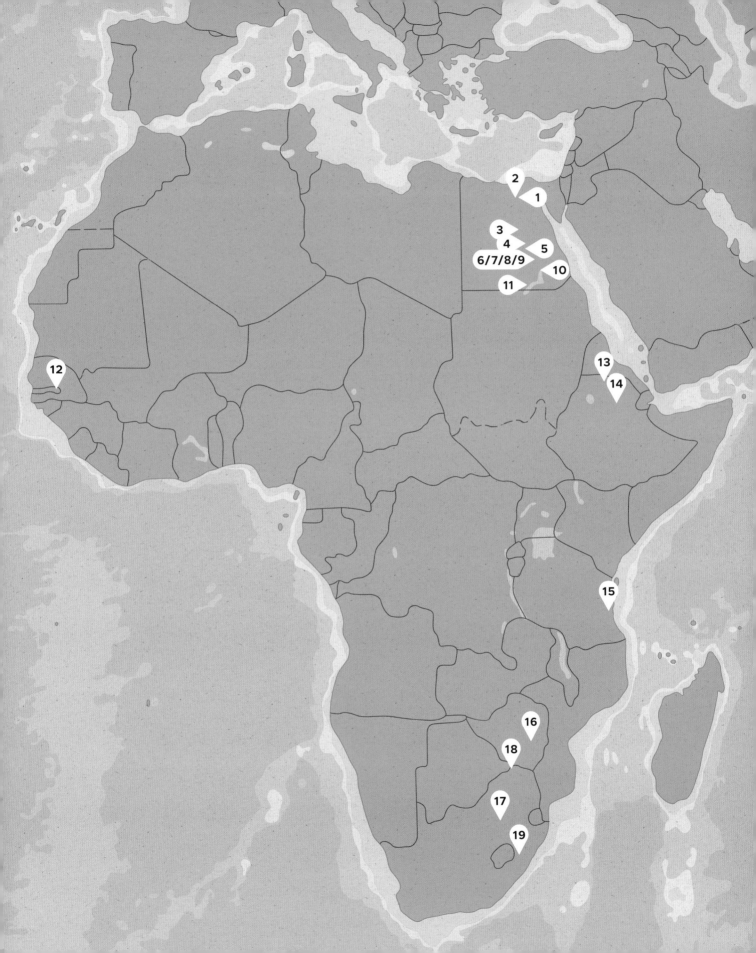

SAKKARA CITY OF THE DEAD

TYPE: CEMETERY • **ARCHITECTURAL STYLE:** PYRAMIDS AND TOMBS
LOCATION: CAIRO, EGYPT • **CONSTRUCTION BEGUN:** CA. 3100 B.C.E.

Rising in the arid landscape of northern Egypt's Western Desert, the Sakkara Step Pyramid was ancient Egypt's first stone building. The work of the innovative architect Imhotep, it is one of fifteen pyramids raised at this site near Heliopolis, ancient cult center of the sun god Ra. The extensive cemetery was used from the Early Dynastic to the Graeco-Roman periods, a timespan of over 3,000 years, but was particularly important during the Old Kingdom (ca. 2686–2160 B.C.E.).

From the 1st Dynasty onward (ca. 3000 B.C.E.), the civil servants who worked in Egypt's first capital city Memphis built mudbrick mastaba tombs in the Sakkara cemetery. Named for the Arabic word *mastaba*, or low bench, these tombs consisted of a rectangular superstructure covering a rock-cut burial chamber. Around the largest mastabas were smaller tombs built for servants who worked for the deceased. During the 2nd Dynasty (ca. 2890–2686 B.C.E.), several kings were buried at Sakkara. Unfortunately, the superstructures of their tombs have been lost.

Although occasionally packed with sand and gravel, the mastaba superstructures were more normally filled with storerooms for grave goods. These conspicuous storerooms proved vulnerable to thieves. By the end of the 1st Dynasty the number of rooms in the superstructure had been reduced in favor of extensive subterranean storage reached by a stairway, and eventually the mastaba became a solid mound. Gradually, stone walls replaced the mudbrick superstructure walls.

Right The "false door" from the tomb of the Old Kingdom priestess Wadjkawes. Visitors to the tomb would leave offerings of food and drink in front of this door.
Opposite The Step Pyramid of the 3rd Dynasty pharaoh Djoser. The world's first monumental stone building.

The Step Pyramid

The royal architect Imhotep designed a remarkable tomb for Djoser, second king of the 3rd Dynasty (r. ca. 2667–48 B.C.E.). Working in limestone cut from a nearby quarry, Imhotep built a solid, square mastaba with corners orientated to the points of the compass. This was subsequently extended outward and upward until, after several intermediate stages, it became a six-step pyramid. As it stands today, Djoser's pyramid measures 197 ft (60 m) high, and has a footprint of 397 x 358 ft (121 x 109 m).

A wide shaft descending from the center of the original mastaba led to Djoser's burial chamber. This small, granite-lined room, too small to house a stone sarcophagus, could only be entered via a 3.3 ft- (1 m-) wide hole in the ceiling. During the funeral the king's body must have been lowered into position, then the hole sealed with a stone plug. A warren of corridors and rooms surrounded the chamber. In the King's Apartment (a modern term employed by archaeologists) over 36,000 curved blue-green faience tiles replicated the reed walls of Djoser' earthly palace.

The Step Pyramid was just one element in Djoser's funerary complex. Around the pyramid was an enclosure defined by a massive limestone wall equipped with fourteen false doors plus one actual entrance. The best-known and most fully restored buildings within this enclosure lie in the southern and eastern sections, and in the area around the pyramid. Here Imhotep created a series of inaccessible symbolic buildings; replicas of Egypt's most important shrines, whose carved stone doors could never be opened by the living. Here, too, was a ritual racetrack where Djoser could, in perpetuity, run to prove his fitness to rule Egypt.

Sakkara in the Late Old Kingdom

In the later part of the Old Kingdom (from the end of Dynasty 4 to the end of Dynasty 6: ca. 2530–2181 B.C.E.), the monumental landscape of Sakkara was greatly expanded by a series of smaller pyramids built by kings who wished to be buried close to Djoser (including the pyramids of Unas, Userkaf, and Teti) and in the expansion of the site to the south (including the pyramids of Pepi I, Merenre, and Pepi II). At the same time, high officials of the royal court built magnificent mastaba tombs, whose walls they covered with reliefs of the highest quality showing the type of afterlife these individuals wished for themselves.

Opposite top An entry to one of several ritual buildings forming part of the funerary complex.

Opposite bottom left The Old Kingdom official Khenu, depicted on his tomb wall in the Unas Causeway cemetery at Sakkara.

Opposite bottom right A stone statue of the pharaoh Djoser.

Below The pyramid and mortuary temple of King Unas

Animal Burials

Not all of the Sakkara burials were human. From the New Kingdom until the Ptolemaic Period (ca. 1550–30 B.C.E.) the sacred Apis bulls were buried in the Serapeum, or bull cemetery. Before the 19th Dynasty reign of Ramesses II (r. ca. 1279–1213 B.C.E.) the mummified bulls were interred in individual tombs. Subsequently they were buried in enormous stone sarcophagi in underground galleries to the northwest of the Step Pyramid.

While the Apis bulls died natural deaths, the millions of animals—including cats, dogs, baboons, and ibises—interred in the catacombs of the sacred animal necropolis were killed and mummified to serve as votive offerings to the gods Bastet, Anubis, and Thoth during the Late and Graeco-Roman periods (664 B.C.E.–395 C.E.).

Travelers wishing to visit Sakkara are advised to take a taxi from Cairo and to ask it to wait, as the journey by public transport is both complicated and slow.

THE GIZA PLATEAU
A ROYAL NECROPOLIS

TYPE: CEMETERY • **ARCHITECTURAL STYLE:** PYRAMIDS
LOCATION: CAIRO, EGYPT • **CONSTRUCTION BEGUN:** 2589 B.C.E.

Intrepid Victorian tourists traveling from Cairo to Giza enjoyed a relaxing carriage ride through twelve peaceful miles (19 km) of fields. Today's visitors face a very different experience. Cairo has expanded so rapidly that the world's most famous monuments loom over the suburbs, and Pyramids Road offers a crowded and polluted introduction to the necropolis. Is the journey worth it? Absolutely. Nothing can match the experience of standing in the shadow of the magnificent pyramids built by Khufu (r. ca. 2589–2566 B.C.E.), his son Khaefre (r. ca. 2558–2532 B.C.E.) and grandson Menkaure (r. ca. 2532–2503 B.C.E.).

Khufu's Great Pyramid

The ancient Giza cemetery lay close by Egypt's first capital city, Memphis. It became a royal necropolis when King Khufu chose Giza as the site for his funerary complex. Today Khufu's Great Pyramid is recognized as the last surviving "Wonder" of the ancient World. The figures are astonishing. The Great Pyramid stands 481 ft (147 m) high, with a slope of fifty-one degrees. Its sides, with an average length of 758 ft (230 m), are orientated almost exactly toward true north, while its base is almost completely flat. The pyramid was once cased in fine limestone that sparkled in the sunlight, but this covering was stripped during the Middle Ages and reused in the building of Cairo. The relatively rough limestone blocks visible today represent the interior masonry.

Inside the Great Pyramid are three chambers linked by passageways. The Subterranean Chamber is an unfinished room of ritual significance. Within the pyramid masonry, the Queen's Chamber was not actually used for a queen's burial; it, too, is a room with an unknown purpose. The topmost room, the King's Chamber, still houses Khufu's impressive red granite sarcophagus. As we cannot see beneath the outer skin of stone, we cannot be certain that there are not more chambers and voids concealed within the masonry. We do know that "air-shafts"—narrow passageways orientated toward the northern pole star and the constellation of Orion—lead from the King's and the Queen's Chambers, and we can guess that these shafts had a ritual rather than practical function.

Khufu's pyramid was just one element in a large funerary complex that included an enclosure wall, a mortuary temple close by the pyramid, and a low-lying valley temple that is now lost under the modern suburb of Nazlet el-Simman. A causeway linked the two temples. Five boat-shaped pits were excavated close to the causeway and mortuary temple, but these were found to be empty when opened. Two narrow, rectangular pits dug parallel to the south side of the pyramid held dismantled wooden boats.

Opposite top The head of the Great Sphinx.
Opposite bottom The three pyramids of the Giza plateau, with three smaller pyramids built for royal women in the foreground.

One of these boats, excavated and restored, is now displayed in the Khufu Boat Museum near the Great Pyramid.

A small subsidiary pyramid lay outside the enclosure wall to the southeast of the main pyramid. Three larger queens' pyramids complete with mortuary chapels lay to the east of the subsidiary pyramid. All three were robbed in antiquity, but a shaft discovered to the east of the Great Pyramid in 1925 has yielded the burial equipment and jewelry of Queen Hetepheres, mother of Khufu.

Khaefre's Pyramid and Sphinx

Khaefre built his funerary complex to the south of the Great Pyramid. His pyramid is smaller than Khufu's, but is built on higher ground and this, together with its slightly steeper angle, makes it appear larger. Khaefre's pyramid had a subterranean burial chamber that was built and roofed in a large, open trench before the solid pyramid was built on top. Today Khaefre's complex is the most complete of the Giza three, and his pyramid is the only one to retain some of its original limestone casing.

The Great Sphinx crouches beside Khaefre's Valley Temple. At 236 ft (72 m) long and 65.6 ft (20 m) tall, it is Egypt's largest statue: its human head—Khaefre's head—is approximately twenty-two times life-sized; its lion's body is disproportionately large. Today the Sphinx is clean-shaven, but in the New Kingdom it gained a braided and curved beard of the type worn by gods and deified kings. As it is carved from a natural rocky outcrop covered in places with a stone block veneer, the Sphinx shows differential weathering due to the limestone strata included in its body.

Left top The reconstructed boat which once formed a part of Khufu's burial equipment.
Left bottom The interior of the valley temple which formed a part of pharaoh Khaefre's funerary complex at Giza.
Opposite top The pyramid built for pharaoh Khaefre.
Opposite bottom Pharaoh Menkaure, escorted by the goddess Hathor (on his right) and a local goddess.

Menkaure's Pyramid

Menkaure's pyramid aligned with those of Khufu and Khaefre although, as space on the plateau was now limited, it was built at a much smaller scale. Perhaps in compensation, the bottom layers of his pyramid were cased in expensive red granite, imported from southern Egypt. The finished pyramid had a height of approximately 213 ft (65 m), a base of 335 x 341 ft (102 x 104 m) and an angle of 51 degrees, 20 minutes. Menkaure's pyramid is built above a subterranean burial chamber and antechamber. The burial chamber yielded a basalt sarcophagus carved with elaborate paneling.

AMARNA HORIZON OF THE ATEN

TYPE: CITY AND ASSOCIATED CEMETERIES • **ARCHITECTURAL STYLE:** ROCK-CUT TOMBS, HOUSES
LOCATION: MIDDLE EGYPT • **CONSTRUCTION BEGUN:** CA. 1350 B.C.E.

Amarna (ancient Akhetaten) was a purpose-built city founded by the "Heretic Pharaoh" Akhenaten (r. ca. 1352–1336 B.C.E.) as a suitable home for his god, the sun disk known as The Aten. Situated in Middle Egypt, equidistant between the northern capital Memphis and the southern capital Thebes, Amarna was built on a virgin site. It was abandoned after just twenty-five years and never reoccupied.

The Aten's new domain—the city, plus its cemeteries and farming land—was defined by a series of "boundary stelae": massive inscriptions carved into the limestone cliffs of the east and west banks of the Nile.

Amarna itself was an elongated city, sandwiched between the river to the west and limestone cliffs to the east. A wide processional road linked its official buildings and ran parallel to the river. The royal family used this road to display themselves to their people.

Archaeologists have given modern names to the various parts of Amarna. The Central City, the religious and administrative heart, included the Great and the Small Aten Temples, the ceremonial Great Palace, the police and army barracks, and a warren of offices. The King's House lay opposite the Great Palace and was linked to it by a mudbrick bridge. To the south of the Central City, the Main City was home to some of Amarna's most influential citizens. Their extensive villas were built next to more humble housing and workshops. To the north lay the Northern Suburb, a less prestigious area, where bureaucrats lived alongside carpenters, and where fishermen and merchants lived within easy reach of the quay. Farther north still was the North City, which included the North Riverside Palace; the private home of the royal family.

Above Little of the Amarna central city remains standing. Here we see a reconstruction of the central temple area.
Opposite top The city of Amarna was surrounded by a series of carved stone stelae.
Opposite bottom A preserved villa at Amarna.

To the east of the city, a walled village was provided for the laborers who worked in Amarna's elite tombs. In contrast to the city proper, the village had a regular plan: seventy-three houses stood in six straight terraced rows facing onto narrow streets. A second worker's settlement, the Stone Village, was situated about a twenty-minute walk from the Workmen's Village.

Tombs and Graves

The rock-cut royal tomb, and a series of subsidiary royal graves, was built in a dry valley or wadi in the cliffs to the east of the city. Locals discovered it sometime during the early 1880s; when archaeologists entered the tomb, it had already been looted.

Two groups of rock-cut tombs, lying to the north (eighteen tombs) and south (twenty-seven tombs) of the royal wadi, were provided for Amarna's elite. Only twenty-four of these tombs were inscribed and none has yielded a mummy, suggesting that few, if any, were ever occupied. The elite decorated their tombs with images of the royal family going about their daily duties.

Amarna's non-elite were buried in a series of cemeteries. Skeletal evidence recovered from these graves indicates that for many, life at Amarna was a harsh regime of hard physical labor and limited food.

The modern city of Minya—easily accessible by road and train—offers a good base for travelers wishing to visit Akhenaten's city.

ABYDOS
EGYPT'S FIRST ROYAL CEMETERY

TYPE: CEMETERY, TEMPLES • **ARCHITECTURAL STYLE:** TOMB COMPLEX
LOCATION: SOUTHERN EGYPT • **CONSTRUCTION BEGUN:** CA. 3100 B.C.E.

The ancient Abydos cemetery, cult center of the funerary god Osiris and home to royal tombs and temples, lies on the desert edge on the west bank of the Nile River, 80 miles (128 km) downstream of modern Luxor, in Egypt. The extensive cemetery was used from predynastic times until the Roman period, a timespan of more than 3,000 years. It has been excavated almost continuously over the past 150 years, with investigations continuing today.

By 3000 B.C.E., the independent city-states lining the Nile River and its delta had united to form one land. The first Egyptian kings ruled from the northern city of Memphis (near modern Cairo) but chose to be buried in the south, at Abydos. They built their mudbrick tombs in a part of the cemetery known today as the Umm el Qa'ab (Arabic for "Mother of Pots") because the surface is covered with millions of ancient potsherds.

Cemetery B on the Umm el Qa'ab housed the tombs built for the Dynasty 0 kings plus the 1st Dynasty tomb complex of Aha. The remaining 1st Dynasty kings, plus Queen Regent Meritneith, built tombs to the south of Cemetery B. Their tombs share a similar plan: a rock-cut burial chamber that is surrounded by storage chambers

Below The New Kingdom temple of Seti I at Abydos is one of the best preserved and most beautifully decorated temples from ancient Egypt.

Opposite top Seti's temple includes two hypostyle halls filled with a forest of huge stone columns.

Opposite bottom The temple of Seti I, seen from the temple gate.

and covered by a low, mudbrick-covered mound that is itself covered by a larger mound. While the first kings of the 2nd Dynasty chose to be buried in northern Egypt, the final two kings of the dynasty returned to Abydos and the Umm el Qa'ab. Their relatively modest tombs were just one element in their wider funerary provision. Less than 1.2 miles (2 km) to the northeast of their Umm el Qa'ab tombs, the 1st and 2nd Dynasty kings built huge rectangular enclosures defined by mudbrick walls. Early Egyptologists interpreted these enclosures as "forts;" today it is realized that they had some unknown ritual purpose.

The 1st Dynasty tomb complexes included subsidiary graves. The deceased—contracted, partially mummified and wrapped in linen—were buried in wooden coffins with their own grave goods, their names engraved on small limestone stelae. The funerary complex of King Djer included 318 of these additional burials. Of the ninety-seven surviving stelae, seventy-six bore female names. It is impossible to determine how theses women died, but it seems likely that they were either murdered or persuaded to commit suicide at the time of the king's death. If this is the case, it was a short-lived ritual. There is no evidence of human sacrifice associated with any other royal burial in ancient Egypt.

The Burial Place of Osiris

By the 12th Dynasty (ca. 1985 B.C.E.) the Umm el Qa'ab was accepted as the last resting place of the mummiform god of the dead Osiris, with the 1st Dynasty tomb of King Djer, suitably embellished, serving as his tomb. The Egyptians had always believed that proximity in death could have beneficial results, and many courtiers chose to be buried close to the pyramids and tombs of their kings. Interment near to the tomb of Osiris was therefore seen as a highly desirable but somewhat impractical option for the masses. Pilgrims flocked to Abydos, where they visited the already ancient tombs, watched the religious processions, and dedicated a stele or statue to the god. Devotees were often buried with a pair of model boats (one to sail upriver and one down) that would allow them to visit Abydos during their afterlife.

The Temples of Seti and the Osireion

Kings, too, wished to be permanently associated with Osiris, and many built temples at Abydos. The most impressive are those built by the first kings of the 19th Dynasty. Seti I (r. ca. 1294–1279 B.C.E.) built a small temple for his father, Ramesses I, and an enormous one

for himself. His son, Ramesses II (r. 1279–1213 B.C.E.), completed Seti's temple and built his own, smaller version. Seti's beautifully decorated and extremely well-preserved limestone temple includes two hypostyle halls and seven chapels dedicated to Osiris, Isis, Horus, Amen-Re, Ra-Horakhty, Ptah, and the deified Seti. One wall is inscribed with a "king list:" an unbroken line of rulers stretching from Menes, the legendary founder of the 1st Dynasty, down to Seti himself. Immediately to the west of his temple, Seti excavated a subterranean cenotaph known today as the Osireion. Here, a room opening off the central hall was shaped like an enormous

sarcophagus. A channel surrounding the hall acted as a moat for groundwater, and in so doing allowed the hall to represent the mound of creation.

Abydos is not conveniently situated for public transport. Travelers are advised to take a taxi from Luxor, and ask it to wait. Most visitors will wish to focus their visit on the Seti temple and Osireion.

Opposite The water-filled interior of the Osireion, a part of the temple of Seti I.

Above On the walls of his Abydos temple, Ramesses II is shown anointing a statue of the god Wennefer (Osiris).

THE TEMPLE OF HATHOR AT **DENDERA**

TYPE: TEMPLE · **ARCHITECTURAL STYLE:** EGYPTIAN
LOCATION: QENA GOVERNORATE, EGYPT · **CONSTRUCTION BEGUN:** CA. 55 B.C.E.

The outer rear wall of the Temple of Hathor offers a rare view of one of the most celebrated of all ancient Egyptian rulers: Cleopatra. A double scene shows her and her son Caesarion making offerings to a line of gods. In the scene on the left they offer to Osiris, his sister-wife Isis, and their son Harsiesis; on the right they offer to Hathor, her son Ihy, and the Osirian triad (Osiris, Isis, and Horus). In the middle of the wall is the head of Hathor.

The town of Dendera (ancient Iunet, Greek Tentyris) is situated on the west bank of the Nile River approximately 37 miles (60 km) north of Luxor, in Egypt. The well-preserved Graeco-Roman temple complex dedicated to the goddess Hathor is to the southwest of the town. Neighboring temples dedicated to Hathor's spouse, Horus, and their son, Ihy, are now lost. Work on the current Hathor complex started during the Ptolemaic Period (305–30 B.C.E.), covering a series of earlier buildings dating back to Egypt's Old Kingdom (2686–2160 B.C.E.). The site also includes a cemetery with tombs dating back to the Early Dynastic Period (ca. 3000–2682 B.C.E.), brick-vaulted Late Period animal catacombs (664–332 B.C.E.), and a Christian basilica dating the fifth Century C.E.

Ptolemy XII had ambitious plans to redesign the, already substantial, 30th Dynasty temple on this site. Unfortunately he died just four years into his building program, leaving his daughter, Cleopatra VII (69–30 B.C.E.), to complete his work. The temple was eventually finished a decade after her death.

Following tradition, the temple is orientated toward the Nile River, which, due to a bend in the river, here flows east–west. In front of the temple are several Roman kiosks and a propylon gateway. A hypostyle hall fronts the temple itself, its twenty-four Hathor-sistrum-style columns

partially revealed by the unusual low screen facade. The hall ceiling displays a colorful chart of the heavens. An inscription confirms that the Roman Emperor Tiberius built this part of the temple in 34–35 C.E.

Beyond the main hypostyle hall, visitors enter a smaller six-columned hall, the "hall of appearances:" here the statue of the goddess would appear during temple rituals. Eleven chapels surround the main sanctuary, each dedicated to a god associated with Hathor. A series of crypts once housed the temple treasures.

In 1821 a carved zodiac ceiling—a map of the sky—was removed from a chapel on the temple roof, dedicated to the commemoration of the resurrection of the god Osiris. While the original ceiling is now displayed in the Louvre Museum, Paris, visitors to the temple today can see a replica of it.

The complex includes two birth houses: temples dedicated to the birth of Hathor's son Ihy. The earlier temple was started during the 30th Dynasty, and completed by the Ptolemies; Augustus and Trajan built the later temple. To the south of the birth houses, a mudbrick sanatorium allowed sick visitors to consult priests, bathe, or drink healing waters drawn from the sacred lake.

Visitors to Dendera are advised to take a taxi from Luxor and ask it to wait, as there is no reliable public transport available.

Opposite top The approach to the temple of Hathor at Dendera.
Opposite bottom Carved at the rear of the temple of Hathor are giant images of Cleopatra VII and her son Caesarion.
Above The temple pronaos, or entrance hall.

KARNAK HOME OF THE HIDDEN ONE

TYPE: TEMPLE COMPLEX · **ARCHITECTURAL STYLE:** TEMPLES AND PYLONS
LOCATION: SOUTHERN EGYPT · **CONSTRUCTION BEGUN:** CA. 2055 B.C.E.

Victorian travel writer Amelia B. Edwards described the Karnak temple complex as "a place that has been much written about and often painted; but of which no writing and no art can convey more than a dwarfed and pallid impression." She was quite right. The complex is a magnificent, multi-period, partially ruined religious site of great size and complexity incorporating temples and chapels to various deities, pylons (gateways), processional routes, and a sacred lake. At its heart lies the vast temple dedicated to Amun-Ra, The Hidden One, patron god of Egypt's New Kingdom. For years the complex was misinterpreted, with early visitors believing that it was a great royal palace.

The ancient Egyptians knew Karnak as Ipet-Swt or "most select of places." Originally a local shrine dedicated to the god Amun, the complex experienced continuous building works from the early Middle Kingdom to Roman times—almost 2,000 years—as successive kings attempted to out-build their predecessors. Unfortunately, many kings also demolished earlier monuments, absorbing the discarded stone blocks within their own constructions. A striking example of this recycling can be seen in the gateway (pylon three) built by the 18th Dynasty King Amenhotep III (r. ca. 1390–1353 B.C.E.). The rubble fill of Amenhotep's gateway has yielded blocks of carved limestone taken from a chapel erected by the Middle Kingdom Senwosret I (r. ca.

1956–1911 B.C.E.). This chapel, known today as the White Chapel, is the most significant remnant of the large, and now almost entirely vanished, Middle Kingdom temple. Today it stands in the open-air museum within the Amun-Ra enclosure. Here, too, stands the quartzite Red Chapel raised by the female pharaoh Hatshepsut (r. ca. 1473–1458); another beautiful building that has been dismantled and reassembled.

Opposite The interior of the hypostyle hall in the temple of Amun-Ra.

Above Looking along the statue-flanked central axis of the Amun-Ra temple at Karnak, towards the hypostyle hall.

Obelisks

Standing alongside the huge buildings, Karnak was graced by a series of granite obelisks erected by early 18th Dynasty kings (ca. 1504–1425 B.C.E.). Obelisks are tall, tapering stones inscribed with royal and religious texts and often entirely or partially covered with gold foil. The stone for these monoliths came from the riverside granite quarries upriver at Aswan. To cut, transport, and erect a large-scale obelisk was both a magnificent technical achievement and an unmistakable mark of powerful kingship.

Amenhotep III at Karnak

The main axis of the Amun-Ra temple was aligned westward, so that it formed part of a processional route linking Karnak with the royal mortuary temples situated across the river on the west bank of the Nile River. It is from the reign of Amenhotep III that the intention to develop the

Amun-Ra temple as the nucleus of a series of related, satellite structures becomes clear. To the south of the Amun-Ra enclosure Amenhotep enlarged a temple enclosure for Mut, wife of Amun-Ra. Mut's temple enclosure was joined to the Amun-Ra enclosure by a second processional axis running south from the Amun-Ra temple via a series of courtyards and pylons. A branch of this southern axis bypassed the Mut enclosure and ran southward along a sphinx-lined road, toward the Luxor temple.

The Hypostyle Hall

The hypostyle hall was started by Ramesses I (r. ca. 1295–1294 B.C.E.) and continued and decorated by his son Seti I (r. ca. 1294–1279). The interior walls were carved with scenes of temple ritual, while the exterior walls were decorated with battle scenes showing Seti in all his military glory. Following Seti's death, his son Ramesses II (r. ca. 1279–1213) completed the hall and named it

Glorious is Ramesses II in the Domain of Amun. The hall now boasted a forest of 134 papyrus-style columns arranged in sixteen rows, the twelve columns in the two central rows standing 80 ft (24 m) high while the outer columns, sixty-one on each side, stood 40 ft (12 m) tall. Dim light filtered through the high, barred clerestory windows creating a cool, dark contrast to the heat and light of the secular world. The workmen were ordered to abandon the delicate raised relief favored by Seti, and to adopt the faster, less elegant sunken relief that characterizes almost all of Ramesses' monuments. The difference in styles must have been obvious, even when covered in layers of paint, and Ramesses later returned to re-carve sections of the raised relief so that it would appear that he had been responsible for the decoration of the entire hall.

Later Building Works

Later kings were unable to build on the same scale as their New Kingdom predecessors, but their interest in Karnak caused them to carry out minor works of repair and improvement in most parts of the temple structure, and they erected smaller temples for "guest" deities within the Amun-Ra enclosure. The last major building project at Karnak was the replacement of the central sanctuary of Amun-Ra with one built by Macedonian King Philip Arrhidaeus (r. 323–317 B.C.E.).

Karnak lies a short stroll northward, along the corniche, from the center of modern Luxor (ancient Thebes), in southern Egypt. The walk is a pleasant one but can be hot and dusty, so visitors might prefer to hire a horse-drawn carriage or taxi and save their energy for sightseeing.

Opposite A series of ram-headed sphinxes which once lined the processional way to the temple.

Right, from top A carving depicting the ram-headed stern of the boat of Amun-Ra. The White Chapel built by Senwosret I. Some of the royal statues found at Karnak.

DEIR EL-MEDINA
A WORKMEN'S VILLAGE

TYPE: VILLAGE • **ARCHITECTURAL STYLE:** STONE HOUSES
LOCATION: SOUTHERN EGYPT • **CONSTRUCTION BEGUN:** CA. 1525 B.C.E.

On the west bank of the Nile River, in a small valley relatively close to the Valley of the Kings, the Valley of the Queens, and Medinet Habu, lie the remains of the New Kingdom workmen's village of Deir el-Medina. Today the village is a well-preserved stone ruin composed of the remains of close-packed multi-room houses surrounded by a wall. The slopes on either side of the village are honeycombed with tombs and chapels for private worship by the villagers. To the north of the village is a failed well known as the "Great Pit." The Ptolemaic Hathor temple, which lies to the northeast of the village, incorporates a 19th Dynasty Hathor chapel.

The original residents knew their village as *pa demi*, simply "the village." The modern name, Deir el-Medina, translates as "Monastery of the Town," and is a reference to the Coptic church and monastery built close by. It has been estimated that, at its peak, the village was home to approximately 200 people. Not all the houses were occupied all the time.

Deir el-Medina was built to house the workmen engaged in the construction and decoration of the royal tombs in the Valley of the Kings, their families, dependents, and servants. The confined nature of the rock-cut tombs meant that they required a small, skilled workforce rather than the thousands who had built the pyramids. It therefore made sound sense to develop a specialized workforce and house them together. To allow easy access to the royal necropolis, the village was situated in the desert more than 164 ft (50 m) above the water table: this caused great problems when it proved impossible to dig a well. Every drop of water had to be taken to the village by donkey. It did prove possible to raise animals and grow crops in small gardens outside the village wall,

but, lacking peasant farmers, Deir el-Medina was a village unable to support itself. The maintenance of the village became one of the costs of royal tomb construction.

When the Valley of the Kings ceased to be the royal cemetery, Deir el-Medina became unviable and the villagers left. The inconvenient desert location prevented any major resettlement at the site, while providing excellent conditions for the preservation of archaeological information. The fact that the houses were partially built of stone, rather than the more usual mudbrick, aided this exceptional preservation.

The Deir el-Medina Houses
The houses were designed and built by the state, with the larger houses close to the village entrance being allocated to the workforce foremen and the scribes. Changes to the original design were permitted, and so by the end of the New Kingdom no two houses were exactly the same. The original houses had no foundations and were built of mudbrick. Later houses had stone rubble foundations, with stone lower courses and mudbrick upper courses.

The roof over the main part of each house was constructed from palm tree trunks and leaves, with the gaps filled with potsherds, and plastered. At up to 8 in (20 cm) thick, the roof was strong enough to form a floor, extending the usable space within the houses.

An Atypical Community

Royal tomb workers were effectively born to the job, as succeeding generations of workmen passed their skills down from father to son. Most Deir el-Medina workmen were born in the village, as were their parents and grandparents before them and, indeed, most of the people they knew. Although they lived in a walled community, and worked on a potentially secret royal project, there is no evidence that they were confined to their village by guards, and a stroll of less than an hour would have taken a workman from the village to the bank of the Nile. This proximity allowed the workers to supplement their state ration by making and selling products both to each other and to their Theban neighbors. These skills included coffin manufacture and decoration, weaving and, of course, tomb building.

When toiling on the royal tomb, the workforce worked two four-hour shifts each day with a lunch break at noon. The working week was spent in the Valley of the Kings, with the men staying overnight in nearby huts. They worked for eight days, returning to the village to rest on the ninth and tenth days (the "weekend"). As every Egyptian month included thirty days, this meant that there were at least six days of rest each month; these were supplemented by official and religious holidays. The huts were situated along the path to the Valley of the Kings. Each included one or two small rooms with a stone sleeping platform against the back wall. They were plastered, painted, and might bear their owner's name.

Visitors to Deir el-Medina are advised to take the Luxor ferry to the west bank, and then either take a forty-five minute walk at a moderate pace, or take a taxi to the site.

Above top View across the village.

Above bottom The reconstruction of the superstructure of a New Kingdom tomb in the form of a little pyramid.

THE VALLEY OF THE KINGS

TYPE: NECROPOLIS • **ARCHITECTURAL STYLE:** ROCK-CUT TOMBS
LOCATION: SOUTHERN EGYPT • **CONSTRUCTION BEGUN:** CA. 1550 B.C.E.

The west bank of the Nile River at Luxor forms one vast cemetery, riddled with tombs of many periods, some royal and some private. During the New Kingdom (Dynasties 18–20; ca. 1550–1069 B.C.E.) Egypt's kings chose to be buried here. Their remote necropolis is today known as the Valley of the Kings.

For more than 1,000 years Egypt's kings had been buried in enormous pyramid complexes raised in the northern desert cemeteries. At the start of the 18th Dynasty everything changed. Kings would now be buried in rock-cut tombs tunneled into the Theban Mountain, with the mountain serving as a natural pyramid. The new necropolis was a part of the vast sacred landscape dedicated to Amun-Ra, incorporating the extensive Karnak temple complex and the smaller Luxor temple.

For nearly 500 years the relatively limited space of the valley was honeycombed with the tombs of virtually every king from the early 18th Dynasty to the end of the 20th Dynasty. Over time the size and complexity of these tombs increased, as did the amount of wall space given over to depictions of the king traversing eternity with the gods. Great kings of the early 18th Dynasty, such as Tuthmosis III (r. 1479–1425 B.C.E.), had rather modest-sized tombs, but the fashion for larger tombs grew through the dynasty. By the beginning of the 19th Dynasty kings such as Seti I (r. 1294–1279 B.C.E.) and Ramesses II (r. 1279–1214 B.C.E.) had magnificent tombs to match their other building achievements. Paradoxically, kings of the later 19th and 20th dynasties—who built relatively little anywhere else—also had large, well-decorated tombs, which were clearly a priority at a time of crisis in royal authority.

Rescuing the Royal Mummies

Toward the end of the New Kingdom, unpredictable Nile levels led to high inflation and food shortages, and Thebes suffered raids by Libyan nomads. The royal tombs faced a sustained threat from well-informed criminal gangs.

Necropolis officials settled on a bold tactic. They opened up the royal tombs and emptied them. They then removed the mummies from their sarcophagi and sent them to workshops where they were stripped of their bandages and jewelry, re-wrapped, labeled, and placed in plain coffins. The mummies were then stored in chambers dotted about the necropolis. From time to time these collections were amalgamated, until there were two major caches: one housed in the family tomb of the High Priest Pinudjem II at Deir el-Bahri and one stored in the valley tomb of Amenhotep II. When, more than 2,000 years later, Western explorers started to investigate the tombs in the Valley of the Kings, they would be mystified by the lack of bodies.

Tutankhamen's Tomb

The only burial to be discovered virtually intact, Tutankhamen's tomb survived because it had been forgotten. Although he had planned to be buried in a splendid royal tomb alongside his grandfather, Amenhotep III, Tutankhamen (r. 1336–1327 B.C.E.) was actually buried in a cramped, non-royal tomb cut into the valley floor. The

accepted explanation is that Tutankhamen died too young to realize his ambitious plans. However, it seems far more likely that Tutankhamen's successor, the elderly Ay, made a strategic swap.

Tutankhamen's tomb was a typical late 18th Dynasty non-royal rock-cut tomb, accessed via a flight of sixteen descending steps. At the bottom of the steps, a doorway opened onto a narrow, sloping passageway leading to a second doorway. This led into a rectangular storeroom, the Antechamber, which allowed access via a sealed doorway to a subsidiary storage chamber, the Annexe. The Burial Chamber was separated from the Antechamber by a plastered dry-stone partition wall that contained a hidden doorway. Opening off the Burial Chamber was a subsidiary storage chamber, the Treasury.

Eighteenth Dynasty royal tombs were traditionally decorated with texts and scenes taken from a collection of religious writings known as the Books of the Underworld. These were provided to help the king on his journey to the afterlife by recalling the nighttime adventure of the sun god Ra. In Tutankhamen's small-scale tomb, the passageway, Antechamber, Annexe, and Treasury remained unplastered and unpainted. Only the Burial Chamber was decorated.

Soon after Tutankhamen's funeral, the valley suffered a spate of robberies and Tutankhamen's tomb was targeted twice. There is little doubt that this would have continued, had nature not intervened. A flash flood deposited a thick sediment that concealed the tomb entrance. Tutankhamen's vanished tomb was quickly forgotten. It was rediscovered by Lord Carnarvon and Howard Carter in 1922.

Travelers wishing to visit the Valley are advised to travel to Luxor by train or plane, then cross the Nile River using the ferry and hire a taxi. Alternatively, for the intrepid, it is possible to hire a bicycle in Luxor.

Above The Valley of the Kings: the remote cemetery used by Egypt's New Kingdom pharaohs.

THE **DEIR EL-BAHRI** BAY TEMPLES

TYPE: TEMPLES • **ARCHITECTURAL STYLE:** EGYPTIAN
LOCATION: LUXOR GOVERNORATE, EGYPT • **CONSTRUCTION BEGUN:** CA. 2004 B.C.E.

Deir el-Bahri is a natural bay in the cliffs on the west bank of the Nile River at Luxor, in Egypt. Its name, literally "Monastery of the North," is a reference to the mudbrick Coptic monastery that was established at the site during the fifth century C.E., and which has since been demolished. Today, the name refers to the bay area and its three temples and, more specifically, to Hatshepsut's mortuary temple. Throughout the Dynastic Age, the Deir el-Bahri bay was strongly associated with the cult of the mother-goddess Hathor in her role as Goddess of the West.

The Temple-Tomb of Mentuhotep II

Nebhepetre Mentuhotep II (r. ca. 2055–2004 B.C.E.) reunited the fragmented Egypt at the start of the Middle Kingdom. A southern warrior, he built a unique terraced funerary complex in the Deir el-Bahri bay. Much of his tomb superstructure has vanished, but it is possible that it was topped by a pyramid.

Holiest of the Holy: Hatshepsut's Temple

Inspired by the example of Mentuhotep II, the female pharaoh Hatshepsut (r. ca. 1473–1458 B.C.E.) built her own mortuary temple, Djeser-djeseru or "Holiest of the Holy" in the Deir el-Bahri bay. Hatshepsut's temple takes the form of three ascending terraces set against the cliff. The tiered porticoes are linked by a broad stairway that rises through the center toward the shrine of Amun. The uppermost level is fronted by a portico whose twenty-four square-cut pillars were each faced by a colossal painted limestone statue of Hatshepsut as the god of the dead, Osiris. The temple was originally accessed through a garden, and defined by a limestone wall.

Djeser-djeseru was a multifunctional temple with a complex of shrines devoted to various deities. In addition to the mortuary chapels provided for Hatshepsut and her

father Tuthmosis I, there were chapels for Hathor and Anubis and an open-roofed chapel for the sun god Ra-Horakhty. The main shrine, which was cut into the cliff, was dedicated to the god Amun. The temple served as the focus of the Amun-based "Feast of the Valley," an annual festival of death and renewal.

Hatshepsut used her stone temple walls to display the highlights of her reign. Visitors to her temple can see the raising of obelisks, the defeat of enemies, trade missions to the land of Punt and, most important of all, the story of her divine birth. Her temple is undergoing restoration, and is now in good condition.

The Temple of Tuthmosis III

Tuthmosis, coruler with, and successor to, Hatshepsut, squeezed a small temple between the other two much larger temples in the Deir el-Bahri bay. Initially it was thought that his temple—Djeser-akhet, or "Holiest of the Horizon"—formed part of his mortuary provision, but now it is realized that this might not be the case. The temple is today a ruin.

Visitors to Deir el-Bahri are advised to take advice in Luxor about buying tickets for the west bank sites. Then, take the Luxor ferry to the west bank, and take a taxi to the bay. A rest house offers facilities to the weary traveller.

Opposite The upper terrace of Hatshepsut's temple is fronted by colossal statues of the female king as the god of the dead Osiris.

Above top The three tiers of Hatshesput's temple merge with the Theban Mountain. The temple sanctuary is cut into the rock.

Above bottom The inspiration for Hatshepsut's temple came from the temple-tomb erected by her Middle Kingdom predecessor, Montuhotep II, as shown here.

ASWAN ANCIENT BORDER TOWN

TYPE: CITY, CEMETERY AND QUARRIES · **ARCHITECTURAL STYLE:** EGYPTIAN
LOCATION: SOUTHERN EGYPT · **CONSTRUCTION BEGUN:** 3000 B.C.E.

For more than 3,000 years Aswan, situated on the First Nile Cataract, was the southern border of ancient Egypt. Beyond Aswan lay Egypt's traditional enemy: Nubia. As a border town—both a frontier garrison and a trading center and customs post—Aswan was always a place of strategic importance. Today it offers visitors a plethora of varied experiences.

Elephantine Island

Elephantine (ancient Yebu) is a granite island measuring 4,900 ft (1,500 m) north–south and 1,640 ft (500 m) at its widest east–west point. It became a single entity when the base level of the Nile River lowered during the First Intermediate Period (ca. 2160–2055 B.C.E.); before this, there were two islands divided by marshland. Today Elephantine is a relatively small element of the large

modern city of Aswan. In ancient times, however, this situation was reversed, with Elephantine being the more important settlement and Aswan (ancient Swnw) a small town on the east bank of the Nile.

The name Elephantine may be a reflection of the elephant-shaped rocks that border the island, or a reference to that fact that Elephantine was the center of the Egyptian ivory trade. The first town developed on Elephantine in late Predynastic/Early Dynastic times (ca. 3100 B.C.E.) with building works continuing into the Roman period (30 B.C.E.–395 C.E.). The Aswan Museum is located at the southern end of the island.

The earliest deity to be associated with Elephantine Island was the goddess Satet, whose Predynastic temple was a grotto situated within a cluster of granite boulders. This temple was expanded and developed in a way that retained its ancient core, but that also saw important additions during the Middle Kingdom (ca. 2055–1650 B.C.E.), New Kingdom (ca. 1550–1069 B.C.E.) and Ptolemaic Period (ca. 305–30 B.C.E.).

By the Middle Kingdom, Satet had acquired a male partner, Khnum, whose temple buildings are now the most striking archaeological remains on Elephantine Island.

There are two nilometers—devices to measure the flow of the Nile River—on Elephantine Island. The better known, a corridor nilometer associated with the Temple of Satis, is one of the oldest nilometers in Egypt. It was reconstructed during the Roman period, and was still in use during the nineteenth century C.E. The other nilometer is located near the Temple of Khnum, opposite the Old Cataract Hotel.

The Qubbet el-Hawa Cemetery

The Qubbet el-Hawa is a high ridge of cliffs on the west bank of the Nile River to the north of Elephantine Island. In the 6th Dynasty (ca. 2345–2181 B.C.E.) the elite of Elephantine cut large rock-cut tombs high into the cliffs, ensuring that they would dominate the landscape, being

visible for miles around. Some of the larger Qubbet el-Hawa tombs are approached via a steep ramp leading directly from the river's edge to their quarried facades.

The decorated interiors of the tombs include traditional scenes showing the deceased receiving offerings and enjoying leisure activities such as fishing and fowling. Their open facades are less conventional: here the deceased had texts carved relating their Nubian adventures and explaining their role in developing trade with Nubia and central Africa beyond. The most unusual text is found on the northern half of the facade of the tomb of the courtier Harkuf. Here we can read a copy of a letter written by the child-pharaoh Pepi II. From this letter we learn how Harkhuf acquired a "dancing dwarf of the god from the land of spirit" as a gift for his young king.

The Aswan Quarries

To the south of Elephantine Island, a series of granite quarries provided stone for statues, obelisks, and sarcophagi. Visitors can still see the "unfinished obelisk," ordered by the female pharaoh Hatshepsut but abandoned in the quarry after it developed a fatal crack. Had it been completed, this obelisk would have stood more than 135 ft (41 m) tall and weighed an estimated 1,000 tons.

The quarry on Sehel Island has yielded a series of graffiti, which includes the work of officials who were either sent on stone-procuring missions to the region, or who were passing through, en route for Nubia. The most famous of these is the Famine Stele—an inscription that dates to the Graeco-Roman period, but claims to record events from the time of the pyramids.

Today, Aswan is easy to access by plane or train from either Cairo or Luxor; it is also possible to take a taxi from Luxor, an option that allows visits to other archaeological sites en route.

Opposite The monuments on Elephantine Island span the entire 3,000 years of the dynastic period.

THE TWIN TEMPLES AT **ABU SIMBEL**

TYPE: ROCK-CUT TEMPLES • **ARCHITECTURAL STYLE:** EGYPTIAN
LOCATION: SOUTHERN EGYPT • **CONSTRUCTION BEGUN:** CA. 1279 B.C.E.

During the thirteenth century B.C.E., the ancient Egyptian pharaoh Ramesses II cut a pair of temples into sandstone cliffs on the west bank of the Nile River. He set them at an angle to each other so that, just twice a year (February and October), the rising sun penetrated the Great Temple and illuminated the four statues sitting in the sanctuary. This is the site of Abu Simbel in Nubia, 40 miles (64 km) to the north of the Second Nile Cataract.

Abu Simbel was a remote spot, far from any sizeable settlement. With no obvious need for temples, it seems likely that Ramesses (r. 1279–1213 B.C.E.) was inspired by the local geography. The facade of the Great Temple was designed to display the king in all his glory. Two colossal statues of the king wearing the double crown of Upper and Lower Egypt sit on either side of the central doorway. An earthquake during Year 30 of Ramesses' reign caused the statue to the north of the entrance to lose an arm (later restored) and the statue to the south to lose its upper body. Between the colossi, the more important members of the royal family are arranged in groups of three. Above the doorway stands Ra-Horakhty, with the goddess Maat by his left leg and the sign for "User" by his right, so that the statue becomes a rebus reading "User-Maat-Ra," the throne name of Ramesses II.

Beyond the facade the temple extends 157 ft (48 m) into the cliff. The first pillared hall is decorated with scenes of Ramesses displaying his military triumphs. The second pillared hall includes images of the divine Ramesses. Beyond the halls, four gods sit in a niche in the sanctuary: Ptah of Memphis, Amen-Re of Thebes, Ra-Horakhty of Heliopolis, and Ramesses of Per-Ramesses.

The Small Temple was built on a much smaller scale than its neighbor, extending only 82 ft (25 m) back into the mountain. This temple was dedicated to a local form of the goddess Hathor, who was strongly identified with Ramesses' consort Nefertari. The facade shows two colossal figures of Nefertari wearing the cow horns and carrying the sistrum of Hathor, and four of Ramesses. The images on the internal walls include scenes of temple ritual, of Hathor the sacred cow and Tawaret the protectors of women in labor. The niche in the sanctuary contains the carved image of Hathor in the form of a cow protecting Ramesses.

Today, this part of ancient Nubia falls within the borders of modern Egypt. Travelers wishing to visit the Abu Simbel temples must journey to Aswan, then either fly or take a long coach journey. Visitors will not, however, be able to see the temples in their original location. When, in 1954, the decision was taken to build the Aswan High Dam, the Abu Simbel temples were threatened by the rising water level. Between 1964 and 1968 the temples, plus sections of the original cliff face, were raised 213 ft (65 m) above their original site to an artificially created environment.

Opposite top The Small Temple of Abu Simbel is decorated with colossal statues of Ramesses II and his consort Nefertari.
Opposite bottom The Great Temple of Abu Simbel, in its new location.

SENEGAMBIAN STONE CIRCLES

TYPE: MEGALITHS • **ARCHITECTURAL STYLE:** N/A • **LOCATION:** SENEGAL AND THE GAMBIA
CONSTRUCTION BEGUN: CA. THIRD CENTURY B.C.E.

Senegal and The Gambia lie at the westernmost point of the African continent. In the area between the Senegal River to the north and the Gambia River to the south are numerous megalithic monuments. Most are stone circles, but some large stones occur singly. Though sometimes referred to as "mini-Stonehenges," they differ because they are associated with burials. Though not securely dated, the first stones probably date from the third century B.C.E. but most date from the later first millennium to the mid-second millennium C.E.

It has been estimated that, in an area of approximately 12,740 sq mi (33,000 sq km), there are more that 1,000 monuments, made up of 29,000 standing stones. Though they occur across the region, about half of the megaliths are found in four concentrations: Wassu and Kerbatch in The Gambia and Sine Ngayene and Wanar in Senegal. They tend to occur in association with watercourses. Today much of the land is open farmland, but historical photos from the early twentieth century show that, at that time, the landscape was woodland; it may have been even more densely vegetated in prehistory.

The megaliths are made of locally quarried laterite rock, worked into cylindrical or polygonal forms and smoothed on one or more sides. Many were erected to form single circles, though double-circle arrangements are also known. Some have single stones outside the circles, known as frontal stones. Especially notable are frontal stones carved into a branching shape, like a "Y," or with parallel branches resembling a lyre and therefore known as "lyre-stones." The stones range in size from less than 39 in (1 m) to 10 ft (3 m) in height.

Given the huge number of megaliths, and because they were made for centuries, few generalizations can be made. There are some differences in the associated grave types—for example, some may initially have been covered by mounds or wooden funerary houses, before the erection of the megaliths. The frontal stones seem to have been a focus of ritual activity, with pottery vessels being placed around them. Numerous complete examples have been excavated; many have a hole bored in the base.

The identity of the makers of the megalithic monuments remains unknown, and documenting and dating the multiple sites are enormous, and ongoing, tasks. Why this megalithic tradition emerged when it did remains unexplained, though it seems likely that it was linked to assertion of identity in the context of early state formation in West Africa.

Opposite Megaliths in a circular formation at Wassu, The Gambia.

Left A lyre stone, carved from laterite rock, from the Kaolack region of Senegal.

Below Concentric stone circles, near Nioro du Rip in Senegal.

Comprising the largest concentration of megalithic monuments in the world, the whole area here is a listed UNESCO World Heritage site. Wherever tourists go in Senegal and The Gambia, the chances are that stone circles exist nearby. Sine Ngayene, in Senegal, is one of the most impressive sites, with fifty-two stone circles, while Wassu, in the Gambia, has more diverse and elaborate examples.

THE KINGDOM OF **AKSUM**

TYPE: CITY • **ARCHITECTURAL STYLE:** AKSUMITE
LOCATION: ETHIOPIA • **CONSTRUCTION BEGUN:** UNKNOWN

Aksum was a thriving polity of the first to seventh centuries C.E. At its height it covered perhaps 390,000 sq mi (1,000,000 sq km) in northern Ethiopia and Eritrea and also extended into southern Arabia. Its capital, also named Aksum, is located on a plateau punctuated by dome-shaped hills and criss-crossed by shallow streams, in the semi-arid Tigray highlands. The Aksumite empire was involved in intercontinental trade through its main seaport, Adulis, on the Red Sea. Among the remains of the city are royal palaces and tombs and, most spectacularly, massive carved monolithic stelae. Aksum was one of relatively few African kingdoms to have a written language.

Though its origins are unclear, this kingdom's original inhabitants belonged to an Iron Age society that already had cultural links with the Arabian Peninsula, across the Red Sea.

The history of Aksum needs to be understood in relation to the decline of Meroe. Meroe was the capital of the kingdom of Kush, on the east bank of the Nile River in the Sudan, and an important urban center from around 700 B.C.E.–300 C.E. It had been founded by rulers of ancient Egypt's 25th Dynasty. After they withdrew, Meroe became increasingly independent of Egyptian political and cultural influence, but achieved great prosperity through extensive trade networks.

Meroe's wealth and power diminished in the first millennium C.E., partly because of over-exploitation of local resources, but also because control of trade had shifted to the southeast, to the kingdom of Aksum. The changing economic landscape was described in a first-century C.E. text, *The Periplus of the Erythraean Sea*. The Aksumites invaded Meroe around 350 C.E., though by that time it was already in terminal decline.

Aksum's exports included agricultural products, ivory, gold, precious stones, salt, and slaves. The kingdom's trade networks stretched into Europe, to Rome and Byzantium, and as far as India. Imports included metal goods, glass, and luxury items such as silks and spices. That the Aksumites minted their own gold, silver, and copper coins from the third century C.E. onward is testament to the center's wealth and its flourishing commercial operations both at home and abroad. Coins bore inscriptions in Greek or in Ge'ez, the Aksumite language. Ezana (325–356 C.E.),

Above Coin with the head of King Aphilas (ruled 300–340 C.E.).
Opposite top The Great Stele (Stele One), representing a 13 story building, may have fallen while being erected.
Opposite bottom The Stele of Aksum was removed to Rome in 1937 but was returned in 2005 and re-erected in 2008.

the ruler of Aksum in the fourth century C.E., adopted Christianity, which replaced the kingdom's older, polytheistic religion. The ancient disk and crescent symbol was replaced on coinage with a Christian cross.

Aksum began to decline around the sixth century C.E. Its end can be attributed to the control of Red Sea trade by the rise of a new and powerful Islamic caliphate in the Arabian Peninsula.

Only a tiny part of the city of Aksum has been scientifically excavated, but it is best known for its architecture, much of it dating to Ezana's reign and

thereafter. Its monumental stelae are especially notable. An older area of the site, known as the Gudit field, contains hundreds of small, more roughly carved stelae that are associated with non-elite burials beneath.

The Northern Stelae Field is where the nobility were buried. Seven huge carved stelae can still be seen. The largest standing stela, at 79 ft (24 m), is the Obelisk of Aksum, which was taken to Rome in 1937 but repatriated to Ethiopia in 2005. Prior to its reinstallation, the largest was King Ezana's stela, which is 69 ft (21 m) tall. The largest of all, at 108 ft (33 m), lies broken on the ground,

perhaps after toppling while being erected. All are carved in imitation of multistory Aksumite stone-and-wood buildings, narrowing toward the top. They display typical Aksumite architectural features, including false windows and doors, with projecting beam ends.

Four tombs dating to the third and fourth centuries C.E. have been found beneath these large stelae. The Tomb of the Brick Arches is a multiroom subterranean complex. The Tomb of the False Door, as the name suggests, had a carefully concealed entrance. Grave goods, including jewelry, glassware, coins, and ivory pieces, provide evidence

of the intercontinental trade on which Aksum thrived.

Tours of the site can be taken from Addis Ababa, and day trips are available from the modern town of Aksum. The site is best visited outside of the rainy season, which extends from around May to September.

Opposite The Tomb of the Brick Arches dates to the fourth century C.E.

Above left The Ezana Stone bears inscriptions in Ge'ez, the Aksumite language, Greek and Sabaean.

Above right The Tomb of the False Door, with the true entrance hidden beneath, was designed to foil grave robbers.

THE ROCK CHURCHES OF **LALIBELA**

TYPE: CHURCHES • **ARCHITECTURAL STYLE:** DIVERSE
LOCATION: ETHIOPIA • **CONSTRUCTION BEGUN:** TWELFTH CENTURY C.E.

For almost 1,000 years, Christian pilgrims and travelers have journeyed to the renowned rock-hewn churches at the holy site of Lalibela, in Tigray, Ethiopia. The eleven churches were sculpted over several centuries, from the soft pink rock of the Lasta Mountains. The most famous of the churches, Biete Giyorgis (referencing St. George, Ethiopia's patron saint), is carved into a striking cruciform shape.

Originally known as Roha, the site is named for Gebre Mesqel Lalibela, (ca. 1162–1221 C.E.), an Ethiopian ruler of the Zagwe dynasty. It is believed that his vision was to build a "new Jerusalem," perhaps after Muslims captured Jerusalem in 1187. The architecture and names of features of the site (such as the Yordanos stream, named for the Jordan River) repeatedly reference Jerusalem. The church of Biete Golgotha ("Biete" meaning "House of") contains replicas of the tombs of Christ and Adam.

The Lalibela churches are monolithic, in that they have been carved out of the mountain so as to be completely detached, and consist of a single block of rock. The church known as Biete Medhane Alem is said to be the largest such rock-hewn structure in the world. The churches in the northern and eastern clusters are linked by underground passageways.

The site is poorly dated and the building chronology is uncertain, partly because the sacred nature of the site has meant that extensive excavations have not been undertaken. Not all of the churches were initially built for purposes of worship. Some (Biete Mercoreos and Biete Gabriel Raphael) seem to incorporate fortifications—perhaps the remains of palaces—that date back to around the seventh century C.E.

The churches are in diverse architectural styles, but several incorporate stylistic details and features (such as windows and doorways with protruding lintels) that mimic those of Aksum, a powerful kingdom in northern Ethiopia that thrived throughout much of the first millennium C.E. Biete Amanuel is a particularly good example of the Aksumite architectural revival at Lalibela. The purpose of these architectural quotations may have been to propagate the idea that Lalibela was as mighty as Aksum had been before it.

The interiors feature semicircular arches, domes, and, sometimes, blind windows (that do not actually open to the outside). Although most of the churches are relatively undecorated inside, some have richly ornamented interiors, including bas-relief sculptures. Biete Maryam has a frieze of horsemen and striking paintings of biblical scenes. Associated structures at the site and nearby include monks' cells and vernacular architecture. The latter, known as Lasta Tukuls, in the nearby village of Lalibela, are two-story houses built from stone.

Lalibela is almost 560 miles (900 km) north of Addis Ababa, and a bus journey takes two days. However, the area is well-served by several airlines that fly to Lalibela airport, where taxis can be hired. Tours of the site that include transfers and, for longer stays, accommodation, are available.

Opposite, from top The interior of Biete Maryam church is richly carved and painted. The monolithic church of Biete Giyorgis is especially notable for its cruciform shape.

THE RUINS OF **KILWA KISIWANI**

TYPE: CITY • **ARCHITECTURAL STYLE:** ISLAMIC
LOCATION: OFF TANZANIA • **CONSTRUCTION BEGUN:** TENTH CENTURY C.E.

In the second millennium C.E. Kilwa Kisiwani was East Africa's most prosperous city-state. The ruins of the once thriving settlement are located on a small island in the Kilwa archipelago off the coast of southern Tanzania, a twenty-minute journey by dhow.

Settlements on the island date to the late first millennium C.E., but it was in the first half of the following millennium, under the Islamic Shirazi sultanate, that Kilwa reached its greatest heights as a wealthy trading center. A UNESCO World Heritage site, its importance lies in its Islamic architecture, as well as the evidence it provides for the growth of Swahili culture.

Under the Kilwa sultanate, the city became a key player in early intercontinental trade with the nearby Arabian Peninsula, but also with places as far afield as India and China. Around the late twelfth century C.E., Kilwa's rulers gained control of the export of African gold, which was exported via the key port of Sofala in Mozambique. Excavations have unearthed unglazed ceramics used by Kilwa's commoners, as well as exotic goods belonging to the wealthy, including items of Chinese celadon ware and Persian faience. Jewelry and textiles were also imported. Kilwa minted its own coins from the eleventh to the fourteenth centuries. A Kilwa coin was found at Great Zimbabwe, testimony to trade links between the two.

The island is home to two important examples of early Islamic architecture: the Great Mosque and the palace of Husuni Kubwa. Until the sixteenth century, the Great Mosque was the largest mosque in sub-Saharan Africa. Today it is the oldest standing mosque in East Africa. Its foundations date to the tenth century C.E., but much of the structure dates to the eleventh and twelfth centuries. It is constructed from blocks of local coral. Notable features include the Northern Prayer Hall, and the building's domed and vaulted ceilings. Writers of early historical texts, such as the Kilwa Chronicle, remarked upon the mosque's impressive Great Dome, a novel architectural phenomenon in East Africa at the time.

Sultan al-Hasan ibn Sulaiman (r. 1310–1333), considerably extended the Great Mosque in the fourteenth century, and commissioned the building of the palace of Husuni Kubwa, which occupies an area of 2 acres (0.8 ha). Though only briefly occupied and never completed, this royal complex included residential quarters with about 100 rooms, private and commercial courtyard areas, and an octagonal pool. Some of the rooms in the residential quarters were richly decorated with carved coral panels, with designs unique to the region.

Kilwa declined in the late 1300s. The settlement, with perhaps 5,000 residents, fell after being invaded by the Portuguese in 1505. Revived briefly a decade later, it was conquered by the rulers of Zanzibar in 1784.

Kilwa is 241 km (150 mi) from Dar es Salaam. Accommodation can be found on the mainland in Kilwa Masoko. Package tours are available, and some hotels organize trips. Visitors can also charter boats at the port.

Opposite, clockwise from bottom left The Great Mosque is one of the few surviving early mosques on the East African coast. The domes of the Great Mosque are among its most notable architectural features. Chinese ceramics found in the palace of Husuni Kubwa provide evidence of long-distance trade relations.

GREAT ZIMBABWE AFRICAN CAPITAL

TYPE: CITY • **ARCHITECTURAL STYLE:** N/A
LOCATION: ZIMBABWE • **CONSTRUCTION BEGUN:** ELEVENTH CENTURY C.E.

Great Zimbabwe is a complex of medieval stone buildings and one of the African continent's most famous ancient settlements. Located in the hills of Masvingo Province in southeastern Zimbabwe, it was the capital of a prosperous African kingdom, with a thriving economy based on cattle and agriculture, the export of gold and ivory and participation in intercontinental trade. The Great Enclosure is the largest structure of its kind in sub-Saharan Africa.

The city attained huge prosperity between the eleventh and fifteenth centuries. The site covers an area of more than 2.7 sq ft (7 sq km), comprises perhaps a thousand residences, and is known for its remarkable granite drystone walling. Its name comes from the Shona word *dzimbabwe*, meaning "stone houses." Also renowned are the Zimbabwe birds, raptor-like soapstone sculptures, of which eight have been found. Believed to be emblems of royal status, they appear on Zimbabwe's flag and coat of arms. As a monument of outstanding universal value, Great Zimbabwe has UNESCO World Heritage Site status.

Great Zimbabwe's buildings occur in three main concentrations: the Hill Ruins, thought to be the oldest; the Great Enclosure, dating to the city's heyday; and the Valley Ruins. Multiple other structures exist, including sinuous outer perimeter walls that in some places are nearly 36 ft (11 m) tall and 19.5 ft (6 m) thick. Some incorporate decorative stonework in a herringbone pattern; others are topped with turret-like structures. Smaller residences and features within dwellings were made of *dhaka* (adobe).

The area was occupied both before and long after its prime, but the main structures date to approximately 1000–1450 C.E. Unscientific excavations in the early twentieth century, and damage to some areas, have complicated the establishment of a firm chronology.

Above The Conical Tower in the Great Enclosure.
Opposite The carved Zimbabwe birds that were taken elsewhere have now been returned, and are housed in a small on-site museum.

Excavations and debates continue. Architectural style sequences, radiocarbon dating of midden materials, and the evidence of imported goods, including oriental ceramics and glass beads, from as far afield as China and Persia, jointly help to date different locations.

The Hill Ruins are the remains of a royal complex that included residences and a ceremonial area. Some of the Zimbabwe birds were probably mounted here. The Great Enclosure, with a circumference of about 820 ft (250 m), was built later, initially with one perimeter wall. A second wall was later built outside it, with a narrow passage between. A celebrated structure within it is the 33 ft (10 m) tall Conical Tower. With no apparent function, it is generally thought to have had symbolic significance. Its shape may reference grain bins, with connotations of good harvests and abundance. The Great Enclosure's function is still debated. Suggestions include that it was a chief's court, a complex for royal wives, or a ceremonial space for female initiation.

The reasons for the city's decline are unclear. Possible environmental factors include overexploitation of resources, climate change, and water shortages. Political instability, shifting trade patterns and the exhaustion of the local gold mines may also be implicated.

Early excavations and colonial-era myths

Great Zimbabwe's fame owes much to the persistent myth that it was a lost city, allegedly built by some vanished race. The settlement first came to European attention through reports by Portuguese travelers and traders in the early 1500s. In 1871 the German geographer Karl Mauch (1837–1875) was shown the ruins. He speculated that the site was linked to the Queen of Sheba. A century later, such speculation about the affiliations of Great Zimbabwe to exotic incomers, such as ancient Phoenicians, Arabs, and Sabaeans, still lingered, tied partly to racist colonial ideologies that maintained that African peoples were incapable of such sophisticated architectural feats.

Excavations in the late nineteenth and early twentieth centuries did little to dismiss these fantasies. In 1905, the first scientific excavations were conducted by David Randall-MacIver (1873–1945), who concluded that the site was of medieval origin, and drew attention to finds linking the site to the forebears of local African peoples. Gertrude Caton Thompson (1888–1985), who excavated at the site in 1929, correctly insisted that all the evidence indicated that the site was built and occupied by the Iron Age ancestors of the Shona people. Research today includes exploring the growth of sociopolitical complexity in sub-Saharan Africa and the global expansion of intercontinental trade networks in the second millennium C.E.

The ruins lie 15 miles (25 km) southeast of the town of Masvingo, close to Lake Mutirikwi, about four hours' drive from Harare on a road that is tarred most of the way. Public transport may be unreliable but there are several companies offering tours, and hotels may assist with transport.

Right Aerial view of the Great Enclosure, with the Conical Tower visible upper right.

THE CRADLE OF HUMANKIND

TYPE: FOSSIL SITES • **ARCHITECTURAL STYLE:** N/A
LOCATION: SOUTH AFRICA • **CONSTRUCTION BEGUN:** N/A

Travelers to the Cradle of Humankind, 30 miles (50 km) northwest of Johannesburg, in South Africa, can experience something of the ancient landscape where our ancestors once lived. Among the hominid sites of global importance are the caves of Sterkfontein, Swartkrans, Kromdraai, and Makapansgat.

The caves are situated in a landscape of rolling hills, in a dolomitic limestone formation that has facilitated excellent preservation of hominid fossils, as well as many other palaeontological remains. A UNESCO World Heritage site, it should not be confused with the equally important fossil sites in East Africa, which are known as the Cradle of Humanity.

Investigations into the Cradle of Humankind sites took off after 1924, when the anatomist Raymond Dart (1893–1988) received boxes of fossils from a limestone quarry at nearby Taung. Among the contents was the fossilized skull of a young primate, including a natural cast of its interior. Dart recognized that this specimen, dubbed the Taung Child, displayed unusual features, including a relatively flat face, and represented a new primate genus. He went on to identify it as a new species of upright-walking hominid and human ancestor, naming it *Australopithecus africanus* (African southern ape).

Controversy raged over Dart's claims before his arguments were accepted, though it is now generally believed that *A. africanus* and humans shared a common ancestor, rather than it being a direct forerunner. However, Dart's initial claims were substantially vindicated by other finds from the Sterkfontein cave system. Mrs. Ples, found in 1947, is an almost complete *A. africanus* skull. Formerly classified as *Plesianthropus transvaalensis*, this find helped to further establish that these specimens had some affiliation with the

human lineage. Another key australopithecine discovery at this site is known as Little Foot. Foot bones examined by Ronald Clarke in the 1990s indicated that the individual walked upright. Further investigations revealed an almost complete skeleton. It is now believed that *A. africanus* lived approximately 3.3–2.1 million years ago (mya).

The nearby site of Kromdraai yielded fossil fragments identified by Robert Broom in 1938 as *Paranthropus robustus*, hominids with large teeth and strong jaws, but small bodies. They are now thought to have lived about 1.8–1.2 mya. These specimens are sometimes considered to be australopithecines, or their close relatives.

Debate also continues regarding other new species identified from finds at the Malapa Cave in the Cradle of Humankind complex since 2010. Six australopithecine individuals (a juvenile, two adults, and three infants) have since been identified and classified as a new species, *A. sediba*. The finds have been dated to no older than two million years. It was proposed by the excavator, Lee Berger, that the specimens are a transitional species, linking *A. africanus* to the early species in the genus Homo. Other palaeoanthropologists believe *A. sediba* is a relative of *A. africanus* but not ancestral to the human line.

Berger has also made headlines with another new species, *Homo naledi*, found in 2013 in yet another area of the Cradle of Humankind, known as the Rising Star

cave system. More than 1,500 fragments, representing the remains of at least fifteen individuals, were recovered. *H. naledi* has a mix of archaic and human features. Its braincase is small, but other anatomical features, such as the feet, are very humanlike. Again opinion is divided, with some experts believing that the fossils relate more closely to early *Homo erectus*. It has also been proposed that these remains give clues to the origin of religious awareness, since they may have been intentionally placed there after death. No other animal bones were found, unlike in most fossil accumulations, but further evidence for deliberate placement is not yet available.

Swartkrans is also famous for the discovery of fragments of burned bone, dating to around 1.5 mya. It has been suggested that these represent the controlled use of fire by an unknown species of hominin. It is likely that some of the bone fragments were burned at temperatures only attainable in a hearth, rather than in a bushfire. Crude stone tools and evidence of cutmarks on some fragments support the idea that the remains are the result of hominin activity and early mastery of fire.

The Cradle of Humankind is easily reached by car from Johannesburg or Pretoria, and can be visited as a day trip. The Sterkfontein Caves are open to visitors. Visitor centers at Maropeng and Sterkfontein provide displays of famous fossils and world-class temporary exhibitions.

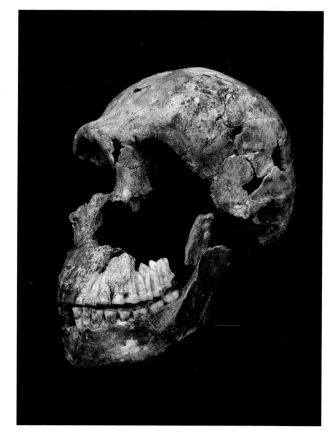

Above top The rolling hills that were once roamed by our human ancestors.

Above bottom The skull of *Homo naledi*, a new species of human discovered in 2013.

MAPUNGUBWE

TYPE: SETTLEMENT • **ARCHITECTURAL STYLE:** N/A
LOCATION: SOUTH AFRICA • **CONSTRUCTION BEGUN:** ELEVENTH CENTURY C.E.

Mapungubwe Hill, situated at the confluence of the Limpopo and Shashe rivers in north-eastern South Africa, was the center of southern Africa's first state. It provides early evidence of social stratification and socio-political complexity. The elite of the kingdom of Mapungubwe lived on the top of the rocky outcrop, while commoners farmed the fertile floodplains below.

Mapungubwe Hill, with its well-preserved remains of the lives of the ruling class, and allied sites in the surrounding savannah bushveld environment, are part of the Mapungubwe Cultural Landscape, a UNESCO World Heritage site. The name is thought to mean "Hill of the Jackal."

The Mapungubwe state probably evolved gradually, in the first four centuries of the second millennium C.E., although signs of evolving complexity, social distinctions, and extensive trade in exotic goods are also seen at other sites in the broader region from about 900 C.E. onward. Excavations began in the 1930s. The discovery of perhaps twenty-seven graves, some containing gold items, created

inevitable excitement. The three graves with gold artifacts contained the remains of two young or middle-aged adults and one older individual (the sex of the skeletons cannot be determined).

The elderly person was interred with more than one hundred gold-wire bangles and another with a gold scepter. All were buried in traditional Iron Age style, in a seated position facing west. Perhaps the most celebrated find is a small, well-preserved golden rhino. It consists of a wooden core that was then covered in thin sheets of gold, secured with gold tacks. The fragmentary remains of two other gold rhinos were also found in the graves. The symbolic significance of the rhino in the Mapungubwe culture is unknown. Other gold grave goods included strings of beads, gold plates, and what may have been a bowl. These items are evidence for the wealth of the Mapungubwe elite, and the place of the kingdom in emergent intercontinental trade networks. Similarly to Great Zimbabwe, this Iron Age culture depended on cattle keeping and agriculture. Exports via the ports on the East African coast would have included gold and ivory. Luxury imports included porcelain from China and glass beads from Persia.

Mapungubwe's decline may have been due to increased aridity around 1300 C.E., with the population dispersing when traditional farming could no longer sustain it. This perhaps contributed to the rise of Great

Zimbabwe to the north, though both kingdoms coexisted as important centers for at least a century.

Mapungubwe National Park is about 310 miles (500 km) north of Johannesburg and Pretoria, along a fully tarred road. It is a 9-hour journey on public transport, so self-drive is recommended. Other local Iron Age and rock art sites in the park can also be visited.

Opposite This small gold-covered rhino was found in one of the elite graves on top of Mapungubwe Hill.

Above The choice of the top of Mapungubwe Hill for the residences of the elite signalled high status, and does not appear to have been for defensive purposes.

GAME PASS SHELTER

TYPE: ROCK SHELTER • **ARCHITECTURAL STYLE:** N/A
LOCATION: SOUTH AFRICA • **CONSTRUCTION BEGUN:** UNDATED

In the foothills of the Drakensberg Mountains of KwaZulu-Natal, about 2.5 hours' drive from Durban, in South Africa, Game Pass Shelter is a painted site containing hundreds of remarkable and well-preserved rock paintings. Collectively, they demonstrate the virtuosity of their makers: hunter-gatherers generically known as the San. The paintings are undated, though it has been speculated that they may be 2,000 years old or more.

Game Pass Shelter is a shallow rock shelter in the Kamberg Nature Reserve. Perhaps the most visually impressive paintings are large-scale images of eland, superimposed on human figures apparently clad in skin cloaks, known as "karosses." Above are four running men, perhaps painted at a different time. The eland are in the shaded polychrome style. This combines several colors, with shading effectively used to convey the animals' bulk and volume. According to historical testimonies, the eland was the antelope most loved by |Kaggen, the trickster-creator of San mythology. Mythical "rain animals," embodiments of the rainstorm, also appeared in eland form.

These paintings were among the earliest San images to be publicized globally, and were reported in *Scientific American* in 1915. At present they are known for the claim that the site is a "Rosetta Stone" for unlocking the meaning of San art. The relevant images are principally an eland with a skull-headed human figure behind it, grasping its tail. Some see the images as clinching evidence that San rock art was the product of shamanic experiences in trance states. According to this hypothesis, the eland was regarded as an animal of potency and shamans in trance believed that they "fused" with the animal. This is supposedly represented by the human figure's crossed legs, which mimic the position of the eland's back legs. The eland, with lowered head, is said to be dying, which shamanists believe is a metaphor for people entering trance states. Among the surrounding images are several therianthropes (figures with both human and animal features).

Many, but not all, specialists accept this interpretation. Heated debate over shamanism as an explanation for both San art and prehistoric art worldwide has raged for decades. In terms of visual analysis, which is always subjective: does the eland have crossed legs, or are they just one in front of the other? Key indigenous testimonies record that spirit rainmakers were asked by the living to capture and magically control rain animals, to make rain fall or perhaps to limit violent storms. Rainmaking is a firmly established theme of San art and the Game Pass composition could equally reference that. Therianthropes may refer to San myths about the First People, who were both human and animal, or represent spirit beings.

Ancient art seldom permits definite interpretations of its "meaning" and San art is no exception. The Game Pass paintings can nevertheless be appreciated for their extraordinary skill and beauty.

The shelter lies high in a ridge, requiring a walk of approximately 2 miles (3 km). Site visits are made in the company of a guide.

Opposite A figure with a skull-like head, probably a spirit being, is shown grasping the tail of an eland.
Right The Kamberg Reserve landscape in the dry winter season.
Below A composition dominated by polychrome paintings of eland.

5

NEAR EAST AND WESTERN ASIA

This huge region contains a tremendous variety of sites, from prehistoric Turkey—notably the utterly remarkable Göbekli Tepe—to the Bible lands, to Iran's grandiose Persepolis, and to the varied riches of India, Pakistan, and Sri Lanka. There are also major sites in Iraq. But perhaps the most famous site, a mecca for archaeology aficionados (as well as Indiana Jones fans) is Petra, where the visitor exiting the narrow Siq comes upon one of the most stunning sights in the world, the rock-cut facade of Al-Khazneh (The Treasury).

Left The rock-cut facade of Al-Khazneh in Petra, Jordan

NEAR EAST AND WESTERN ASIA
LOCATIONS

GÖBEKLI TEPE
CONGREGATING IN A SACRED SPACE

TYPE: RELIGIOUS COMPLEX • **ARCHITECTURAL STYLE:** PPNA (PREPOTTERY NEOLITHIC A)
LOCATION: ŞANLIURFA PROVINCE, TURKEY • **CONSTRUCTION BEGUN:** CA. 9600 B.C.E.

High in the Germus mountains in southeastern Turkey is a mound that in the 1990s was found to cover the world's earliest known sanctuary: Göbekli Tepe. Massive monolithic pillars, some more than 16 ft (5 m) high, bear witness to the astonishing engineering achievements of our ancestors, armed only with stone tools, muscle, willpower, and the ability to cooperate.

Distant from a water source, this was never a settlement but, it seems, a place visited periodically by large groups of people congregating for a purpose. This included the creation of remarkable ritual structures—an enormous undertaking, repeated at intervals.

Excavations have uncovered a number of stone circles, 40–100 ft (10–30 m) in diameter, consecutively constructed and deliberately infilled after a period of use; geophysical survey of the mound suggests that there are twenty or more. Ten to twelve T-shaped pillars were erected around a circular space and connected by stone walls and benches set in clay mortar. In the circle's center, two much larger T-shaped pillars were erected, facing each other. The floor, cut from bedrock, was given a smooth finish or covered with burnished burned-lime plaster.

Many of the pillars are richly decorated with designs in low relief. Features carved on some hint that they were intended as abstract representations of humans (or anthropomorphic deities): hands and arms, a stole across the upper body, a belt with a fox-skin loincloth hanging from it. The horizontal crossbar may represent the figure's head, although there are never facial features.

Most carvings are of creatures. In one circle, snakes predominate among the designs, and they are present in almost all circles. Foxes are also frequently shown, and are the most common creature on circle B's stones. In circle C wild boar are in the majority. Many different creatures appear in circle D, as well as in other circles. Some of the creatures selected for depiction moved between different worlds—birds, occupying land and sky; reptiles, water and land; ducks, which often occur, belonging to all three worlds. Vultures, hovering on the threshold between life and death, are frequently shown. Others epitomize power and danger: predators, carnivores, and creatures noted for their ferocity, such as boar and aurochs (wild cattle). All are male, sometimes ithyphallic so that there is no doubt as to their sex. Some of these, particularly boars and felines (lions or leopards), also appear as three-dimensional sculptures.

Other elements feature in the designs: for example, what appear to be wicker baskets with handles, arranged in a line. It seems likely that these compositions have a mythological content forever lost to us, as well as a ritual significance whose dramatic power is still palpable even though we cannot penetrate its meaning.

Each circle seems to have been used for a while, the wall and benches being renewed by constructing another circle inside, until eventually it was deliberately filled in and a new circle constructed. In the final period of the site,

instead of circles, much smaller rectangular enclosures were built, around 10 x 13 ft (3 x 4 m) in size. These had far fewer T-shaped pillars, which were much smaller, around 5 ft (1.5 m) high, and generally undecorated, though the designs that occur were still the same.

Gathering and Feasting

The circles began to be constructed an astonishing 11,000 years ago, around 9600 B.C.E. At this time West Asia was home both to hunter-gatherers—many living in permanent settlements—and to early farmers. Although Göbekli Tepe lies within the region in which cereals were first domesticated, there is no indication that the builders of these circles were farmers: the finds here include masses of wild animal bones, indicating the importance of hunting to these people. Feasting was too: whatever brought groups of people here, in numbers large enough to quarry and move these stones the quarter mile (0.4 km) to where they were erected, it involved communal celebration as well as shared labor and rituals. Residues in large troughs found here

suggest that these were used for brewing beer, probably from the wild wheat that grew in dense stands in the region. The abundant wild harvest and the plentiful game drawn by it may explain why people chose this area to congregate.

Although Göbekli Tepe is unique, it is not culturally isolated. Within the same region are several settlements, such as Nevali Çori, with communal, probably ritual enclosures containing smaller T-shaped pillars. Some of the carved designs from Göbekli Tepe's stones reappear on small decorated objects found in settlements throughout the region. And whatever the belief system behind this astonishing monumental shrine, it seems to have rooted deeply, since much of its iconography can still be traced at Çatalhöyük, 2,000 years later.

The World Heritage site of Göbekli Tepe can be accessed by public transport from the town of Sanliufa, 32 miles (40 km) away.

Above Circle C, with circles A and B behind and part of circle D visible in the foreground.

LIFE IN NEOLITHIC **ÇATALHÖYÜK**

TYPE: SETTLEMENT • **ARCHITECTURAL STYLE:** NEOLITHIC
LOCATION: KONYA PROVINCE, TURKEY • **CONSTRUCTION BEGUN:** CA. 7400 B.C.E.

An enormous mound rises above Turkey's Konya plain: 9,000 years ago this was a huge settlement of tightly packed mudbrick houses, home to between 1,000 and 8,000 people. Yet this was not a city, not even a town, but seemingly a village improbably magnified, held together and managed by its inhabitants through kinship ties, links to shared history, and beliefs and rituals held in common though practiced privately.

Or so archaeologists have come to believe over recent decades. Çatalhöyük, discovered in 1958 and partially excavated in 1961–1965, saw intensive investigation by excavators and a team of wide-ranging archaeological specialists in 1993–2017, and its final story has yet to be written.

Farming settlements had begun to appear in central Anatolia in the Prepottery Neolithic (PPN) period, and around 7400 B.C.E. people settled at Çatalhöyük near the Çarşamba River, above the level of spring floods. The settlement grew massively, and was for more than a millennium the only major settlement on the Konya Plain.

Although some early houses shared party walls, typical buildings at Çatalhöyük were freestanding, though with mere inches between them. Ladders led to the rooftops, across which, in the absence of ground-level alleyways, people moved around the settlement. Rubbish was thrown into occasional open spaces between blocks of houses and into middens on the settlement's edge. Roof openings, again with ladders, gave access to the house interiors.

A domed clay oven and a hearth, the house's cooking and heating facilities, stood immediately beneath the roof hole, against the south wall, allowing the smoke to escape upward. Clustered around the hearth were various useful objects: wooden bowls; clay balls, to be heated in the fire, then used to

roast grain; a stash of obsidian (volcanic glass) ready to make sharp tools as required. Babies and very small children were buried in this part of the house. Brick and plaster platforms occupied much of the interior space, used for sleeping and for sitting at work, making basketry, stone and bone tools, stone or clay figurines, beads, and other objects. Pottery making began around 7000 B.C.E. The first pots were very simple, later ones more useful; all were undecorated.

Below Excavations in progress at Çatalhöyük, showing plastered walls and benches containing burial pits.

Right The interior of a house—a reconstruction based on what was found in the excavations.

A low doorway led into a side room where food was stored in large clay bins, wooden bowls, baskets, and textile bags. Supplies included cultivated wheat, barley, and pulses, and wild plants such as nuts and berries from the nearby uplands, and wetland plants from the marshy area by the river. Eggs were collected from wild birds. Meat also contributed to the diet: mainly from domestic sheep and goats, but also beef and wild game, including plentiful wildfowl. By 6500 B.C.E. milk, from cattle, sheep, and goats, was processed to make cheese, curds, or yoghurt.

Oak and juniper beams carried the clay and reed roof, and wooden posts reinforced the brick walls. White plaster, frequently renewed, covered floors and walls. Some walls featured painted designs, focusing on dangerous animals, emphasizing claws, fangs, and horns. Huge bulls are a favorite subject, often baited by tiny figures—human dominance over nature's violence seems the central theme. In some houses bulls' horns or skulls were attached to the walls or benches, often modeled into heads with plaster.

Ancestral Ties

Houses were probably the scene of domestic rituals in which these decorations played a part. Their placement particularly in the north part of rooms suggests that rituals focused on the ancestors, for it is here that benches most often cover burials. It was originally thought that the dead were buried within the houses, but recent research suggests that, at least in some cases, houses were built over the place where burials had previously been laid.

Maintenance of links with the family or lineage's past seem to be a guiding principle of life at Çatalhöyük. Houses lasted around forty-five to ninety years, and were then renewed. Roof beams and important fixtures, such as the bulls' skulls and horns, were carefully removed and stored and the upper walls demolished, the debris being used to infill the lower part of the house, creating a solid surface on which to construct a new house, generally to the same plan.

Late in Çatalhöyük's life people began to move away and, by around 6000 B.C.E., it was largely abandoned. Some people had, however, moved only to the opposite side of the river, where they built a new, rather different settlement, in which the houses—more widely spaced—had external buttresses and a large room with a central hearth, surrounded by smaller rooms. The inhabitants no longer painted their walls, but exuberantly painted their pottery. This much smaller village lasted only around 500 years. The site was reoccupied briefly during the Late Bronze Age and later by a substantial Hellenistic to Byzantine settlement.

Protected by a roof, the excavated portion of this World Heritage site now forms part of an impressive visitor complex with excellent on-site information. Visitors can reach the site by public transport or taxi from nearby Konya.

Opposite top An aerial view of Çatalhöyük's mound.
Opposite bottom A wall painting of a massive bull, surrounded by human figures who appear to be baiting it.
Above Low benches in building 77. One, surrounded by cattle horns set in plaster, covers a burial.

WELL-WATERED **JERICHO**

TYPE: PREHISTORIC WALLED SETTLEMENT AND LATER PALACES • **ARCHITECTURAL STYLE:** NEOLITHIC
LOCATION: JORDAN VALLEY, WEST BANK, PALESTINE • **CONSTRUCTION BEGUN:** CA. 10,000 B.C.E.

Jericho (Tell es-Sultan), in the arid western Jordan Valley of Palestine, has enjoyed an
exceptionally long history of settlement due to its favorable oasis location on an alluvial fan
made fertile by runoff from the adjacent mountains and watered by the 'Ain es-Sultan spring.
Famed in Classical times for growing dates and balsam, and rich in market gardens today, it is
one of a handful of settlements where the beginnings of agriculture have been traced.

Although hunter-gatherers usually move seasonally
to obtain food, in some parts of early postglacial West
Asia the availability of storable resources such as cereals
and nuts enabled some groups to occupy permanent
settlements. Among these was Jericho, where by around
10,000 B.C.E. people were living in mud-walled huts, also
hunting gazelle and waterfowl.

By around 8500 B.C.E., they were building more
substantial semisubterranean houses, probably with domed
clay roofs, and planting barley and emmer wheat, which

developed new "domestic" characteristics: agriculture had begun here. This increased the quantity of available food enabling the community to grow substantially—estimates for Jericho's population in this Prepottery Neolithic A (PPNA) period range from 500 to 2,000. Exchange networks with other communities brought in materials from far away, including obsidian (volcanic glass) from Turkey, greenstone from Sinai, and shells from the Red Sea.

The settlement's most remarkable and surprising feature is the stone wall that its inhabitants built around it. Originally more than 16 ft (5 m) high, it was 5 ft (1.5 m) thick, and would have taken at least 1,400 man-days to construct. It was not, as originally believed, defensive, since there were no external threats at that time; it may have protected the settlement against flooding, and would have represented an ostentatious undertaking that engaged the whole community. A massive tower was built immediately inside the wall, solid but with an internal stair giving access to a summit from which the whole surrounding area could be viewed. It survives to a height of 25 ft (7.75 m), its base diameter measuring 28 ft (8.5 m).

The later, PPNB, period saw major changes. The villagers began herding sheep and goats, domesticated elsewhere in West Asia, and building rectangular mudbrick houses with plastered floors, subdivided into several rooms.

As in PPNA, the dead were usually buried under house floors, and their skulls were sometimes retrieved after the body had decayed. However, now skulls were sometimes coated with plaster and painted, modeling living features, with shells for eyes. Perhaps as part of an ancestor cult, they were then kept on display within the houses, before eventually being reburied in caches, as were large human clay statuettes.

Jericho was abandoned after the PPN period, but later reoccupied. A substantial, massively fortified city in the Bronze Age, it was destroyed by fire around 1550 B.C.E. It later re-emerged as a prosperous town. In the final centuries B.C.E. Jericho Valley became a royal estate. The kings of Judaea built a winter palace on Wadi Qelt south of Jericho, which Herod (r. 40–4 B.C.E.) elaborated with fine reception areas, swimming pools, bathhouses, and gardens.

A magnificent Ummayyad palace was built north of the oasis in the eighth century C.E. Material from this and Tell es-Sultan is displayed in Jerusalem's Rockefeller Museum; the Palestinians are now establishing museums at Jericho itself.

All these sites lie close to the modern town, and are best visited in the cooler winter months.

Opposite A view of Jericho's tell (settlement mound)
Above Aerial view of Herod's palace, including a tiled hall, pillared courtyard, and bathhouse.

UNDER THE CITY OF **JERUSALEM**

TYPE: CITY WITH WATER SUPPLY TUNNELS • **ARCHITECTURAL STYLE:** BRONZE AGE AND IRON AGE
LOCATION: JERUSALEM, ISRAEL AND WEST BANK • **CONSTRUCTION BEGUN:** CA. 3500 B.C.E.

At the heart of the vibrant modern city of Jerusalem, reminders of its richly layered past are everywhere to be seen. People have lived here more for than 5,000 years—but traces of Jerusalem's earliest history are largely hidden beneath the superimposed buildings of later ages, to be glimpsed —and lovingly investigated and preserved—whenever areas are cleared for new construction.

Ancient occupation focused on two hills and the intervening valley: the Eastern Hill, the heart of early settlement, and the western hill (Mount Zion) onto which settlement periodically expanded. The Gihon Spring, in a cave on the southeast slopes, was the only perennial water source.

Early settlement, beginning in the late fourth millennium B.C.E., was on the southern spur of the Eastern Hill, where third-millennium houses and an early second-millennium wall have been found. Two massive towers protecting the Gihon Spring may be contemporary with the wall. In the late second millennium B.C.E., stepped terraces were constructed on the northeastern slopes, incorporating massive retaining walls and stone rubble-filled boxes. These supported a platform extending the level ground on the spur's northern summit, where the local rulers' palace may have been built. In later centuries houses were built on these terraces.

No remains have been traced of the Jebusite city captured by King David in the tenth century B.C.E., but David's wall may follow its defenses. David's son Solomon extended the city north to include the Temple Mount where he built his palace and the First Temple. As this area was completely cleared by Herod (r. 40–4 B.C.E.) when he remodeled the Second Temple, knowledge of Solomon's temple depends upon Biblical descriptions, supplemented by archaeological evidence of contemporary temple construction elsewhere.

Jerusalem expanded onto the western hill in the eight and seventh centuries B.C.E., when the kingdom was divided into Israel and Judah. Remains of houses from this period have been found, as have cemeteries of rock-cut tombs in the surrounding hills. Many such tombs, some with magnificently decorated facades, also survive from later times. In 721 B.C.E. the city's population grew as refugees fled the Assyrian conquest of Israel. The Assyrians now threatened Judah. King Hezekiah of Judah therefore strengthened and extended the city's defensive wall to surround the entire settled area.

A secure water supply was essential in times of siege. At some earlier date a 134.5 ft (41 m) tunnel had been cut through the rock from inside the city to a 40.4 ft-(12.3 m-) deep well, Warren's Shaft, supplied through a channel from the Gihon Spring. This gave protected, but labor-intensive, access to water. Hezekiah undertook a magnificent feat of engineering, creating a rock-cut tunnel 0.3 miles (0.5 km) long, leading water from the Gihon Spring to a new reservoir, the Siloam Pool, south of the hill within the extended city walls.

The city successfully withstood an Assyrian siege in 701 B.C.E., but fell in 587 B.C.E. to the Babylonians, who sacked the city and deported its leading citizens. When the Persians conquered Babylon in 539 B.C.E., the exiled Jews returned home and over subsequent centuries, with

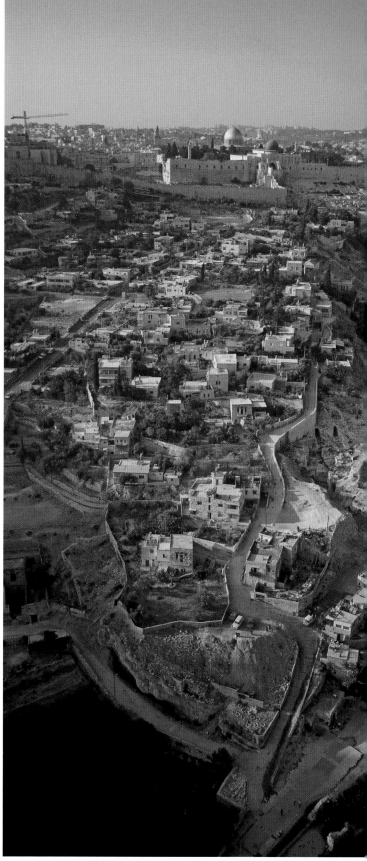

many changes of ruling regime, the city revived and grew: excavated remains include substantial wealthy houses, streets, an aqueduct, industrial facilities, and workshops. The doomed Jewish Revolt of 67–70 C.E., however, ended in the Romans' destruction of the city.

Some of Jerusalem's ancient remains can be seen by wandering around the Old City, the City of David, and adjacent areas. There are organized tours of the major sights, including the impressive underground water tunnels.

Clockwise from top Impressive family tombs with columned facades. An aerial view of the eastern hill: in the foreground, the spur where early settlement focused. Warren's Shaft, which gave access to water.

THE ROSE-RED CITY OF **PETRA**

TYPE: URBAN • **ARCHITECTURAL STYLE:** CLASSICAL WITH LOCAL VARIATIONS
LOCATION: JORDAN • **CONSTRUCTION BEGUN:** FIRST CENTURY B.C.E.

The Nabatean city of Petra, known as Selah in Aramaic, is located in Jordan, among
the mountains to the east of the Wadi Araba that runs from the bottom of the Dead
Sea to the port of Aqaba. The setting of the city within a series of wadis suggested the
nineteenth-century description by John W. Burgon, dean of Chichester Cathedral, in his
prize-winning poem of 1845 as "rose-red city half as old as time." Burgon himself had
not even been to Petra and had relied on descriptions made by early travelers.

Petra lies 146 miles (235 km) to the south of Amman, and 78 miles (125 km) northeast of Aqaba. The site is usually approached through a narrow gorge, el Siq, which reveals the monumental Al-Khazneh. This two-storyed facade, 128 ft (39 m) high, in the Classical Corinthian style is cut into the rock face. Inside are three main rooms, and the function of the structure seems to have been that of a temple. Farther into the city, in the Outer Siq, is the classical theater, perhaps constructed in the early second century C.E.; the upper part of the seating is cut through an earlier Nabataean street. The stage building, in the Roman style, was erected in front of the auditorium.

At the center of the city, on the south side of the Wadi Musa, was a colonnaded street, an urban feature that became very popular in the provinces of the Eastern Roman Empire. At the eastern end was a monumental fountain or nymphaeum that was fed by a water system running through the Siq. On the south side of the colonnade was a series of markets fronted by small structures that are likely to have served as shops. The large sanctuary on the south side of the colonnaded street was entered through a monumental gateway, or propylon, that contained a stairway leading to the precinct placed on an upper level. It seems to have been enlarged during the first century C.E.

At the western end of the colonnaded street, the Temenos Gate, with three arches in a local Nabataean style, led into a sanctuary area, at the end of which is a square temple known as the Qasr al-Bint. It was approached by a flight of steps that led into a portico. Behind this was a rectangular room, with two smaller rooms behind. The earliest structure probably dates from the end of the first century B.C.E., suggested by an inscription of King Aretas IV (9 B.C.E.–40 C.E.) that was placed in the temenos. The temple appears to have been rebuilt in the second century C.E.

Mausolea were cut into the sides of wadis surrounding the city and were often given classical facades. Some probably date to the Hellenistic period, and one is identified as the tomb of a second-century C.E. Roman provincial governor of Arabia, T. Aninius Sextius Florentinus. One of the finest tombs is known as the Deir: it had two stories 125 ft (38 m) high, and the facade is 131 ft (40 m) wide. The Bab al-Siq Triclinium is laid out as if in the form of a classical dining room with benches on three sides of the room. It is placed immediately below the cliff face of the Obelisk Tomb, with four relief obelisks carved in the facade.

There are public buses as well as coach tours to Petra from Amman and Aqaba. There is a visitor center for Petra in Wadi Musa where accommodation can be found. Strong boots are advised.

Opposite The rock-cut monument known as the Deir. It dates to the mid-first century C.E.

Above, from left The second-century C.E. theater with cuttings at the top from buildings that were destroyed in its construction. The Great Temple with gateway leading from the colonnaded street.

UR A CITY AT THE DAWN OF URBAN LIFE

TYPE: CITY WITH SACRED PRECINCT INCLUDING ZIGGURAT • **ARCHITECTURAL STYLE:** SUMERIAN
LOCATION: TELL EL-MUQAYYAR, DHI QAR GOVERNORATE, IRAQ • **CONSTRUCTION BEGUN:** CA. 4000 B.C.E.

A towering ziggurat surrounded by mudbrick ruins and desert at Tell el-Muqayyar
in southern Iraq gives a misleading impression of ancient Ur. Once a huge walled
metropolis built on elevated ground in marshy plains, Ur was flanked by a branch of the
Euphrates River that connected it to the nearby northern shores of the Gulf, providing
river and sea links that enabled it to trade throughout West Asia and beyond.

Trade was a major source of Ur's prosperity, as rich
finds from its Royal Cemetery attest. Often identified
as the Biblical Garden of Eden, this fertile region,
rich in fish, date palms, and marsh resources, was
inhabited by at least the sixth millennium B.C.E. Major
excavations conducted at Ur in 1920–1934 by Sir
Leonard Woolley (1880–1960) revealed 6,000 years of
occupation. Developing into a city in the Early Dynastic
period (earlier third millennium B.C.E.), it saw its heyday
under the Ur III dynasty who ruled all of southern
Mesopotamia 2112–2004 B.C.E., but it continued to
flourish thereafter as a major religious and cultural
center. An eastward shift in the Euphrates' course during
the Persian period caused Ur's eventual abandonment.

Sumer, the southern part of southern Mesopotamia,
was where urban life first began. Ur was one of its leading
Early Dynastic cities, distinguished by the extraordinary
discoveries in its large cemetery, in use around 2600–2300
B.C.E. Many people buried here were accompanied by objects
made from exotic materials, including gold, carnelian from
the Indus region, and lapis lazuli from Afghanistan. Sixteen
graves were exceptional: the principal burial was laid within
a vaulted chamber with wonderful offerings such as jewelry
and musical instruments decorated with precious materials;
others (in one case sixty-eight) were buried in the associated

grave pit, also with fine grave goods. Whether these
individuals were sacrificed is still debated, as is the identity
of the principals, though they are often regarded as royalty.

The Sumerian cities were united by Sargon of Akkad
(r. ca. 2334–2284 B.C.E.) around 2334 B.C.E. Woolley's
excavations focused largely on the sacred precinct of
the city's patron deity, Nanna (Sin), where he uncovered
buildings including the giparu where Nanna's priestess
(Sargon's daughter) lived, along with her staff and those of
Ningal, the moon god's wife. This included a courtyard,
domestic and public rooms, a chapel, and archives.

Ur III kings significantly remodeled the precinct and were probably buried in the vaulted mausolea just outside its walls. They built the ziggurat that still dominates the site (repaired and partially reconstructed by Saddam Hussein): a three-tiered stepped pyramid, originally crowned by a temple. The ziggurat's mudbrick core was covered by a thick outer shell of baked brick decorated with buttresses and recesses, with bitumen as mortar. A triple staircase provided access to the upper tiers.

The ziggurat was the main structure within a separately walled inner precinct dedicated to Nanna. After Ur was sacked in 2004 B.C.E. and the center of power moved farther north, Nanna's shrine continued to attract worshippers for many centuries. The surrounding city, Mesopotamia's cultural capital under Ur III, also enjoyed continuing prestige as a center of learning. Woolley uncovered a large area of closely packed second-millennium-B.C.E. streets of one- or two-story buildings with internal courtyards overlooked by balconies—houses, workshops, chapels and, in at least one case, a school.

Local guides can help the visitor to interpret the ruins. Ur should be visited from Nasiriyah, 13 miles (20 km) away, where the local museum displays finds from the city. The spectacular objects from the Royal Cemetery, however, are in London's British Museum and Pennsylania's University Museum in Philadelphia.

Opposite Inside one of the vaulted underground tombs of the Ur III kings near the sacred precinct.

Below The first ziggurat, built by King Ur-Nammu (r. 2112–2095 B.C.E.), founder of the Ur III empire.

BABYLON THE MIGHTY CITY

TYPE: IMPERIAL CAPITAL CITY • **ARCHITECTURAL STYLE:** BABYLONIAN
LOCATION: HILLAH, BABIL PROVINCE, IRAQ • **CONSTRUCTION BEGUN:** THIRD MILLENNIUM B.C.E.

Infamous to the Jews, who suffered a hated exile there, and famed by the Greeks as home to Wonders of the World, Babylon has never been forgotten through the ages. Today it is both famous for its extraordinary remains and infamous for the "theme-park" reconstruction of parts of the city by Iraq's former dictator, Saddam Hussein.

A minor town in the third millennium B.C.E., Babylon grew prosperous in the early second millennium after a favorable shift in the course of the Euphrates River brought local agricultural wealth. In the competitive environment after the Ur III empire fell in 2004 B.C.E., Babylon's shrewd and aggressive kings began carving out a wider realm. The greatest, Hammurabi (r. 1792–1750 B.C.E.), created an empire stretching from the Gulf to Mari on the middle Euphrates, though under his less able successors this quickly shrank. Babylonia (southern Mesopotamia) had regained international power by the later second millennium. It eventually fell subject to its northern neighbor and former competitor, Assyria,

Opposite, from top Polychrome glazed bricks were used to create the magnificent bas-relief images of bulls and dragons on the Ishtar Gate and lions along the Processional Way at Babylon.

Below Saddam Hussein's "reconstruction" of the Southern Palace, built over Babylon's excavated foundations.

Within the City Walls

Babylon's most prominent monument, reaching toward the heavens, was the ziggurat of Marduk, Etemenanki, (popularly known as the Tower of Babel). Constructed on a square base with sides 300 ft (92 m) long, this stepped pyramid originally stood 300 ft (92 m) high. It probably had seven tiers and was surmounted by a temple complex, the main cella dedicated to Babylon's patron deity, Marduk, with chapels to other major gods. Later destruction and brick quarrying have left only its foundations, marked by a water-filled hole.

Etemenanki stood within a huge precinct raised on a high platform and surrounded by a massive wall as protection against flooding by the Euphrates River, on whose eastern bank lay all the city's most important buildings. Immediately to its south was Esagila, Marduk's temple, home to his golden statue and its attendants. Chapels within its precinct accommodated statues of other gods when they visited Marduk for the New Year Festival. A grand Processional Way, along which the gods' statues were carried, led from the temple past the royal palaces to the Festival house outside the city.

The southern palace, in the northwest corner of the eastern inner city, was begun by Nabupolassar and completed by Nebuchadrezzar. Residential and official rooms surrounded a massive central throne room, its facade decorated with a magnificent frieze in glazed brick, brilliant lapis-lazuli blue its predominent color. Along its foot prowled lions, sacred to Ishtar, goddess of love and war; above them towered palm-tree columns, surrounded by an elaborate floral border. Nebuchadrezzar added a larger palace immediately north of the inner city wall.

The Processional Way passed through the Ishtar Gate east of the palaces. This gate and the wall along the slab-paved road beyond were decorated with colorful glazed-brick friezes. The city's crowning glory, these can now be seen in Berlin's Pergamon Museum; Babylon itself has an inferior replica erected by Saddam. Along the walls were Ishtar's lions, while the gate was covered with lines

but inherited Assyria's vast empire when Assyrian authority collapsed around 612 B.C.E. The Babylonian king Nabupolassar (r. 626–605 B.C.E.) and his son Nebuchadrezzar II (r. 604–562 B.C.E.) devoted themselves to rebuilding, extending, and embellishing Babylon, replacing mudbrick structures with more solid baked-brick architecture, often of impressive monumentality: what survives of Babylon is mainly their work.

Impressively massive defensive walls surrounded the city and reached their apogee under Nebuchadrezzar. Two thick walls, separated by a raised military roadway, surrounded the inner city; an outer wall, added in the twelfth century B.C.E., trebled the land enclosed within the city to 3 sq mi (7.8 sq km) and a wide moat surrounded both sets of walls. The Euphrates River divided the city into a major eastern and a suburban western half. Nebuchadrezzar strengthened the embankments and added a massive baked-brick bulwark at the northern corner, to protect the city against the river.

of bulls, representing the storm god Adad, and dragons (*mushusshu*), symbolizing Marduk.

The last Babylonian king, Nabonidus (r. 555–539 B.C.E.) further embellished the city, as did his son, Belshazzar, who acted as regent during his father's ten-year residence in the Arabian city of Taima. The New Year Festival, all-important for the city and nation's spiritual well-being, required the king's presence: popular dissatisfaction at the ten-year hiatus in its performance may have contributed to the ease with which Cyrus, the Persian king, captured Babylon in 539 B.C.E. The city prospered under Cyrus' rule and later, but became a ruin in Sassanian times. The Greeks wrote much about its former glories, which according to Herodotus included the famous Hanging Gardens. These have never been located, despite extensive searching—and it now seems likely that Herodotus confused their location: his description closely matches the royal gardens built by the Assyrian king Sennacherib at his capital, Nineveh.

Visitors to Babylon can get an impression of the ancient city from the surviving ruins and valuable information from local guides, though Saddam's reconstructions, on original foundations, somewhat mar the experience.

Opposite Earlier, unglazed courses of bricks in the Ishtar Gate, exposed during excavation.

Right The Processional Way (top) and Ishtar Gate (bottom), reconstructed in Berlin's Pergamon Museum from original bricks, contrast starkly with Saddam's in situ modern walls (center).

PERSIAN SPLENDOR IN **PERSEPOLIS**

TYPE: IMPERIAL CEREMONIAL AND ADMINISTRATIVE CAPITAL • **ARCHITECTURAL STYLE:**
ACHAEMENID **LOCATION:** FARS PROVINCE, IRAN • **CONSTRUCTION BEGUN:** 515 B.C.E.

In 539 B.C.E. the Persian King Cyrus the Great (r. 559–530 B.C.E.) conquered Babylon. The empire
Cyrus forged—extended by his successors Cambyses and Darius to reach from the Balkans and
Egypt to the Indus—was the largest world had yet seen. Parsa (Persepolis—modern Takht-e
Jamshid, Fars Province, Iran) was created by Darius around 515 B.C.E. as one of the empire's capitals.
Built on a vast walled terrace, its magnificent columned halls commanded the Marvdasht plain,
their glories echoed by the columned facades of royal tombs cut into the hill behind.

This was the ceremonial and official heart of a city
that sprawled across the plain. Little is known of the
residential, commercial, and other areas that once lay here,
since archaeological investigations have concentrated
almost exclusively on the terrace buildings. The king and
his court occupied Persepolis for part of the year, moving
between here and Susa (their winter residence in Elam),
Babylon, and their upland summer palace at Ecbatana in
northwestern Iran.

Imperial Grandeur

Climbing an imposing staircase, the visitor to Persepolis
entered the royal center through a monumental entrance,
the Gate of All Nations. Two enormous bull statues fronted
the gateway, through which the visitor entered a hall in
which benches could accommodate 100 people awaiting
their turn to pass through the matching inner gateway onto
a walled road that led to the eastern side of the terrace. Here
another imposing gateway, unfinished, led into a courtyard
giving access through a pillared portico to the Hall of 100
Columns, the venue for public ceremonies drawing officials
(probably military personnel) from all over the empire.
Two doorways opened on each side, those on the north and
south showing the king seated on his throne, supported by

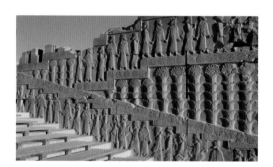

Above, from top Reliefs carved on the
platform of the Apadana: delegates of subject
nations bring tribute, while richly clad Persian
and Median nobles mount the stair.

Right view across Persepolis: on the far side the
Apadana (left) and Gate of All Nations (center.)

rows of figures representing the empire's subject nations, with the winged figure of the supreme god Ahuramazda above. On the jambs of the west and east doorways, carvings depicted the king, or a hero figure, subduing a lionlike mythical beast with an eagle's wings and a scorpion's tail.

From the Gate of All Nations, an alternative exit to the south led into the courtyard of Persepolis' chief public building, the Apadana. This vast pillared hall was surrounded on three sides by porticos. The stone columns, of which a number still stand, had stepped square bases within the hall and bell-shaped bases in the porticos. Their massive stone capitals (protomes) were carved with pairs of animal forequarters—bulls, lions, griffins, and human-headed bulls—shown back to back, the saddle between them supporting huge cedar beams that carried the timber and plaster roof. Mudbrick walls between massive corner towers separated the hall from the porticos, stone-framed windows shedding light into the interior. The towers' facades bore faience tiles with geometric and floral designs.

The Apadana stood on a platform approached by monumental stairs on the north and east sides. The panels fronting the stairs are carved with Persian and Median guards and combat scenes of a lion attacking a bull, while the sides of the stairs show processions of figures, on one side Persian and Median nobles, attendants, and guards,

on the other delegates from twenty-three subject nations bearing tribute, such as fine textiles, gold vessels and jewelry, exotic animals, and horses. Delegates from these nations probably assembled here on important ceremonial or official occasions—the hall could accommodate 10,000 people.

Widespread Inspiration

Craftsmen from across the empire were employed on these buildings: texts mention Egyptian, Ionian, Syrian, and Babylonian workers. Elements of the architecture and decoration also draw on foreign sources—monumental bull sculptures and figural reliefs hark back to the decoration of Assyrian palaces, the use of architectural glazed bricks to Babylonia, columned halls to Media—but these are reinterpreted to create a distinctive Persian style, with a very different message: harmony and multicultural unity under the beneficent control of the universal monarch, beloved and watched over by God.

The southern half of the complex contained smaller buildings of a similar design, all probably public—ceremonial or official—rather than residential in purpose. Several, including the Central Building (perhaps a ceremonial meeting place for the aristocracy), had stairs decorated with Persian and Median nobles and with priests or servants bearing food, drink, and live animals. A large complex with many rooms south of the Hall of 100 Columns is known as the Treasury: this held rich offerings brought to Persepolis in tribute. Little remains of these treasures.

In 330 B.C.E., during his whirlwind conquest of the mighty Persian empire, Alexander the Great (356–323 B.C.E.) set fire to Persepolis–either an act of reckless drunken vandalism or deliberate revenge for the Persians' sack of Athens 150 years earlier. He and his soldiers thoroughly looted the city. Enough remained of the monuments, however, to excite visitors and antiquarians over the centuries and in the early twentieth century it was excavated and its spectacular treasures revealed. These magnificent ruins can be reached by taxi from Marvdasht, the nearest town. There is a good site museum and local guides can provide information. Material from this World Heritage site can also be seen in the National Museum in Tehran.

Opposite, from left The rock-cut tomb of Artaxerxes III (r. 358-338 B.C.E) overlooking Persepolis. A griffin protome (column capital) from the Apadana.

Below A magnificent man-headed bull fronts Xerxes' Gate of All Nations.

MOHENJO DARO AND INDUS CIVILIZATION

TYPE: CITY • **ARCHITECTURAL STYLE:** HARAPPAN
LOCATION: LARKANA DISTRICT, SINDH, PAKISTAN • **CONSTRUCTION BEGUN:** 2600 B.C.E.

The ruined city of Mohenjo Daro is an imposing sight, rising above the lush green fields of the Indus plain in Sindh, Pakistan. Silt deposited by the river's annual floods has steadily raised the floodplain: four thousand years ago the city towered above it, built on walled platforms more than 20 ft (6 m) high. Houses stood two or three stories tall, and the stark brick walls seen today were originally plastered and gaily painted.

Mohenjo Daro was the largest city of the Indus (Harappan) civilization, forgotten by posterity and unknown until a century ago. Farming villages had appeared in the Indus plains and adjacent regions during the fourth millennium B.C.E. Some grew into towns and, by 2600 B.C.E., into cities.

But perhaps not Mohenjo Daro—evidence suggests that this was a deliberate foundation on virgin soil around 2600 B.C.E., a planned city, located at the very center of the Indus realms and at the crossroads between routes along the Indus River and overland north into Baluchistan. The alluvial plain, though agriculturally productive, was a challenging environment for settlement, exposed to frequent massive river floods. In order to live here safely, the city's builders created enormous foundation platforms of mudbricks encased in a solid baked-brick protective walls.

Lower Town

In the residential area of the city, the main streets were aligned to the cardinal directions using astronomical sightings lined up with landscape features. Wide main streets were crossed by narrower side streets off which the houses opened, their windowless facades and entrance passages keeping the interiors free from street dust. Much of daily life, such as food preparation and craft activities, took place in the courtyard, off which rooms opened; a stair led to the upper story(ies) and roof, where people might sleep. Houses often had a latrine and most had a bathroom, paved with close-fitting baked bricks covered with polished plaster. Wastewater was carried away through terracotta drainpipes connected to brick street drains and left the city through brick culverts. Clean water came from around 700 private and public wells, built of tightly fitting wedge-shaped bricks. The sophisticated provision and disposal of water was a remarkable feature of the Indus civilization.

Many craft activities took place throughout the city, some within domestic workshops or houses, such as textile making, others clustered in industrial quarters of the city, such as pottery manufacture and stoneworking, and the most polluting on the outskirts. City workshops made copper and bronze into tools, vessels, and occasionally sculptures, and silver and gold into jewelry, sometimes combined with other materials. Jewelry was also made from faience, pottery, shell, ivory, gemstones, and other materials. Bead making was a craft in which the Harappans excelled, their skills displayed in exceptionally long carnelian beads and microscopic steatite beads. Steatite was also made into exquisite seals, bearing a brief inscription and an image, usually of a single animal.

Public Architecture

The buildings on the higher, western ("Citadel") mound strongly contrast with the residential and industrial buildings of the Lower Town. Most famous is the Great

Bath, a rectangular pool 39 ft (12 m) long by 23 ft (7 m) wide and 8 ft (2.4 m) deep, entered down steps from either end. It was completely watertight, constructed of layers of closely fitted baked bricks, mudbrick, and bitumen. It was emptied through a large drain with a magnificent corbeled vault. Built in the center of a complex to which access seemed, by its layout, restricted, this probably served a religious purpose. Nearby were rows of bathrooms and a large two-story building with many small rooms, perhaps administrative. Adjacent to the Great Bath lay the so-called Granary, not suitable for storing grain but possibly a warehouse. Farther south were other large buildings.

Who ran the Indus state? No clear signs of rulers, such as palaces or rich burials, or of religious leaders have been found at Mohenjo Daro (or elsewhere). Nevertheless, the efficiency with which fine raw materials and good-quality manufactured goods from different regions were distributed suggests a system answerable to some authority. This is reinforced by the use of weights conforming to a strictly maintained standard. Overseas trade also flourished, reaching from Afghanistan to Mesopotamia.

The Decline of the Indus Civilization

Around 1800 B.C.E. urban life declined and the hallmark Indus cultural uniformity ceased, although farming villages continued to prosper, particularly in Gujarat and the eastern region. There were probably many causes of this change. The decline is marked at Mohenjo Daro by the appearance of very inferior houses and skeletons apparently dumped in abandoned houses rather than decently buried, perhaps victims of epidemic disease, a known hazard in densely packed cities: if so, this may have been one reason for the cessation of Harappan urban life.

Mohenjo Daro is best visited in the cooler winter months, by taking an organized tour or making a day trip from Larkana. Visitors can wander along streets and into houses still standing above head height. Many of the beautiful artifacts from the city can be seen in the excellent site museum.

Above The Great Bath, set within the courtyard of a larger complex with bathrooms and upstairs rooms.

THE COSMOPOLITAN METROPOLIS OF **TAXILA**

TYPE: CITY AND SURROUNDING RELIGIOUS ESTABLISHMENTS • **ARCHITECTURAL STYLE:** GANDHARAN
LOCATION: PUNJAB, PAKISTAN • **CONSTRUCTION BEGUN:** CA. SIXTH CENTURY B.C.E.

Strategically located for trade, the great city of Taxila in Gandhara (northern Punjab, Pakistan) also enjoyed great agricultural prosperity. Three successive major settlements and many extramural religious complexes are spread through the valley and into its surrounding hills. History records Taxila's participation in many encounters between east and west in the later centuries B.C.E. and early C.E., and its art and architecture exemplify the outstanding results of this cultural cross-fertilization.

Mesolithic hunter-gatherers occupied caves in the hills, and farmers settled in the valley by the fourth millennium B.C.E. In the late sixth century B.C.E., a substantial settlement (the Bhir Mound) was built in the southeast of the valley. Excavated material attests to contacts with states developing in the Ganges Valley, supporting literary evidence that Gandhara was one of the Early Historic Indian kingdoms that traded, made alliances, and fought with each other in this period. Farther west, the Persian (Achaemenid) empire was expanding, and Taxila probably came under its control around this time. When Alexander the Great (356–323 B.C.E.) conquered the Achaemenid empire and reached India in 326 B.C.E., Taxila's king voluntarily allied with him. However, no material that can be linked to the Persians or to Alexander's visit has been identified here.

In the power vacuum following Alexander's brief incursion, the region fell, in 311 B.C.E., to Chandragupta Maurya (r. ca. 321–297 B.C.E.), ruler of the expanding Mauryan empire. The Mauryas had begun as rulers of the central Gangetic state of Magadha. By the time of Chandragupta's grandson, Ashoka (r. ca. 268–ca. 232 B.C.E.), they controlled almost all the Indian subcontinent.

Opposite, from top Aerial view of the Dharmarajika stupa, ringed by small stupas and chapels, with others beyond. Detail of the main stupa's typical Kushan masonry, with decorative niches.

Above A small stupa in one of the courtyards of a private house on Sirkap's main street.

Taxila became the Mauryas' northern capital, and during his father's reign Ashoka was viceroy here. Most buildings uncovered in the Bhir Mound belong to this period. Houses generally had a central courtyard off which rooms opened; many contained ring wells for drainage. A pillared hall in the west of the city may have been a Hindu shrine.

After the Mauryan empire fell in 185 B.C.E., the Gandhara region came under the control of competing Indo-Greek kingdoms. In the mid-second century B.C.E. the Indo-Greeks built a new city, Sirkap, following the grid street layout characteristic of planned Greek cities. Although Gandhara and Taxila changed hands repeatedly in subsequent centuries, coming under the control of Indianized invaders from Central Asia (Shakas), Iran (Indo-Parthians), and Central Asia again (Kushans), Sirkap's citizens maintained its regular plan: wide main streets and smaller lanes, dividing it into blocks of spacious stone-masonry houses with workshops, administrative buildings, shrines, and shops. A walled acropolis on high ground in the city's south contained official buildings, including a probable ruler's palace. The excavated remains belong mainly to the Indo-Parthian and Kushan periods, when the city was reconstructed after serious earthquake damage in 30 C.E. In the late first century C.E., the Kushans built a new city, Sirsukh, in the valley's north.

Crossroads of Trade and Culture

Finds from Sirkap vividly reflect the city's important role as a crossroads in international trade, linking states in India with the major east–west route from China to Rome, the routes dividing in Gandhara to run overland or down the Indus and thence across the sea. Sirkap's merchants received Roman and Alexandrian glassware, silver vessels, engraved gems, bronze statuary, and wine, and transmitted goods such as Chinese silks and Afghan lapis lazuli, and Indian spices and ivory furniture decorations.

The cosmopolitan nature of Sirkap's population is reflected in the religions attested here by literary and archaeological evidence, including Jainism, Vaishnavite Hinduism, Greek cults, perhaps Zoroastrianism, and possibly Christianity. But most religious structures in the city and the valley beyond were Buddhist. These included the magnificent Dharmarajika stupa, 2 miles (3.2 km) east of Sirkap. Traditionally founded by Ashoka, it reached its present form in the second century C.E. The large central stupa, faced with carved limestone blocks, stands on a platform, surrounded by many small stupas and chapels.

The Jaulian monastery was constructed in the hills 7 miles (11 km) from Taxila, enabling the monks to enjoy tranquility for contemplation while remaining close enough to the city to obtain the alms on which they depended. The monastery had two stories, its cells surrounding a central courtyard with a verandah. An adjacent enclosure held a large stupa surrounded by small votive stupas, their plinths copiously decorated with fine stucco reliefs of Buddhas and Bodhisattvas.

Stucco decorations on the valley's many stupas and monasteries are echoed by a wealth of carvings in schist and figures in terracotta, all exemplifying the magnificent Gandharan art style. This combined the naturalism of Greek art with decorative elements and subjects from traditional Indian art. In addition to majestic statues of the Buddha, there were lively scenes from his life.

In 460 C.E. Taxila was sacked by the White Huns (Hephthalites)—destroyed buildings, scattered skeletons, and hoards of precious objects concealed and never recovered all bear witness to this disaster.

Taxila's cities and many religious sites are scattered through the valley around the modern town, so visitors are recommended to hire local transport and a guide to enjoy this World Heritage site to the full. Visit the excellent museum too.

Opposite, from top Diverse religious architecture at Taxila: the Dharmarajika stupa; and the temple of the Double-headed Eagle, decorated with both Greek and Indian architectural forms.

THE ROCK ART OF **BHIMBETKA**

TYPE: ROCK SHELTERS WITH PAINTINGS • **ARCHITECTURAL STYLE:** MESOLITHIC TO MEDIEVAL
LOCATION: RAISEN DISTRICT, MADHYA PRADESH, INDIA • **CONSTRUCTION BEGUN:** N/A

Massive rock shelters carved by eroding winds from the rocks of Bhimbetka and neighboring hills near Bhopal in central India conceal hundreds of ancient paintings, some more than 10,000 years old. Discovered by V. S. Wakankar (1919–1988) in 1957, these reveal in intimate detail the lives of hunter-gatherers who drew on the rich plant and animal resources of the surrounding teak forests.

Excavations exposing stone tools, other everyday material, and human burials revealed that these rock shelters were already being occupied more than 100,000 years ago and were still in use in medieval times. Elegant green paintings seem to be the earliest, probably painted in the late Palaeolithic period. A great range of paintings in brown, black, sometimes white, and especially red show scenes from the daily lives of the later Mesolithic hunter-gatherers, or depict the animals they knew—many, such as antelope, tiger, and deer still present, while others, such as Indian lion, rhino, and wild buffalo no longer inhabit this region. Some creatures are shown in outline, others with their bodies colored, decorated with geometric patterns, or showing their insides, as in an X-ray. People are most commonly shown as stick figures or with a triangular torso infilled with crisscross lines, wearing small items of clothing.

The Bhimbetka paintings give an extraordinarily detailed picture of forager existence. Hunters armed with spears, slings, and bows work together, encircling ferocious wild buffalo or boar or pursuing herds of deer. Women set traps, club lizards, and team up to catch rats, some driving them from their burrows into nets held by others. Women also gather fruit in baskets and dig tubers. Men in boats set nets for fish. One person collects honey from a treetop, with bees buzzing furiously around.

Bhimbetka's people are also shown at leisure. Men in headdresses, with streamers on their knees and elbows, dance in a long line arm-in-arm, accompanied by drummers, while an appreciative audience of women and children watch. At other times, they separate into family groups, eating together, preparing food, or making and mending tools.

While in many parts of the world the advent of farming destroyed or marginalized the hunter-gatherer way of life, in India mutually beneficial relationships

developed between many farming communities and their forager neighbors: hunter-gatherers had the skills, knowledge, and opportunities to exploit wild resources inaccessible to settled farmers. The people of Bhimbetka may have supplied farmers with honey, game, wild silk, fish, dye and food plants, herbal medicines, and other forest resources, exchanging these for grain, pottery, and copper tools. After around 2500 B.C.E., such objects appear both in the excavated rock shelters and in the paintings, along with depictions of domestic cattle, sheep, and goats. Such harmonious collaboration continued into recent times.

By the late centuries B.C.E., the paintings include observed outsiders, such as soldiers armed with swords, spears, and shields, mounted on horses or elephants or driving chariots.

Battle scenes occur: here, the fighters armed with bows and arrows may be the hunter-gatherers themselves.

While the modern Adivasi inhabitants of villages around Bhimbetka—descendants of the local forager tribes—are farmers nowadays, growing crops and keeping livestock, they still hunt and gather forest produce, maintaining some part of their traditional way of life.

Bhimbetka's World Heritage archaeological park contains fifteen rock shelters, with good interpretation boards. It is best visited in the cooler winter months. Access by public transport is difficult but organized tours are available.

Opposite A terrifying Mesolithic scene—a tiny man is pursued by an enormous boar with horns.

Above Later painting of armed and armored soldiers on foot and on horseback, one with an elaborate saddlecloth.

CAVE TEMPLES AND MONASTERIES AT **AJANTA**

TYPE: ROCK-CUT CAVE TEMPLES AND MONASTERIES • **ARCHITECTURAL STYLE:** SHUNGA AND VAKATAKA
LOCATION: AURANGABAD DISTRICT, INDIA • **CONSTRUCTION BEGUN:** SECOND CENTURY B.C.E.

In 1819 army officers hunting in western India pursued a tiger into a beautiful, secluded gorge of the Waghora River—and stumbled across one of the greatest treasures of Buddhist art and architecture. Here, carved into the rock-face, were thirty cave temples and monasteries, where Buddhist monks had lived and worshipped, serenely detached from the outside world. A steep stair connected each cave to the river below. Originally decorated with sculptures and polychrome paintings, the caves have suffered the ravages of time, but what remains is breathtaking.

Buddhism developed in India around the sixth century B.C.E. Dependent on alms, during the rainy season Buddhist monks also needed shelter. Lay devotees gained spiritual merit by providing places for them to stay: through time, these developed into monasteries, with associated temples, where monks lived permanently. Some were created as rock-cut caves, faithfully reproducing in stone the details of freestanding structures originally built in wood.

Two cave temples and four monasteries were created at Ajanta between the second century B.C.E. and first century C.E. The temples took the form of an apsidal hall with vaulted ceiling, pillars separating the nave and apse from the aisles that formed a continuous passage round which the devotee could circumambulate, an important practice in Buddhist and other Indian worship. In the apse stood a small stupa (relic mound), symbolizing the Buddha. A great horseshoe-shaped chaitya arch framed a window that lit the interior, while many smaller arches decorated the rest of the facade. Monasteries were laid out as a central hall, used for congregation, off which the monks' cells opened on three sides. Originally both monasteries and temples were painted, though scant trace now remains.

Around 462 C.E., in the peaceful reign of the Vakataka king Harisena (r. 460–478 C.E.), a spectacular burst of new activity began at Ajanta, during which wealthy Buddhist lay devotees, including merchants and royal officials, sponsored the creation of three temples and many monasteries. These follow the general form of earlier examples, but with significant changes. A substantial pillared verandah now formed the entrance to each cave. Small shrines were added within the monasteries. Most strikingly, these later caves are covered with sculptured decoration, closely integrated with paintings. Images of the Buddha occupy the most significant

positions in the decorative scheme—alone, accompanied by attendants or Bodhisattvas (future Buddhas), or in significant scenes from his life—on the front of stupas, in panels above pillars, and on facades. These uplifting formal images contrast with more relaxed, exuberant *jataka* stories, scenes from the life of former incarnations of the Buddha, where the moral message did not prevent the artists vividly depicting aspects of everyday life: the extravagant comforts of the royal court, the bustle of towns, the tranquility of rural existence, or the adventures of seafaring merchants.

Though construction at Ajanta ceased around 480 C.E., leaving some caves unfinished, the monasteries continued to flourish for centuries. Merchants and other travelers (often Buddhist patrons) were welcomed there as visitors.

Modern visitors can reach the valley by public transport from Aurangabad. Stairs and walkways connect the caves at different levels. The magnificent scenery enhances the experience of visiting the wonderful art and architecture of this World Heritage site.

Opposite The elaborately carved interior of cave temple 26 (fifth century C.E.). Its stupa bears a seated figure of Buddha.

Above, clockwise from top A general view of part of Ajanta's valley. The rear wall and ceiling of monastery Cave 2. The damaged but still impressive facade of temple cave 26.

VIJAYANAGARA CITY OF VICTORY

TYPE: IMPERIAL CAPITAL CITY • **ARCHITECTURAL STYLE:** VIJAYANAGARA • **LOCATION:** HAMPI, BELLARY DISTRICT, KARNATAKA, INDIA • **CONSTRUCTION BEGUN:** CA. NINTH CENTURY C.E.

From the top of Matanga Hill at Hampi in South India's Bellary district, an extraordinary panorama can be seen: a city that was once reputedly the largest in the world. Clusters of magnificent palaces and temples, defensive walls, and canals follow the great Tungabhadra River and emerge at intervals across an extraordinary landscape of ancient hills shaped by erosion so that enormous boulders lie scattered or rest precariously one on another, as if thrown around by giants. Paddy fields paint the land a brilliant green where once there were innumerable houses, shops, shrines, and reservoirs. This is Vijayanagara, City of Victory, capital for two centuries of an empire that encompassed almost all South India.

In the early fourteenth century, local Hindu chiefs successfully resisted the threatened Muslim conquest of southern India. They established their base at Vijayanagara in 1336, gradually gained hegemony over South India and repelled their Muslim neighbors. To do so, they created an efficient standing army with cavalry and elephant troops, enlarged at need with levies from their subordinate kingdoms and equipped with the latest handguns and cannon. They encouraged trade to acquire fine cavalry horses from Arabia; trade brought the kingdom great wealth.

Prosperity also followed investment in hydraulic works: great reservoirs, dams, wells, and a network of canals and aqueducts that supplied water for highly productive agriculture, and for domestic use and ritual bathing. By their religious patronage, the kings made Vijayanagara the spiritual heart of the empire. Vijayanagara was itself a holy place, sacred mythology written into its landscape, and the kings enhanced its sacred spaces with shrines and art.

The Sacred Center

The kings expanded an important temple that had stood by the Tungabhadra River since the ninth century, attracting pilgrims (as it still does today). This was dedicated to Virapaksha, an avatar of Shiva who rewarded the exceptional pious devotion of a local girl, Pampa, by marrying her. Annual festivals celebrating their marriage took place in the temple, with processions through the city's Sacred Center, a long paved colonnaded street lined with temples, smaller shrines and the fine stone houses of the elite. Localities linked to Pampa were venerated.

The Royal Center

Vijayanagara was also identified with the mythological monkey kingdom, Kishkindha, where Rama (an incarnation of Vishnu) spent time while seeking his abducted wife, Sita: many features of the landscape were venerated for their association with key episodes in his sojourn. The Royal Center, a complex divided into public buildings and royal residential quarters, lay at the heart of the city and at its very heart was the Hazara Rama temple, dedicated to Rama. Its temple and enclosure walls are richly decorated with relief carvings of scenes from Rama's story.

Other reliefs depict processions of elephants, horses, soldiers, musicians, dancing girls, and other participants in the annual nine-day Mahanavami festival, the principal event of the year, attended by military commanders and rulers from across the empire. A Great Platform within the Royal Center was used as the royal viewing platform during this festival. It is richly decorated with scenes from everyday life, as well as animals and the life of Vijayanagara's kings.

Other notable buildings within the Royal Center included the Lotus Mahal, an octagonal two-story pavilion (probably a council chamber), and the vast Elephant Stables overlooking a parade ground. Both are in an architectural style, developed at Vijayanagara, that combined elements of traditional Hindu and contemporary Islamic design.

Vitthala Temple

One of the finest of the city's many monuments was the Vitthala temple, in the northeast, not far from the river. The work mainly of Krishnadevaraya I (r. 1509–1530), the city's greatest architectural patron, the temple lay within an enclosure with three massive tiered and elaborately ornamented gateways (*gopuras*). Dedicated to Vitthala, an avatar of Vishnu, its base is carved with reliefs of horses and their attendants, its stairs flanked by elephant and *yali* (horned lion) balustrades. Two successive entrance halls, with slender columns around stone piers and pillars in the form of rearing yalis, lead into the main shrine: a stunningly beautiful creation. Smaller surrounding shrines include one dedicated to Garuda, Vishnu's mount, in the unusual form of a *ratha* (wooden temple chariot, used to carry the god in procession), every detail lovingly translated into stone.

Opposite The main temple (foreground) and the Kalyana Mandapa in the Vitthala temple complex.

A catastrophic defeat

The Vijayanagara empire reached the height of its power under Krishnadevaraya and his successor Achyutaraya (r. 1530–1542). Tragically, in 1565 Vijayanagara's armies were heavily defeated at the battle of Talikota. Its kings fled to southern Andhra Pradesh, ruling a much-diminished state until 1664; others seized parts of the empire, and the city was sacked for six months. Thereafter Vijayanagara was largely abandoned, though many of its suburbs endured as villages or towns, and the Virapaksha temple remained a place of pilgrimage. Since 1980 intensive survey, clearance, excavation, and restoration work have brought renewed life to this astonishing monumental landscape.

Although auto rickshaws can be hired to tour the different locations within the Vijayanagara metropolis, to experience the wonders of this World Heritage site to the full, visitors should wander round on foot or by bicycle, taking several days, and perhaps hiring the services of an official guide.

Opposite, clockwise from top Pillared halls and shrines set into the vast boulder landscape. In the Royal Center, intricately carved granite pillars with elaborate capitals support the Hazara Rama temple's porch.

Below View east from Matanga Hill: Tiruvengalanatha temple, part of the extensive Sacred Center.

THE VENERATED CITY
OF **ANURADHAPURA**

TYPE: CITY WITH MONASTERIES, STUPAS, AND RESERVOIRS • **ARCHITECTURAL STYLE:** ANURADHAPURA (EARLY HISTORIC) • **LOCATION:** ANURADHAPURA DISTRICT, SRI LANKA • **CONSTRUCTION BEGUN:** CA. 900 B.C.E.

Sri Lanka's capital for 1,500 years, Anuradhapura today is a sacred landscape of towering stupas surrounded by monastic ruins, with traces of the ancient city at its heart. Huge reservoirs and smaller pools reflect the central importance of water here, deep in Sri Lanka's Dry Zone.

Hunter-gatherers inhabited this island for more than 30,000 years. The settlements of rice farmers (traditionally from western India) appear in the earlier first millennium B.C.E. These include Anuradhapura, by the fourth century B.C.E. a walled city of well-built houses on regular streets.

In 246 B.C.E., the Mauryan emperor Ashoka (r. ca. 268–ca. 232 B.C.E.) sent his son Mahinda on a successful mission to introduce Buddhism to Sri Lanka. Anuradhapura's king,

Devanampiyatissa (r. 250–210 B.C.E.), donated his royal pleasure garden to establish a monastery, Mahavihara, where he built a stupa, Thuparama, to enshrine precious relics given by Mahinda—the Buddha's collarbone and begging bowl. Ashoka's daughter Sanghamitta, who founded a Buddhist nunnery at Anuradhapura, brought a cutting from the sacred Bodhi (pipal) tree beneath which the Buddha had gained enlightenment. Planted in the

Mahavihara grounds, this Mahabodhi tree still thrives, and is an object of great veneration.

Within the city Devanampiyatissa constructed an alms hall, Mahapali, where he provided the monks with cooked rice, served from a huge stone trough that still stands here. Later kings continued this practice—a visiting Buddhist pilgrim, Faxian (ca. 337–ca. 422 C.E), reported that 6,000 monks were fed here daily.

King Dutthagamini (r. 161–137 B.C.E.), who expelled South Indian invaders and united the island in 161 B.C.E., was also a generous patron to the Mahavihara. His finest creation was the Great Stupa (Ruvanveli Dagoba; like other stupas at Anuradhapura, this has been heavily restored). His nephew Vattagamini built the vast Abhayagiri Dagoba. Enlarged by later rulers, it achieved its present height of 360 ft (110 m) in the second century C.E. Vattagamini also founded the surrounding Abhayagirivihara, for monks of the growing Mahayana Buddhist sect since Mahavihara's monks followed the traditional Theravadin doctrine. Over subsequent centuries various kings favored one or other of these sects: for example, Mahasena (274–301 C.E.) seized Mahavihara land to establish a new Mahayana monastery, Jetavanavihara, for which he built another vast stupa, the Jetavanaramaya. This originally stood at 394 ft (120 m), though it is now only 233 ft (71 m) high.

The ancient Sri Lankans were skilled hydraulic engineers, building networks of canals and reservoirs from early times to supply the water for irrigation and domestic use required for life in the low-rainfall Dry Zone. Bathing, for pleasure and for ritual purposes, played an important part in life at Anuradhapura, and some of the finest surviving art and architecture is associated with pools, such as the magnificent Kuttam Pokuna within the Abhayagirivihara and the Isurumuniya pool with its delightful carvings of elephants playing in the water.

In 1017 Cholas from South India sacked Anuradhapura. The capital shifted to Polonnaruwa, abandoning Anuradhapura to the jungle, though it never lost its sanctity. Since the nineteenth century its important buildings have been cleared and some have been reconstructed.

Visitors to this World Heritage site can stay in the modern town, where the Archaeological Museum is located, and use local public transport, rickshaws, or bicycles to visit the old city, the many monasteries, and the beautiful surrounding scenery.

Opposite The Ruvanveli Dagoba reflected in nearby Basawakkulamawewa, Anuradhapura's earliest reservoir.
Above, from left The vast Jetavanaramaya stupa. A semi-circular threshold slab (moonstone), decorated with auspicious symbols to bring prosperity.

6

FAR EAST
AND OCEANIA

This vast area is inevitably dominated by China, with its tremendous Great Wall, its terracotta army—one of the most incredible discoveries in the history of archaeology—and its major tombs, some of them with remarkably well-preserved bodies and grave goods. But Japan and Korea also offer some remarkable sites such as the city of Gyeongju and the keyhole-shaped tombs. In Australia, archaeological research is a relatively recent development, but it offers some interesting sites and an enormous wealth of wonderful rock art. In Oceania, by far the greatest attraction is Easter Island— the entire island can be considered an archaeological site, justly famed for its hundreds of stone platforms and statues.

Left The Great Wall of China, one of the most famous monuments in the world.

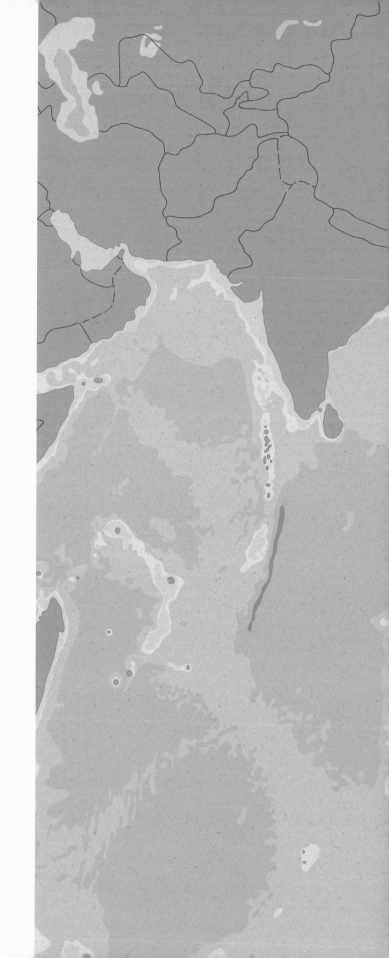

FAR EAST
AND OCEANIA
LOCATIONS

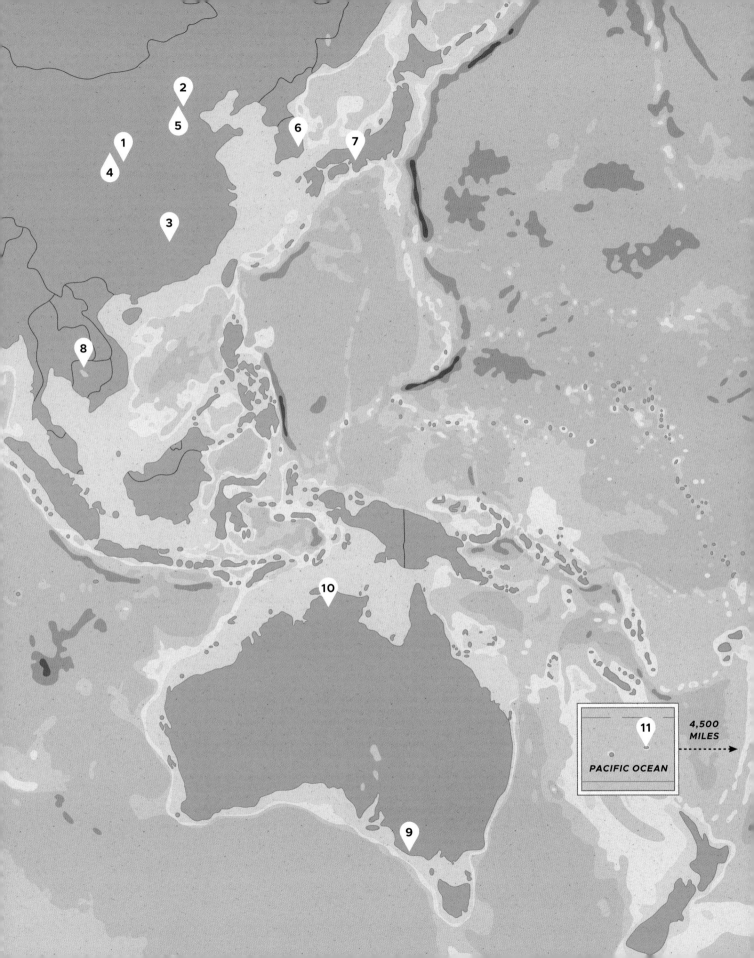

4,500
MILES

PACIFIC OCEAN

THE MAUSOLEUM OF THE
FIRST EMPEROR OF CHINA

TYPE: MAUSOLEUM • **ARCHITECTURAL STYLE:** QIN DYNASTY (221–206 B.C.E.)
LOCATION: XI'AN, SHAANXI PROVINCE, NORTH CENTRAL CHINA • **CONSTRUCTION BEGUN:** 246 B.C.E.

It was long known that the pyramid-shaped Mount Li contained the tomb of the First Emperor of China, Qin Shi Huangdi (r. 221–210 B.C.E.), but it was not until March 1974 that farmers came across red fired bricks while digging a well. The underground vault yielded thousands of terracotta warriors and horses in battle formation in trenchlike corridors, soon to be known as the Terracotta Army.

The emperor had chosen the ideal location for his last resting place during his lifetime, and more than 700,000 workers from all over the unified empire slaved away in order to construct the subterranean tomb complex ahead of his death. The imperial tomb complex—together with burial mound, burial pits, and sites of ritual constructions—includes more than 600 sites within the property area of 21.8 sq mi (56.25 sq km). Since 1987 it has been on the UNESCO World Heritage List. Extensive excavations have been carried out, and today the area offers some of the greatest insights into the world of ancient China.

The Secret of the Tomb and the Burial Pits

The emperor's tomb remains untouched. According to the Records of the Historian Sima Qian (ca. 145–ca. 87 B.C.E.) a system of crossbows triggered by movement protect the tomb owner and his valuable grave goods. Rivers and lakes of mercury, a ceiling with star constellations, and eternally burning whale-oil lamps evoke a remarkable image of the emperor's underground realm.

While this chamber still awaits excavation, several burial pits and architectural structures are open to the public. The largest pit, No. 1, is sheltered in a large hangar-like building,

with a rectangular groundplan—756 x 203 ft (230 x 62 m) in an east–west direction—and five access ramps. Ten ramparts divide the pit into eleven corridors, opening out onto two transverse galleries with approximately 6,000 terracotta warriors (only 2,000 are on display) representing the main strike force in the battle formation. A vanguard of three rows of archers is followed by the main force of soldiers standing in battle formation, and infantry. Although the almost life-sized figures are mostly gray, patches of paint show that the garments of the warriors were originally brightly colored. Their weaponry, including crossbows, spears, swords, and dagger axes, was looted early on, leaving behind only a small quantity of bronze artifacts, such as arrowheads.

Pits No. 2 and No. 3 shared the same fate. In Pit No.2, 1,300 warriors, kneeling and standing archers, cavalrymen, and mid-ranking officers with horses were partly destroyed. Pit No. 3 is the smallest. With only seventy-two warriors and horses, it is believed to be the headquarters for the high-ranking officers.

Recently, excavations of more than 400 graves and pits around the tomb have revealed terracotta dancers, musicians, acrobats, and rare bronze birds and animals. The lifelike forms of cranes, swans, and geese were

arranged on either side of a trench, which was originally filled with water and constituted an artificial subterranean stream. Also, a fair number of stone suits of armor came to light, with plates of limestone pierced at the edges and joined together with wires.

The Making of the Terracotta Army

So far, 180 pits containing burial goods have been discovered—funerary figures made up the most significant part of the assemblage. As no comparable sculptures ever existed in China before, it is difficult to imagine how the life-sized terracotta warriors, acrobats, and horses weighing as much as 330 lb (150 kg) were produced. There must have been a central place for the production of high-quality clay, and the modeling by hand of the various body parts, such as heads, arms and hands, and legs and feet, as well as armor. No two figures are identical: the facial expressions, hairstyles, headwear, armor, and footwear are unique. The names of local craftsmen and supervisors testify to the fact that there was a serial production line.

For a visit of the large site allow at least one day. To get to the site, a tourist bus, on line 5 starting from Xi'an railway station, takes one hour (to avoid crowds, arrival around 10 a.m. is recommended). The Museum of the Terracotta Army, with pits 1-3, is a must see. For an in-depth visit, a shuttle bus connects to Lishan Garden which includes the emperor's tomb and accessory pits.

Above Horses and warriors stood guard to protect the First Emperor. Today, they are part of the museum complex.

THE GREAT WALL

TYPE: DEFENSIVE WALL · **ARCHITECTURAL STYLE:** QIN DYNASTY (221-206 B.C.E.),
HAN DYNASTY (206 B.C.E.-220 C.E.), MING DYNASTY (1368-1644)
LOCATION: NORTH CHINA AND CENTRAL PLAINS · **CONSTRUCTION BEGUN:** QIN DYNASTY (221-206 B.C.E.)

When Yang Liwei, China's first man in space, returned to Earth, he reported: "The scenery was very beautiful, but I did not see the Great Wall." It was one of the great myths that the largest man-made structure could be spotted from the moon with the naked eye. But due to the fact that the wall is of almost the same color as the surrounding soil, it is only visible from the International Space Station using a strong telephoto lens.

The Great Wall stretches along an east–west line across the northern borders of China from the Lop Lake in the west to Dandong in the east, crossing nine provinces and municipalities. The term "ten thousand li" (3,100 miles/5,000 kilometres) in length is used as a metaphor to describe an "invincible force and insurmountable barrier."

In 2012, after four years of tremendous archaeological survey and investigation, the actual length was finally revealed: 13,170.69 miles (21,196.18 km).

The practice of using walls as a defensive work began when China's warring states contended with, and tried to annex, one another during the time of known as the

Left Watchtowers are the keypart of the military constructions.

Opposite The Great wall was an integrated military defensive system fortesses for command posts and logistics.

Spring and Autumn Period (772–481 B.C.E.). Yet those walls did not stop the army of the strongest state of Qin from defeating all other kingdoms in the third century B.C.E. to complete the unification of the empire. The First Emperor of China, Qin Shi Huangdi (221–210 B.C.E.), connected the existing walls. He dispatched his general Meng Tian (d. 210 B.C.E.) to lead an army of 300,000 men to expel northern invaders. Meng Tian was also charged with extending the defensive line. Thousands of men under forced labor constructed the Great Wall following the natural contours of the land, utilizing the narrow defiles. Some parts of the landscape did not allow a continuous structure, so natural barriers such as mountain ridges were used to link parts of the wall.

After the fall of the Qin dynasty the Great Wall had a troubled history. The following Han dynasty (206 B.C.E.–220 C.E.) mainly extended the Great Wall to the west and also the northeast. Further beacon and smoke towers were built for long-distance communication with the troops. Centuries later the most enthusiastic

Constructing the Wall

The amount of work put into building the Great Wall was enormous. In the era of the Qin dynasty, mainly soldiers, farmers, and convicts were forced to do the hard labor. Local resources were called upon for the transport of the large volume of materials required for construction, an extremely challenging enterprise. Stones from the mountains formed passages over mountain ranges and rammed-earth walls crossed the lowlands. Building the rammed-earth walls was as simple as it was effective. A temporary frame made of wooden planks served as a mold for the desired shape and dimension of a wall section. A damp mixture of sand, gravel, and clay—in layers of 3–6 in (7–15 cm)—was then compacted to around 50 percent of its original height. Once this had dried out, the planks of the frame were raised, and the process repeated. Within the structure, builders erected watchtowers with signal fires, troop barracks, and garrison stations. Later, the Ming dynasty builders used bricks and stones instead.

It took a millennium to build the Great Wall. It is one of the world's most famous landmarks and the most recognizable symbol of China. In 1987 it was designated as a UNESCO World Heritage site.

Major efforts are currently underway to preserve the endangered parts of the wall, threatened by the forces of both nature and mankind. Since part of the Wall was opened to the public in 1952, the number of visitors has exceeded hundreds of millions of visitors. The most famous and closest sections north of the capital of Beijing are Badaling and Mutianyu and these can be visited easily. Jinshanling, which is half restored and half wild, is said to be the most beautiful section of the wall and is also known as the "photographers paradise." Visitors can hike all the way to the section of Simatai in the west or take a cable car from the front gate to the Jinshan Tower.

wall builders were the emperors of the Ming dynasty (1368–1644). During a period of almost 270 years they carried out massive repairs, virtually turning it into a new Great Wall. For a long period, the northern border enjoyed peace and stability. It was not until March 15, 1644, that the wall finally failed to withstand the pressure of the invaders and the Ming dynasty came to an end.

Above The height of the Great Wall is 16–26 ft (5–8 m). Parts of the wall were built along ridges to make it look taller. and turned it into an almost impenetrable fortification.

THE SECRETS OF THE
MAWANGDUI TOMBS

TYPE: TOMBS · **ARCHITECTURAL STYLE:** EARLY WESTERN HAN DYNASTY (206–168 B.C.E.)
LOCATION: CHANGSHA, HUNAN PROVINCE, SOUTH CENTRAL CHINA
CONSTRUCTION BEGUN: SECOND CENTURY B.C.E.

The discovery of a Han dynasty tomb at Mawangdui, a hill site in the southern Chinese city of Changsha, Hunan province, in 1972, created an archaeological sensation. Workers digging for an air-raid shelter for the local hospital at the hill of Mawangdui, encountered a wooden structure made of large cypress planks. Work at the tomb from 1972–1974 proved it to be one of the most important archaeological excavations of the twentieth century.

The tomb was one of three buried in a vertical pit and surrounded by charcoal—weighing about 11,000 lb (5,000 kg)—in the case of tomb No. 1—and white clay, which led to the near-perfect preservation of the grave goods and one body. Nested, lacquered, and complete with 3,000 burial objects, the coffins gave great insight into the funerary tradition of the Han dynasty. The largest tomb, No. 1, belonged to Xin Zhui (213–163 B.C.E.), wife of Li Cang, who was prime minister of the Changsha kingdom. He died in 186 B.C.E. and was buried in tomb No. 2. A third tomb belonged to their son Li Xi, who died shortly before his mother. While Li Cang's tomb was severely damaged by the construction of the other tombs and also heavily plundered, those of the wife and son remained untouched for more than 2,000 years.

Archaeologists were stunned when they opened the innermost coffin in tomb No. 1: wrapped in twenty layers of silk, they found an almost intact female corpse, the first discovered in China. Xin Zhui's body was identified by a wooden seal, and was in exceptional condition, showing no signs of decomposition. An autopsy revealed that she was in her fifties when she died from a coronary heart attack.

Left More than 700 lacquered items with intricate patterns show the delicate workmanship of the Han dynastic manufacturers.

Opposite The outer wooden chamber of the tomb.

The three tombs yielded a stunning array of luxury materials. The nearly 1,400 grave goods in Xin Zhui's tomb included exquisite painted wooden coffins, silk tapestries, bamboo objects, pottery vessels, musical instruments (including a mouth organ and a twenty-five-string zither), and wooden figures. Ritual bronze vessels, silk textiles, food, clothing, cash, household items such as screens and mats, and toiletries provide important insights into the development of technology and the sophisticated art of the Han dynasty. Some of Xin Zhui's personal belongings and funeral gifts were carefully packed in bamboo hampers, while others were placed individually or in sets. Wooden labels attached to some of the hampers and an inventory written on wooden or bamboo slips provided terminology for the funeral goods.

Luxury for the Afterlife

More than 700 exquisite lacquer sets and single items display superb craftsmanship. Eating and drinking vessels, cosmetic items, and boxes and games are exceptionally well preserved and decorated with ornate motifs. A so-called *liubo* chess set includes the most complete set of pieces for this game that has ever been excavated in China.

The finds also included a comprehensive range of sumptuous silks and garments, openwork silk, silk gauze, embroidery, and cottons. Most famous is the almost translucent gauze gown with a straight lapel and diagonal hem. The total surface area of the garment is 28 sq ft (2.6 sq m) and it weighs only 1.7 oz (48 g). This delicate fabric was described by the people of the Han dynasty as "light as clouds and mist."

The contents of the excavated silk documents and wooden manuscripts were very diverse, including historical anecdotes, philosophical prose, divinatory texts, and topographic maps. Medical compendia were among Xin Zhui's favorite books, including the earliest instructions on Qigong exercises, best explained as the "ancient mastery of energy." Celestial events were of special interest in Han dynastic life, and are depicted in a special map showing twenty-nine comets with head and tail and their specific names. Altogether more than fifty manuscripts served as a personal underground library.

A T-shaped silken tomb banner (the so-called *feiyi*, the flying garment), which was carried at the front of her

funeral procession, was laid over Xin Zhui's innermost coffin at the burial. This delicate silk banner has been carefully restored. Colorful drawings show Xin Zhui ascending to the heavenly realm. The banner is divided into three parts: the underworld guarded by felines and twin-like male figures, the human sphere with a female person representing Xin Zhui and her servants, and occupying the upper part of the "T," the red sun with a raven and the crescent moon, with the crow representing the cope of heaven. It is one of the best-preserved banners ever found in a tomb.

Today, visitors to this site will see only the tomb shaft. But the newly built Hunan Province Museum in the center of Changsha has a special gallery, the Mawangdui Han Dynasty Tomb Exhibition, which is solely dedicated to these important finds. It provides an insight into the highly sophisticated burial architecture including a reconstruction of tomb No. 1 with a multimedia show. Finally, the delicately lacquered coffins lead to a separate enclosed part of the exhibition that has the well-preserved body of Xin Zhui.

IMPERIAL MAUSOLEUMS OF THE **TANG DYNASTY**

TYPE: MAUSOLEUM • **ARCHITECTURAL STYLE:** TANG DYNASTY (618–907 C.E.)
LOCATION: XI'AN, SHAANXI PROVINCE, NORTHWEST CHINA • **CONSTRUCTION BEGUN:** SEVENTH CENTURY C.E.

North of the ancient center of power, Chang'an (today's Xi'an), eighteen imperial tombs of the cosmopolitan Tang dynasty (618–907 C.E.) lie scattered across the Guangzhong plain, the area "between the mountain passes." This region is known as China's Valley of the Kings, because it is also the location of the mausoleum of the emperors of the Western Han (206 B.C.E.–6 C.E.) and hundreds of satellite tombs belonging to the members of the imperial families, leading civilians, and military officials.

After centuries of fragmentation and several short-lived dynasties, China was successfully unified and ruled by the powerful Tang dynasty emperors for almost 300 years. Whenever possible, Tang emperors started building their last resting places in their lifetimes using geomancers to help choose the right location. The emperors were buried under mountains, using the natural endowment as a tumulus at the center of the complex.

Mausoleum of Emperor Taizong

Zhaoling, the largest mausoleum, belonged to the second Tang ruler, emperor Taizong (r. 626–649 C.E.). He oversaw one of China's greatest periods of political and cultural accomplishments. His tomb complex, with around 190 satellite tombs of the imperial family members, covered more than 85 sq mi (220 sq km), thus occupying more space than the ancient capital Chang'an. Excavations of the so-called spirit path leading to the tomb brought to light six reliefs featuring Taizong's favorite stallion and fourteen foreign envoys, testimony to his international relations along the Silk Road.

A Joint Burial

Emperor Gaozong (r. 628–638 C.E.) and his wife Wu Zetian (r. 624–705 C.E.) are buried together in Qianling mausoleum. After the sudden death of her husband, Wu Zetian, a controversial figure in dynastic history, ascended the throne. She is the only woman ever to have formally ruled a Chinese dynasty. The mausoleum is unlooted and still awaits excavation. Chinese archaeologists uncovered four gates, parts of the inner wall, and parts of the outer wall surrounding the tomb together with remnants of houses of the people who were probably safeguarding the tomb. They also excavated foundations of the Sacrificial Hall, a Pavilion, and the Hall of Ministers. Visitors today can follow the spirit path that leads to the emperor's tomb lined with 124 stone statues. His favorite stallions, horses and winged horses, mighty lions, grooms with

Opposite Two groups of now headless mourners stand guard at the Qianling maosoleum.

Above Only three pairs of stone guards leading the saddled horses have survived at Qianling.

horses, officials, and foreign envoys line up for his funeral procession. Amazingly, ostriches can also be seen along the pathway. History has it that these flightless birds, which are not native to China, were first presented to the Tang court by a khan of the Western Turks in 620 C.E. At the end of the spirit path the great gateway opens up to the tomb entrance. Statues of sixty-one foreign envoys dressed in long robes, almost all of them decapitated, are marked with their individual name and the country they represent.

The Satellite Tombs

Three satellite tombs of the imperial family members have been excavated and are open to the public. They comprise the last resting places of Prince Zhanghuai, Crown Prince Yide, and Princess Yongtai. Empress Wu Zetian, mother and grandmother to the three, put them to death and it was only after Wu's death that they received a proper funeral. The walls of the three tombs are decorated with exquisite murals showing typical scenes of Tang court life such as beautiful maidservants, nobles playing polo on horseback, and members of the imperial family receiving foreign guests. Princess Yongtai's tomb is now a museum with more than 4,300 historical relics excavated from the three tombs. Visitors can admire the original murals in the Historical Museum in Xi'an.

MING IMPERIAL TOMBS

TYPE: MAUSOLEUM • **ARCHITECTURAL STYLE:** MING DYNASTY (1368–1644 C.E.)
LOCATION: BEIJING, HEBEI PROVINCE, NORTHERN CHINA • **CONSTRUCTION BEGUN:** FIFTEENTH CENTURY C.E.

In 1409, Yongle (r. 1402–1424), started to build his last resting place at the southern foot of the Tianshou Mountain. He selected the site, surrounded by trees and crossed by a river, according to Chinese geomancy traditions (*feng shui*). The beautiful scenery was also an excellent choice from a military perspective, with the surrounding mountains providing a natural defense.

In the 230 years that followed, a total of thirteen Ming emperors followed Yongle's paradigm. Covering more than 46 sq mi (120 sq km), the area features not only the imperial mausoleums but also those of twenty-three empresses, two princes, and more than thirty imperial concubines. The largest is Yongle's Changling tomb, followed by the Dingling tomb of the thirteenth Ming emperor, Wanli (r. 1572–1620), whose underground palace has been excavated. The smallest is the Zhaoling tomb of the twelfth Ming emperor, Longqing (r. 1567–1572). A visit to the site starts at the 4.3 mile (7 km) spirit path lined with twenty-four animal statues including lions, camels, and elephants, and twelve officials. The so-called Red Gate, a three-arched gateway, serves as an entrance to the tomb complex. The Shengde Stone Memorial archway, a stele pavilion, the Dragon and Phoenix gate, and a five-arch bridge offer a glimpse of the imperial ambitions and might of the Ming rulers.

Changling tomb is the only tomb in the complex to have been scientifically excavated, and visitors can reach the burial chamber itself. Emperor Yongle built Beijing's Forbidden City and sent Admiral Zheng He to explore the Maritime Silk Road to Southeast Asia, Ceylon, India, and as far as the Arabian Peninsula. According to legend it took five years to complete the tomb, and eighteen years to build the huge Ling'en hall (Hall of Eminent Favor) in front of the tomb, which covered 21,000 sq ft (1,956 sq m). Today visitors are still impressed by the thirty-two pillars that support the roof. Each pillar is made from a single tree trunk of Chinese cedar, transported from the southern provinces to Beijing. The tomb itself contained more than 3,000 precious funeral objects.

Emperor Wanli ruled his empire for forty-eight years, the longest reign in the Ming dynasty. Historical records show that the costs for the Dingling tomb

exceeded eight million taels (equivalent to 300 tons) of silver, the sum of two years imperial tax income during that time. The excavation of the tomb took place in 1957 and a museum was established in 1959. The intact tomb had a subterranean palace with five chambers some 88.6 ft (27 m) below ground. The rear chamber held the coffins of Emperor Wanli and his two wives, together with twenty-six red-lacquered boxes containing more than 3,000 funerary goods, such as silk, textiles, and porcelain. Storing the objects was a big problem at that time. His tomb suffered a sad fate: the Cultural Revolution started in 1966, making scientific excavation and preservation impossible for more than ten years. Most of the objects were lost during this unstable period.

Zhaoling tomb belonged to Emperor Longqing and his three empresses and concubines. The tomb area was first built in 1538 but underwent major repairs after that. In 1989 the tomb was restored to its original appearance. The two square courtyards in front of the tomb and the entire aboveground architecture are accessible to the public.

In 2000 and 2003 the imperial cemetery was placed on the UNESCO World Heritage List and three tombs have been open to the public since 2008.

Opposite Officials and animals border the spirit path. The mythological creature *xiezhi* kept the evil spirits away.

Above The so-called Soul Tower marks the innermost entrance to the Changling tomb.

GYEONGJU MUSEUM WITHOUT WALLS

TYPE: ROYAL CITY WITH TOMBS, TEMPLES AND PALACE • **ARCHITECTURAL STYLE:** SILLA KINGDOM
(57 B.C.E.–935 C.E.) • **LOCATION:** GYEONGJU CITY, GYEONGSANGBUK PROVINCE, SOUTH KOREA
CONSTRUCTION BEGUN: SIXTH CENTURY B.C.E.

Gyeongju is a city in the far southeastern corner of South Korea's Gyeongsanbuk province, on the coast of the Sea of Japan. Low mountains and small rivers are characteristic for the picturesque landscape. Visitors to this vibrant place leave with a impression of the living culture and history of the ancient Silla kingdom. The city and neighboring areas have more tombs, temples, pagodas, Buddhist rock carvings, and palaces with gardens than any other area in South Korea.

Gyeongju was once the political, economic, and cultural center of the Silla kingdom. It developed into a cosmopolitan city, with intensive cultural interactions with the Tang dynasty in China, as well as the ancient kingdoms of Japan and Southeast Asia. Buddhism flourished and brought social and cultural changes. Gyeongju is home to thirty-one National Treasures and has been a UNESCO World Heritage Site since the year 2000.

Most impressive is the Tumuli Park in the center of the city, home to twenty-three large burial mounds of Silla monarchs and their family members. From the outside, the tombs look more like small grassy hillocks. Most of them have been excavated and resealed, and only one is open to the public. The Tomb of the Heavenly Horse (Cheonmachong), dating from around the end of the fifth–early sixth centuries C.E. underwent excavation in 1973. It is named for the winged horse painted on a birchbark saddle-flap. It measures 44 ft (13 m) high by 154 ft (47 m) in diameter, and contained a double wooden coffin covered with gravel. Facsimiles of some of the 140 funerary objects, such as the golden crown, jade ornaments, weaponry, metal vessels, lacquerware, and ceramics are exhibited. A Syrian blue glass cup is evidence for international cultural exchange during the Silla period.

Opposite The Anapji park area is illuminated in the evenings, with occasional public concerts and theater performances.

Above Impressive ancient Korean architecture awaits visitors around every corner.

Southeast of the Tumuli Park is the adjacent Wolsong Park, in which visitors can admire the oldest existing astronomical observatory in East Asia. The bottle-shaped building is called Cheomsongdae (Observe the Stars Platform) and was built by Queen Seondeok between 632 and 646 C.E. It is 29 ft (9 m) high and constructed of 364 stone blocks in twenty-seven courses, corresponding approximately to the days of the lunar year.

Farther south in the park, a magnificent royal palace complex built by King Munmu in 674 C.E., can only be imagined today. The buildings burned down in 935 C.E. and the surrounding park, with its exquisite garden and exotic animals was abandoned. In 1974–1975 excavation was carried out of the so-called Anapji garden (the Pond of Wild Geese and Ducks) and four palace buildings. The investigation revealed that the pond and the structures nearby had once belonged to the East Palace of the Crown Prince, site of royal state banquets and the reception of foreign ambassadors. The original name of the pond was Wolji (The Pond that reflects the Moon). Today only a few pavilions have been rebuilt, and the pond with its stone embankment restored. A selection of the more than 33,000 excavated objects from the pond, including pottery, Buddhist statues, iron objects, and roof tiles can be seen in the nearby Museum as well as in the Gyeongju National Museum.

Additional Sites

In the vicinity of Gyeongju, the Gyeongju National Park with Mount Namsan (South Mountain) covers an area of 6,550 acres (2,650 ha). Its wooded mountains are famous for Buddhist remains—122 temples, 53 stone statues, 64 stone pagodas, and 16 stone lanterns border the path into the park, reflecting the long history of Buddhism in this area.

Just 10 miles (16 km) southeast of the city center is the famous Bulguksa, the World of Buddha Temple, referred to as the epitome of Buddhist architecture. Founded in 553 C.E. and rebuilt in 751 C.E. by the chief minister Kim Daesong (700–774), it was destroyed in the sixteenth century. Today's architecture mainly dates back to the eighteenth century. Two bridges guide visitors to the Daeungjeon Hall (the Hall of the Great Enlightenment), dated 1765. Two pagodas have survived the destruction,

while other halls, such as the Hall for the Avalokitesvara (Goddess of Mercy), were constructed more recently. The temple area was designated UNESCO World Heritage in 1995, and is still a living monastery.

Close to, and part of, the monastery in the mountains is the world-famous and UNESCO-listed Buddhist grotto Seokguram (Stone Grotto Hermitage). The grotto, with its huge Buddha statue surrounded by forty-one guardians and deities, was completed in 774 C.E. Huge blocks of granite create the most refined Buddha Shakyamuni sitting in a domed circular chamber.

Opposite, from left The "World of Buddha Temple" (Bulguksa) is located at the foot of the Tohamsa Mountain. From the observatory, astronomers made observations all year round.

Above Colorful painted wooden beams with dragon heads are characteristic for the indigenous Korean construction methods.

DAISENRYO KOFUN LAST RESTING PLACE OF EMPEROR NINTOKU

TYPE: TOMB • **ARCHITECTURAL STYLE:** KOFUN PERIOD STYLE
LOCATION: SAKAI, OSAKA PREFECTURE, JAPAN • **CONSTRUCTION BEGUN:** FIFTH CENTURY C.E.

Visitors to the panoramic observatory in the Sakai City Hall complex will enjoy not only a grand view across the growing city of Sakai. They will also be able to survey the immense burial mound of the Daisenryo Kofun, believed to be the final resting place of Emperor Nintoku. He was supposedly the sixteenth emperor of Japan, believed to have reigned from 319–399 C.E., but his life and also his reign are shrouded in myth. The tomb complex with its keyhole-shaped structure measures 1,500 ft (457 m) long, 900 ft (274 m) wide, and 115 ft (35 m) high, and is enclosed by three moats. It is the largest tomb in Japan and the third-largest tomb in the world, surpassed only by the Pyramid of Giza in Egypt and the Mausoleum of the First Emperor of China.

Daisenryo Tomb

The city of Sakai is located in Osaka Prefecture on the edge of Osaka Bay and the mouth of the Yamato River. Since medieval times it was one of Japan's largest and most important seaports. Today Sakai is the second-largest city in Osaka prefecture, after the city of Osaka itself. In the heart of the bustling urban center, with its dense population and crowded living quarters, the

Daisenryo Kofun stands out with its gigantic tumulus. The mound is built with three levels and an area for religious ceremonies. When seen from above, the keyhole structure can be identified with a quadrilateral area and a directly abutting circular mound. The tomb itself is surrounded by three concentric moats with a circumference of 1.7 miles (2.8 km). Thanks to archaeological findings and written sources, the construction of the tomb is estimated to date to the mid–fifth century C.E. Legend has it that it took sixteen years and 2,000 labourers to complete this huge mausoleum.

Despite being the largest mausoleum in Japan, very little is known about Nintoku's tomb chamber. Tourists, archaeologists, and even royalty can only go as far as a bridge over the second moat. Nobody has crossed the inner moat since a storm damaged the lower part of the tomb in 1872. Subsequent restoration brought to light many artifacts, including helmets, a glass bowl, and clay figures known as *haniwa*. Since then, because kofun are considered sacred sites, further excavations have been prohibited.

Mozu Kofun Tombs

The Daisenryo Kofun is one of forty-nine burial mounds of different shapes and sizes in Sakai, known collectively as the Mozu Kofun Tombs and designated a UNESCO World Heritage Site in 2019. A *kofun*, literally meaning "ancient tomb," was built for a wealthy leader or member of the aristocracy during the eponymous Kofun Period (250–538 C.E.). The tombs display a highly sophisticated funeral system. They also reflect the growth of social and economic hierarchies and wealth in Japan during the Kofun era.

After viewing the Daisenryo Kofun from the top floor of the Sakai City Hall, visitors should take the time to experience the area of the Daisen Park, either walking or cycling. A walking path leads around the tomb into the park with wooded areas and three moats to explore. A visit during the cherry blossom season in the spring is highly recommended. A single circuit is 1.7 miles (2.8 km) in length and may take fifty minutes to cover on foot. In addition, the Sakai City Museum offers an insight into Kofun history and culture.

Opposite The gate to the tomb itself is closed for all visitors.
Above The park area lies in the center of Sakai and can be visited all year round.

TEMPLES OF CAMBODIA
ANGKOR WAT AND ANGKOR THOM

TYPE: TEMPLES AND ROYAL CAPITAL • **ARCHITECTURAL STYLE:** KHMER STYLE
LOCATION: NORTH OF SIEM REAP, SIEM REAP PROVINCE, CAMBODIA
CONSTRUCTION BEGUN: TWELFTH CENTURY C.E.

"...In the province still bearing the name Ongkor [Angkor]...there are ruins of such grandeur, remains of structures which must have been raised at such an immense cost of labor, that, at the first view, one is filled with profound admiration..." When the French explorer Henri Mouhet (1826–1861) visited Angkor in the late nineteenth century he found many, though not all, of the area's stone temples abandoned and overgrown. Today Angkor is the most popular and most visited area of Cambodia and is truly an absolute must-see.

The word "angkor" derives from a Sanskrit term meaning "the holy city." It was the capital of Southeast Asia's Khmer empire from the ninth to the fifteenth centuries C.E., a bustling place with temples, monuments, reservoirs, and irrigation systems. Today Angkor is one of the most important archaeological sites in Southeast Asia. It is located north of Siem Reap, about 150 miles (240 km) northwest of today's Cambodian capital Phnom Penh. The whole area stretches over more than 155 sq mi (440 sq km) including the surrounding forests, city foundations, and the remains of the mighty Khmer empire, the temples of Angkor Wat and Angkor Thom.

Angkor Wat, The Temple city

Angkor Wat is a good starting point for a visit on a small or grand circuit, the two circular routes that lead visitors through the archaeological park of Angkor with its temples, and the royal city of Angkor Thom. Angkor Wat is the largest religious building in the world, occupying a total area of 500 acres (200 ha) with a surrounding moat, defining a perimeter of more than 3 miles (5 km). The construction

of Angkor Wat as the state temple and political center of the empire began in the first half of the twelfth century during the reign of King Suryavarman II (r. 1113–1150). This was the heyday of cultural, religious, and artistic development of the Khmer civilization, that occupied the heartland in the lower Mekong valley. The construction took an estimated thirty years to complete. The Khmer had developed and refined their own architectural style using sandstone. Thousands of people must have worked on the temple, where elephants were used to move the massive stone blocks coming from the nearby mountain ranges. Like most temples built during the Khmer empire, Angkor Wat began as a Hindu temple and became a Buddhist temple by the end of the twelfth century. Thus, the central complex has thousands of bas-reliefs representing important deities and figures in the Hindu and Buddhist religions, and also a

Opposite, from top The "Temple of the Many Faces" is one of the highlights for photographers all over the world. Nature had long reclaimed part of the temple, creating a mystical, mysterious atmosphere throughout the complex.

depiction of Emperor Suryavarman II entering the city. As Angkor Wat is the main landmark of Cambodia, the temple is depicted on the national flag. Since 1992 it has been a UNESCO World Heritage site.

Angkor Thom, The Great City

Leaving Angkor Wat, visitors follow the circuit route to the south gate of Angkor Thom, the new royal capital. Approaching the gate entrance stone sculptures of fifty-four gods and fifty-four demons flank the causeway. Angkor Thom was built by Jayavarman VII (1181–1201)

who finally proclaimed Buddhism as the state religion. Temples and towers were erected within a framework of massive walls. Most famous is the Bayon Temple in the center of the city, which was also known as the "temple with many faces." The fifty-four towers and 216 faces of Bodhisattva Avalokiteshvara ("the Lord who gazes down to the world"), facing in all four directions, are best visited after sunrise and also in the afternoon.

Near the temple, the Terrace of the Elephant, an 8 ft- (2.5 m-) high and 984 ft- (300 m-) long platform with five staircases, was once the place for the royal family to attend

processing and parades. Bas-relief sculptures of elephants, horses, lions, dancers, and warriors, together with sculptures of elephant heads with long trunks, are popular photo motifs.

Located just outside of Angkor Thom, following the small circuit route, visitors will come across Ta Prohm, one of the most interesting temples. In the twentieth century archaeologists decided to leave this temple untouched, conserving it minimally. Overgrown by huge tropical trees and embraced by their roots, the spot was the ideal location for the film *Tomb Raider*. A flashlight and compass are very useful when visiting Ta Prohm.

Visitors to Angkor will hardly be able to visit the whole area in one day. But if there is only a day to experience the site, Angkor Wat, the South Gate of Angkor Thom, Bayon Temple, the Terrace of the Elephants, and Ta Prohm are the most important spots to visit. As a preparation for a visit, the Angkor National Museum in Siem Reap is a good way to delve into Khmer history and culture.

Above Sunrise and sunset at both palaces, here Angkor Thom, will leave deep impressions of this magical spot.

BUDJ BIM CULTURAL LANDSCAPE

TYPE: AQUACULTURE SYSTEM • **ARCHITECTURAL STYLE:** N/A
LOCATION: VICTORIA, AUSTRALIA • **CONSTRUCTION BEGUN:** 6,000–7,000 B.C.E.

The remains of channels, weirs, ponds, and stone houses occur throughout the rugged landscape of Western Victoria, and point to a sophisticated aquaculture system developed by the Gunditjmara people more than 8,000 years ago. Particularly well-preserved complexes occur at Tae Rak (Lake Condah), Kurtonitj, on Killara (Darlot Creek), and Tyrendarra. These areas, together with Budj Bim itself (the extinct volcano, Mount Eccles) and the Lake Condah Mission site, make up the World Heritage listed Budj Bim Cultural Landscape.

About 30,000 years ago the Gunditjmara people would have witnessed the eruption of Budj Bim (Mount Eccles). Lava from the volcano flowed south and west for more than 30 miles (50 km), creating this distinctive landscape of lakes and wetlands. The Gunditjmara call it Tungatt Mirring, or stone country, and describe how the ancestral being, Budj Bim, transformed himself into the Budj Bim landscape.

It was within this landscape that the Gunditjmara used their detailed knowledge of seasonal changes in water levels to build a system of stone weirs, channels, and ponds to manage and direct water flow in order to harvest eels and other fish. These, they would catch in wicker basket traps placed in the channels or at gaps in weirs, or hold in ponds. This aquaculture system produced an abundance

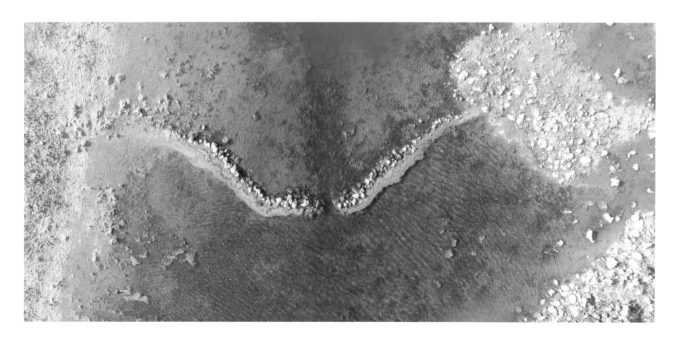

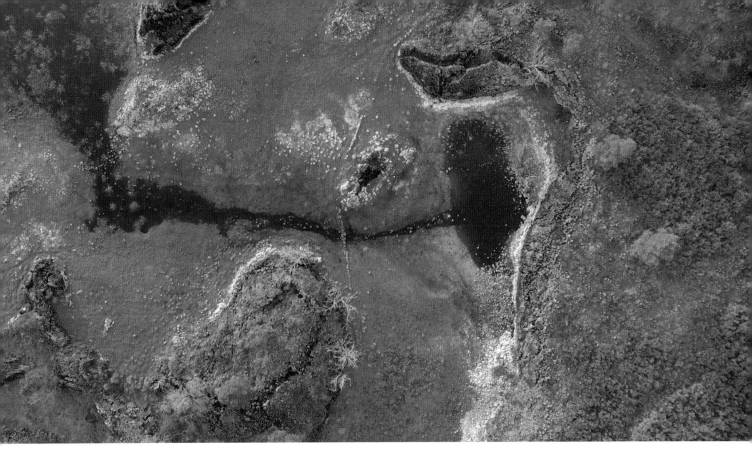

of resources that supported large seasonal gatherings. Surplus eels were smoked and dried for storage and trade.

Archaeological features of this type are difficult to date and the system probably grew in size and complexity through many generations. So far, the oldest firm evidence for channel building comes from the Muldoons Trap Complex at the southwest edge of Tae Rak (Lake Condah). This maze of channels, extending at least 1,150 ft (350 m) caught the late winter-early spring floodwaters from Tae Rak. The Gunditjmara would have placed basket traps along the channels to catch eels, and would have directed surplus water into a natural sinkhole at the western end of the complex. Here, excavation showed an early phase of channel construction by removing basalt bedrock blocks about 6,600 years ago. The channel walls were rebuilt between 300 and 800 years ago.

Beside the aquaculture complex, hundreds of other ancient stone structures occupy the Budj Bim landscape. Many of these are the foundations of huts that would once have had domed roofs covered with turf. They often occur in groups of five or more. This has led to the suggestion that these were permanently occupied villages. However, it is more likely that they were used seasonally as base camps. Perhaps the Gunditjmara visited different parts of the system as water levels changed throughout the year. What is clear is that eel farming in the Budj Bim landscape supported a large and settled population by the 1840s.

European settlers found it difficult to penetrate the rugged rocky landscape of Budj Bim. It thus became a center of Gunditjmara resistance and a base for a decade of guerrilla warfare against the invaders, known as the Eumeralla War.

The return of the area to the Gunditjmara has seen the beginnings of restoration of the original wetlands after more than a century of agriculture and a new life for the aquaculture systems. The traditional owners are developing plans for sustainable tourism and interpretation at key locations in the Budj Bim cultural landscape while also offering a range of guided tours and cultural experiences.

Opposite A weir at Tae Rak (Lake Condah), showing the opening for a wicker trap.

Above A channel carries the water from Tae Rak (Lake Condah) to a holding pond.

ABORIGINAL ART IN
KAKADU NATIONAL PARK

TYPE: ABORIGINAL ROCK ART • **ARCHITECTURAL STYLE:** N/A **LOCATION:** NORTHERN TERRITORY, AUSTRALIA • **CONSTRUCTION BEGUN** EVIDENCE OF OCCUPATION DATES BACK ABOUT 60,000 YEARS

Famous for its natural beauty, rich wildlife, and extraordinary rock art, Kakadu National Park, in Australia's Northern Territory, is one of the continent's best-known tourist destinations. The spectacular sandstone cliffs of Kakadu are home to one of the largest and most diverse concentrations of rock art in the world. They also harbor the oldest archaeological evidence for human occupation in Australia.

The Traditional Owners, known as Bininj/Mungguy, maintain a deep spiritual connection to the country and the rock art documents their creation stories and lifeways over thousands of years. In the national park itself about 5,000 sites have been documented, but there are undoubtedly many more and the whole region is rich in art.

Kakadu covers nearly 7,700 sq mi (20,000 sq km) of wetlands, rocky hills, or "stone country," and the sandstone cliffs and gorges of the western Arnhem Land escarpment. The rich natural resources of the area have sustained Aboriginal people for thousands of years. Several rock shelters contain archaeological evidence dating back to the last ice age, while at Madjedbebe occupation dates back some 60,000 years—the oldest site so far identified in Australia. The recent archaeological excavations at Madjedbebe have produced the oldest evidence for ground-edge hatchets and seed grinding in the world.

Determining the age of the rock art is very difficult. In sites with more than one style, studying the order of different layers of painting can provide relative ages. Subject matter also gives clues to dating. For example, animals now extinct in the area, such as the thylacine (Tasmanian tiger) and the Tasmanian devil are portrayed in the older art. A fragment of painted rock found in excavations at Nawarla Gabarnmang dates back 27,000 years and is the oldest dated art in the area. However, finds of ocher crayons in the earliest levels of sites such as Madjedbebe and Nawarla Gabarnmang, suggest that the tradition of art goes back to the first colonization of the Australian continent, more than 60,000 years ago.

The many different styles of art in Kakadu sites clearly vary through time, and also regionally. The environment here has changed substantially over the long period of Aboriginal occupation. During the last ice age, before about 8,000 years ago, the climate was much drier and sea levels lower. Some of the older art at Kakadu has many naturalistic depictions of land animals and dynamic portrayals of human figures. As sea levels rose at the end of the last ice age estuarine conditions, including mangrove swamps, developed as far inland as the Arnhem Land escarpment. Over the last 4,000 years these gradually transformed from saltwater estuaries to freshwater floodplains. Portrayals of land animals become much less common and are replaced by fish and saltwater crocodiles. The colorful X-ray style is

Opposite Ancestral creative beings at Anbangbang Gallery, Nourlangie Rock.

prominent during this period. These paintings show internal organs and bones of the subject within an outline silhouette. Many paintings from this time portray ancestral creation figures that are significant in the mythology of Bininj/ Mungguy groups in the area today.

By about 1,500 years ago, increasing numbers of large sites on the floodplains show that the rich resources of the freshwater wetlands supported a large and growing Aboriginal population. In the rock art, depictions of activities such as goose hunting and wetland species reflect the shift to a way of life increasingly focused on freshwater wetlands. The X-ray style continues, although the outline is now divided into decorative zones rather than a representation of internal structures. After contact with Europeans, as well as painting traditional images, the Bininj/Mungguy painted European subjects such as sailing ships, steel axes, and guns.

Nayombolmi, who died in 1967, was one of the last artists known to paint on rock in the region. More than 600 paintings are attributed to him. The best documented of them is a panel at the Anbangbang Gallery, Nourlangie Rock, painted by Nayombolmi and Djimongurr in the 1963/64 wet season. The tradition of rock painting finally ceased in Kakadu sometime in the 1970s, but local Bininj/ Mungguy artists continue to use the same motifs and styles in other media including bark painting.

The Kakadu National Park World Heritage site is 133 km (82 miles) east of Darwin. Anbangbang is one of the many rock art sites that can be visited in the park. Two interpretation centers in the park explain Aboriginal culture and the landscape, display the work of local artists and feature cultural workshops.

Opposite, from top Fish painted in X-ray style. The frieze of running figures is painted in one of the older styles present in Kakadu National Park.

Below The Arnhem Land sandstone escarpment, with its many rock art sites, dominates the Kakadu landscape.

MOAI AND BIRDMEN ON **EASTER ISLAND**

TYPE: ISLAND • **ARCHITECTURAL STYLE:** N/A
LOCATION: THE SOUTHERN PACIFIC • **CONSTRUCTION BEGUN:** 1000-1500 C.E.

One of the most remote pieces of permanently inhabited land in the world, Easter Island offers the visitor two utterly unique and world-class sites—the statue quarry and the birdman village—and the richest rock art in the Pacific.

Roughly triangular in shape, Easter Island is entirely volcanic in origin, and covers just 66 sq mi (171 sq km) in the South Pacific. The island is now generally known as Rapa Nui (Big Rapa), and is so remote that it is extremely unlikely that it was ever colonized more than once by

people: the archaeological record indicates a single unbroken development of culture from the first settlers until the arrival of Europeans.

A variety of evidence suggests that people first came here from eastern Polynesia in the early centuries of the

Common Era. Having arrived, they were trapped here, and the island constituted their whole world. Their first known contact with the rest of humanity came on Easter Sunday (April 5) 1722, when Dutch navigator Jacob Roggeveen (1659–1729) encountered the island, and gave it its popular name. Subsequent eighteenth-century visitors included Captain Cook (1728–1779).

The Island's Statues

All of the early accounts of Easter Island marvel at the huge statues and wonder how such a primitive people could move and erect them on an island with no timber. Archaeological investigation of the island came into its own in 1955, when an expedition led by Thor Heyerdahl (1914–2002) brought in professional archaeologists. They carried out the first stratigraphic excavations and obtained the first radiocarbon dates, but also conducted experiments in carving, moving, and erecting statues.

However, it was analyses of pollen obtained in cores from the sediments at the bottom of the freshwater lakes in the island's volcanic craters that led British palaeobotanist John Flenley in the 1980s to discover that the island was originally covered by a rainforest dominated by a species of huge palm tree. It was to this island—totally different in appearance from that of today—that there came a group of Polynesian voyagers bringing with them the domestic animals and food plants with which they transformed the environment of so many Polynesian islands. The colonists set about changing the landscape—making clearings in the forest to plant their crops—and constructed small, simple *ahu* (stone platforms) of normal Polynesian type, with small, crude statues upon or in front of them.

In the next phase, ca. 1000–1500, vast efforts went into the construction of more and bigger ceremonial platforms (cores of rubble encased with stone slabs) and hundreds of large statues. The population must have increased, perhaps quite rapidly, leading to greater pressure on the supply of

Opposite One of the *moai* at Tongariki, with the cliffs of the Poike Peninsula in the background.

Above The restored platform of Tongariki, the biggest on the island, with 15 *moai* standing on it.

land, and the need for increasing quantities of food. The decline of the forest, as land was cleared, can be seen in the record of pollen from the crater swamps. But the increasing pace and quantity of statue carving required ever greater quantities of timber for rollers and levers.

Using basalt picks, Easter Island's inhabitants carved more than 1,000 *moai* (statues), nearly all of them in the soft, volcanic tuff of the Rano Raraku crater. All were variations on a theme, a human figure with a prominent, angular nose and chin, and often elongated perforated ears. The bodies, which end at the abdomen, have arms held tightly to the sides, and hands held in front, with long fingertips meeting a stylized loincloth. The *moai* represent ancestors.

The islanders transported more than 230 *moai* considerable distances from the quarry to platforms around the edge of the island, where they erected them with their backs to the sea, watching over the villages around each platform. At the most prestigious platforms, they gave the statues a *pukao* or topknot of red scoria, raised and placed on the head, and eyes of white coral, which they inserted at certain times to "activate" a statue's *mana*, or spiritual power. The quarry at Rano Raraku still contains almost 400 statues on, and around, its inner and outer slopes, in every stage of manufacture. One of them, El Gigante, is more than 65.5 ft (20 m) long and, if completed, would have weighed up to 270 tons.

The Birdman Tradition

In the final phase of the island's prehistory, the islanders ceased to carve statues, cremation gave way to burial, and the manufacture in huge quantities of *mataa*, spearheads and daggers of obsidian, a sharp, black, volcanic glass shattered 1,000 years of peaceful coexistence. Conflict led to the toppling of the statues and the islanders abandoned the earlier religion and social system based on ancestor worship in favor of one featuring a warrior elite. An annual chief or "birdman" was chosen each year in a race at the ceremonial village of Orongo, whose drystone corbeled houses perch high on the cliff separating the great Rano Kau crater from the ocean. Each candidate had a young man to represent him. Every spring, the competitors had to descend the sheer 985 ft (300 m) cliff, then swim over 0.6 mile (1 km) on a bunch of reeds to the largest and outermost islet, Motu Nui, where they awaited the arrival of a migratory seabird, the sooty tern. The aim was to find its first egg. The winner swam back with the egg securely held in a headband, and his master became the new sacred birdman. Orongo's rich rock art is festooned with carvings of the birdmen, sometimes holding the egg, which symbolized fertility. This system was still developing when the Europeans turned up, and ended with the arrival of missionaries in the 1860s.

The causes of the island's decline and change are probably complex, but the major factor is clearly human colonization. By 1722, when Europeans arrived, the population had been reduced to around 2,000, living in poverty amid the ruins of their former culture. Subsequent slave-raids and epidemics eventually reduced the population to just over 100, wiping out almost all of the ruling and priestly elite who could have provided so much information. Instead scholars have had to build up a picture from the stunted testimony of the descendants of these few survivors, and from archaeological and palaeoenvironmental investigations.

Today Easter Island is best visited by plane, although some cruise ships do call there.

Opposite The restored "royal" platform at Anakena, showing the red pukao placed on the moai's heads.

Above, from top The finished statues at the Rano Raraku quarry are often erroneously called "heads" but are complete statues buried in sediment up to the neck. One *moai* at Ahu Tahai has had eyes permanently inserted for tourist photos.

INDEX

CREDITS

Paul Bahn is a prehistorian who has written and edited a wide variety of books, and who lectures on numerous archaeological tours.
Covalanas · Côa Valley · Easter Island

Caroline Bird is a consultant archaeologist and independent researcher, currently based in Perth, Western Australia.
Budj Bim · Kakadu National Park

Peter Bogucki is dean for undergraduate affairs of the School of Engineering and Applied Science at Princeton University and an archaeologist specializing in European prehistory.
Tanum · Gamla Uppsala · King Harald Bluetooth's Fortresses · The Boyne Valley · Stonehenge · Carnac · Hochdorf · Hallstatt · Biskupin

Philip Duke is an Emeritus Professor of Anthropology and a Fellow of the Society of Antiquaries, with degrees from the universities of Cambridge and Calgary.
Head-Smashed-In Buffalo Jump · L'Anse-aux-Meadows · Chaco Canyon · Mesa Verde · Little Bighorn · Cahokia · Serpent Mound

David Gill is Professor of Archaeological Heritage, and Honorary Research Fellow in the School of History at the University of East Anglia (UEA).
Hadrian's Wall · Rome · Pompeii and Herculaneum · Athens · Olympia · Corinth · Delphi · Pergamon · Petra

Jane McIntosh studied and taught archaeology at Cambridge, specialising in the Indus civilization, and has written extensively on aspects of the world's past.
Göbekli Tepe · Çatalhöyük · Jericho · Jerusalem · Ur · Babylon · Persepolis · Mohenjo Daro · Taxila · Bhimbetka · Ajanta · Vijayanagara · Anuradhapura

Elena Miklashevich is a researcher in the Palaeoart Centre of the Institute of Archaeology, Russian Academy of Science (Moscow) and vice-president of the Siberian Association for Prehistoric Art Research.
Novgorod · Khakasia · Oglakhty Mountains · Tomskaya Pisanitsa

Georgina Muskett is an Honorary Research Fellow at the University of Liverpool and Honorary Research Associate at National Museums Liverpool.
Akrotiri · Mycenae · Gournia · Knossos

Paul Pettitt is Professor of Palaeolithic Archaeology at Durham University, UK. He researches the European Middle and Upper Palaeolithic.
Sierra de Atapuerca · Neanderthal

Patricia Plunket is now an independent scholar after thirty-three years as Professor of Mesoamerican Archaeology at the Universidad de las Américas Puebla, Mexico.
Teotihuacan · Monte Albán · Tikal · Copán · Palenque · Toniná · Chichén Itzá · Mitla · Xochicalco · Tenochtitlan

Margareta Prüch studied Sinology and Far Eastern Art History in Bonn, Beijing and Heidelberg, where she is now affiliated as a Research Associate. She has worked as curator, lecturer and author. Her research interests mainly focus on the dynastic periods of China, Korea and Japan, specializing in Chinese Zhou- to Han-period tombs and material culture.
Terracotta Army · The Great Wall · Mawangdui Tombs · Tang imperial tombs · Ming imperial tombs · Gyeongju · Daisenryo Kofun · Angkor Thom and Angkor Wat

Anne Solomon is an archaeologist specialising in rock art, hunter-gatherer prehistory and the ethnographies of the Khoisan peoples of southern Africa.
Senegambian · Aksum · Lalibela · Kilwa Kisiwani · Great Zimbabwe · Cradle of Humankind · Mapungubwe · Game Pass Shelter

Henry Tantaleán studied archaeology at San Marcos National University. He got his Master's and Ph.D. in Prehistoric Archaeology at the Universidad Autónoma de Barcelona, Spain. Currently, he is a full professor at San Marcos National University.
Machu Picchu · Chan Chan · Chavín de Huántar · Moche Huacas del Sol and La Luna · Pachacamac · Caral · Sipán · Nazca Lines · Tiwanaku

Joyce Tyldesley is Reader in Egyptology at the University of Manchester, UK, where she teaches a suite of online programmes to students worldwide.
Sakkara · Giza Plateau · Amarna · Abydos · Dendera · Karnak · Deir el-Medina · Valley of the Kings · Deir el-Bahri · Aswan · Abu Simbel